Swift

Apprentice:

Fundamentals

By the Kodeco Team

Ehab Amer, Alexis Gallagher, Matt Galloway & Eli Ganim

Swift Apprentice: Fundamentals

Ehab Amer, Alexis Gallagher, Matt Galloway & Eli Ganim

Copyright ©2023 Kodeco Inc.

ISBN: 978-1-950325-82-5

Table of Contents

Chapter 10: Regex 219

Section III: Building Your Own Types 237

Chapter 11: Structures 239

Chapter 12: Properties 253

Book License

By purchasing *Swift Apprentice: Fundamentals*, you have the following license:

- You are allowed to use and/or modify the source code in *Swift Apprentice: Fundamentals* in as many apps as you want, with no attribution required.

- You are allowed to use and/or modify all art, images and designs that are included in *Swift Apprentice: Fundamentals* in as many apps as you want, but must include this attribution line somewhere inside your app: "Artwork/images/designs: from *Swift Apprentice: Fundamentals*, available at www.kodeco.com".

- The source code included in *Swift Apprentice: Fundamentals* is for your personal use only. You are NOT allowed to distribute or sell the source code in *Swift Apprentice: Fundamentals* without prior authorization.

- This book is for your personal use only. You are NOT allowed to reproduce or transmit any part of this book by any means, electronic or mechanical, including photocopying, recording, etc. without previous authorization. You may not sell digital versions of this book or distribute them to friends, coworkers or students without prior authorization. They need to purchase their own copies.

All materials provided with this book are provided on an "as is" basis, without warranty of any kind, express or implied, including but not limited to the warranties of merchantability, fitness for a particular purpose and noninfringement. In no event shall the authors or copyright holders be liable for any claim, damages or other liability, whether in an action of contract, tort or otherwise, arising from, out of or in connection with the software or the use or other dealings in the software.

All trademarks and registered trademarks appearing in this guide are the properties of their respective owners.

Before You Begin

This section tells you a few things you need to know before you get started, such as what you'll need for hardware and software, where to find the project files for this book and more.

What You Need

To follow along with the tutorials in this book, you'll need the following:

- **A Mac running macOS Monterey 12.5 or later.** with the latest point release and security patches installed. This is so you can install the latest version of the required development tool: Xcode.

- **Xcode 14.2 or later.** Xcode is the main development tool for writing code in Swift. You need Xcode 14.2 at a minimum, since that version includes Swift 5.7 Xcode playgrounds. You can download the latest version of Xcode for free from the Mac App Store, here: apple.co/1FLn51R

If you haven't installed the latest version of Xcode, be sure to do that before continuing with the book. The code covered in this book depends on Swift 5.7 and Xcode 14.2 — you may get lost if you try to work with an older version or work outside the playground environment that this book assumes.

Book Source Code & Forums

Book Source Code

The materials for this book are all available in the GitHub repository here:

- https://github.com/kodecocodes/saf-materials/tree/editions/1.0

You can download the entire set of materials for the book from that page.

Forum

We've also set up an official forum for the book at https://forums.kodeco.com/c/books/swift-apprentice-fundamentals. This is a great place to ask questions about the book or to submit any errors you may find.

"Thanks to my family for their unconditional support, and my beautiful Merche for being a wonderful blessing."

— *Ehab Amer*

"To my wife and kids – Ringae, Odysseus, and Kallisto."

— *Alexis Gallagher*

"To my amazing family who keep putting up with me spending my spare hours writing books like this."

— *Matt Galloway*

"To my loved ones: Moriah, Lia and Ari."

— *Eli Ganim*

About the Authors

 **Ehab Amer** is an author of this book. He is a very enthusiastic Lead iOS developer with a very diverse experience, from building games to enterprise applications and POCs, especially when exploring new technologies. In his spare time, TV shows take the majority, followed by video games. When away from the screen, he goes with his friends for escape room experiences or to explore the underwater world through diving.

 **Alexis Gallagher** is an author of this book. He's worked in consulting, science, iOS development, startup management, and theater. Perhaps the only software engineer in San Francisco who was born there, he lives there now with his family, and works at Google on machine learning research and applications.

 **Matt Galloway** is an author of this book. He is a software engineer with a passion for excellence. He stumbled into iOS programming when it first was a thing, and he has never looked back. When not coding, he likes to brew his own beer.

 **Eli Ganim** is an author of this book. He is a Software Engineer who's passionate about teaching, writing and sharing knowledge with others. He lives in Israel with his wife and kids.

About the Editors

Kirk Ericson is an editor of this book. Kirk has worked as a copy editor, reporter and columnist for three daily newspapers in the real Washington. He lives in Olympia.

Walter Tyree is a technical editor of this book. By day he runs the tiniest of technology consulting companies. He writes software and also gives talks and writes articles for others to learn how to write software. After hours, he likes to knit and bake bread, play with his dog, and dance with his wife. You can find him at his company website (www.tyreeapps.com).

Steven Van Impe is a technical editor of this book. Steven is a computer science lecturer at the University College of Ghent, Belgium, an author at Programming with Swift: Fundamentals (https://www.pwsacademy.org), and an open-source contributor to projects that support cross-platform adoption of Swift. You can contact Steven on Twitter at @pwsacademy (https://twitter.com/pwsacademy) and various Slack and Discord channels.

Ray Fix is the final pass editor of this book. During the day, Ray works on next-generation microscopes made for iPad at Discover Echo Inc. in San Diego, California. He enjoys learning new things and is excited about math, data, visualization, machine learning and computer vision. Swift is his problem-solving language of choice. Twitter: @rayfix (https://twitter.com/rayfix).

Introduction

By Ray Fix

Welcome to the Swift Apprentice: Fundamentals, fully updated for Xcode 14.2 and Swift 5.7! This book was derived from the first three sections of the Swift Apprentice, Seventh Edition. It expands on the core concepts the are vital to a solid understanding of the Swift language.

In the last eight years, Swift has gone from a secret project at Apple, Inc. to a full-blown, open-source, community-driven language. It continues to refine its core goal of being a general-purpose language that supports safety, speed and expressiveness.

Despite its progressive, industrial-strength nature, Swift is an excellent choice for the beginning programmer since Xcode offers a sandbox-type environment where you can directly execute Swift statements to try out various language features without creating a whole app first.

Developers worldwide use Swift to build thousands of amazing apps for iOS, iPadOS, macOS, tvOS and watchOS. Swift is also in server-side technology on non-Apple platforms. That means what you learn in this book will be extremely useful as you expand your development skills and possibly work as a developer someday.

You'll learn about basic things like constants, values, operations and types, and move up to more intermediate concepts like data structures, classes and enumerations. Finally, you'll finish off by getting in-depth knowledge about protocol extensions, custom operators, protocol-oriented programming and generics. Swift lets you create beautiful abstractions to solve real-world problems that you will learn about in this book.

Swift is also a lot of fun! It's easy to try out small snippets of code as you test new ideas. Programming is a hands-on experience, and Swift makes it fast and easy to follow along with this book and explore on your own.

Who This Book Is For

If you're a complete beginner at programming, this is the book for you! There are short exercises and challenges throughout the book to give you some programming practice and test your knowledge along the way.

If you want to get right into iOS app development while learning bits of the Swift language as you go, we recommend *SwiftUI by Tutorials* by the raywenderlich.com team. SwiftUI is so approachable that you may have even *built* a simple app or two with some sample code. As you go through this book, you may be wondering why you don't see some of the syntaxes that appear in an elementary SwiftUI app. These include @State and @ObservedObject property wrappers, opaque return types and result builders. While property wrappers and opaque return types are eventually covered, they are advanced language features and require quite a bit of background to understand their inner workings. Using them, fortunately, is easy, and *SwiftUI by Tutorials* will show you how to do that.

How to Use This Book

Each chapter of this book presents theory and Swift code to demonstrate the practical applications of what you're learning.

Since this is a book for beginners, we suggest reading it in order the first time. After that, the book will make an excellent reference for you to return to and refresh your memory on particular topics.

All the code in this book is platform-neutral; it isn't specific to iOS, macOS or any other platform. The code runs in **playgrounds**, which you'll learn about in the very first chapter.

As you read through the book, you can follow along and type the code into a playground. That means you'll be able to experiment with the code by making changes and see the results immediately.

Throughout the book, you'll find **mini-exercises**, which are short exercises about the topic at hand. At the end of each chapter, there are also **challenges**. These are either programming questions or more extended coding exercises to test your knowledge. You'll get the most out of this book if you follow along with these exercises and challenges.

What's in Store

This book consists of three sections. Each section has a short introduction that describes its chapters, their topics and the overarching themes of the section. Here's a brief overview of the book's sections:

Section I: Swift Basics

The book's first section starts at the beginning of the computing environment: first, how computers work, and then, how Swift's playgrounds feature works. With those logistics out of the way, you'll take a tour of the fundamentals of the Swift language and learn the basics of managing data, structuring your code, performing simple operations and calculations, working with types.

Section II: Collection Types

Stored data is a core component of any app, whether it's a list of friends in your social networking app or a set of unlockable characters in your hit game. In this section, you'll learn how to store collections of data in Swift.

Section III: Building Your Own Types

Swift comes with basic building blocks, but its real power is in the custom things you can build to model parts of your app. Swift has no idea about playable characters and monsters and power-ups — these are things you need to build yourself! You'll see how to organize your types with protocols and learn how to use generics to make your code more reusable.

Acknowledgments

We want to thank many people for their assistance in making this book possible:

- **Janie Clayton** For her previous work on the first, second and third editions of *Swift Apprentice*.

- **Erik Kerber** For his previous work on the first and second editions of *Swift Apprentice*.

- **Ben Morrow** For his previous work on the first seven editions of *Swift Apprentice*.

- **Cosmin Pupăză** For his previous work on the fifth, sixth and seventh editions of *Swift Apprentice*.

- **Our families:** For bearing with us in this crazy time as we worked all hours of the night to get this book ready for publication!

- **Everyone at Apple:** For creating an exciting new programming language that we can use everywhere!

- **The Swift Community**: For all the people, both inside and outside of Apple, who have worked very hard to make Swift the best computer language in the world.

- And most importantly, **the readers of Kodeco — especially you!** Thank you so much for reading our site and purchasing this book. Your continued readership and support are what make all of this possible!

Section I: Swift Basics

The chapters in this section will introduce you to the very basics of programming in Swift. From the fundamentals of how computers work up to language structures, you'll cover enough of the language to be able to work with data and organize your code's behavior.

The section begins with some groundwork to get you started.Once you have the basic data types in your head, it'll be time to *do* things with that data, and finally, you'll learn about an essential data type, optionals, that let you express potentially missing data.

These fundamentals will get you Swiftly on your way, and before you know it, you'll be ready for the more advanced topics that follow. Let's get started!

Chapter 1: Expressions, Variables & Constants

By Matt Galloway

Welcome to the book! In this first chapter, you're going to learn a few basics. You'll learn how code works first. Then you'll learn about the tools you'll use to write Swift code.

You'll then start your adventure into Swift by learning some basics, such as code comments, arithmetic operations, constants and variables. These are some of the fundamental building blocks of any language, and Swift is no different.

First, you'll cover the basic workings of computers because it pays to have a grounding before you get into more complicated aspects of programming.

How a Computer Works

You may not believe me when I say it, but a computer is not very smart on its own. The power of a computer comes mostly from how people like you and me program it. If you want to harness the power of a computer successfully — and I assume you do if you're reading this book — it's important to understand how computers work.

It may also surprise you to learn that computers themselves are rather simple machines. At the heart of a computer is a **Central Processing Unit (CPU)**. This component is essentially a math machine. It performs addition, subtraction, and other arithmetical operations on numbers. Everything you see when you operate your computer is built upon a CPU crunching numbers many millions of times per second. Isn't it amazing what can come from just numbers?

The CPU stores the numbers it acts upon in small memory units called **registers**. The CPU can read numbers into registers from the computer's main memory, known as **Random Access Memory (RAM)**. It can also write the number stored in a register back into RAM. This capability allows the CPU to work with large amounts of data that wouldn't all fit in the bank of registers.

Here is a diagram of how this works:

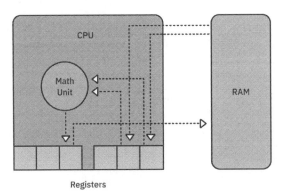

Registers

As the CPU pulls values from RAM into its registers, it uses those values in its math unit and stores the results back in another register.

Each time the CPU makes an addition, a subtraction, a read from RAM or a write to RAM, it's executing a single **instruction**. Each computer program does its work by running thousands to millions of simple instructions. A complex computer program such as your operating system, macOS (yes, that's a computer program too!), consists of millions of instructions.

It's entirely possible to write individual instructions to tell a computer what to do, but it would be immensely time-consuming and tedious for all but the simplest programs. After all, most computer programs aim to do much more than simple math — computer programs let you surf the Internet, manipulate images, and chat with your friends.

Instead of writing individual instructions, you write **source code** (or just code) in a specific **programming language**, which in your case will be Swift. This code is put through a computer program called a **compiler**, which converts the code into those small machine instructions the CPU knows how to execute. Each line of code you write will turn into many instructions — some lines could end up being tens of instructions!

Representing Numbers

As you know by now, numbers are a computer's bread and butter, the fundamental basis of everything it does. Whatever information you send to the compiler will eventually become a number. For example, each character within a block of text is represented by a number. You'll learn more about this in Chapter 2, "Types & Operations", which delves into types, including **strings**, the computer term for a text block.

Images are no exception. In a computer, each image is also represented by a series of numbers. An image consists of thousands or millions of picture elements called **pixels**, where each pixel is a solid color. If you look closely at your computer screen, you can make out these blocks. That is unless you have a particularly high-resolution display with incredibly small pixels! Each of these solid color pixels is usually represented by three numbers: one for the amount of red, one for the amount of green and one for the amount of blue. For example, an entirely red pixel would be 100% red, 0% green and 0% blue.

The numbers the CPU works with are notably different from those you are used to. When dealing with numbers in day-to-day life, you work with them in **base 10**, otherwise known as the **decimal** system. Having used this numerical system for so long, you intuitively understand how it works. So that you can appreciate the CPU's point of view, consider how base 10 works.

The decimal or base 10 number **423** contains **three units, two tens** and **four hundreds**:

1000	100	10	1
0	4	2	3

In the base 10 system, each digit of a number can have a value of 0, 1, 2, 3, 4, 5, 6, 7, 8 or 9, giving a total of 10 possible values for each digit. Yep, that's why it's called base 10! But the actual value of each digit depends on its position within the number. Moving from right to left, each digit gets multiplied by an increasing power of 10. So the multiplier for the far-right position is 10 to the power of 0, which is 1. Moving to the left, the next multiplier is 10 to the power of 1, which is 10. Moving again to the left, the next multiplier is 10 to the power of 2, which is 100. And so on.

This means each digit has a value ten times that of the digit to its right. The number **423** is equal to the following:

```
(0 * 1000) + (4 * 100) + (2 * 10) + (3 * 1) = 423
```

Binary Numbers

Because you've been trained to operate in base 10, you don't have to think about how to read most numbers — it feels quite natural. But to a computer, base 10 is way too complicated! Computers are simple-minded, remember? They like to work with base 2.

Base 2 is often called **binary**, which you've likely heard of before. Base 2 has only two options for each digit: 0 or 1.

Almost all modern computers use binary because, at the physical level, it's easiest to handle only two options for each digit. In digital electronic circuitry, which is mostly what comprises a computer, the presence of an electrical voltage is 1 and the absence is 0 — that's base 2!

> **Note:** There have been computers, both real and imagined, that use the ternary numeral system, which has three possible values instead of two. Computer scientists, engineers and dedicated hackers continue to explore the possibilities of a base-3 computer. See https://en.wikipedia.org/wiki/Ternary_computer and http://hackaday.com/tag/ternary-computer/.

Here's a representation of the base 2 number 1101:

8	4	2	1
1	1	0	1

In the base 10 number system, the place values increase by a factor of 10: 1, 10, 100, 1000, etc. In base 2, they increase by a factor of 2: 1, 2, 4, 8, 16, etc. The general rule is to multiply each digit by an increasing power of the base number — in this case, powers of 2 — moving from right to left.

So the far-right digit represents (1 * 2^0), which is (1 * 1), which is 1. The next digit to the left represents (0 * 2^1), which is (0 * 2), which is 0. In the illustration above, you can see the powers of 2 on top of the blocks.

Put another way, every power of 2 either is (1) or isn't (0) present as a component of a binary number. The decimal version of a binary number is the sum of all the powers of 2 that make up that number. So the binary number 1101 is equal to:

```
(1 * 8) + (1 * 4) + (0 * 2) + (1 * 1) = 13
```

And if you wanted to convert the base 10 number 423 into binary, you would simply need to break down 423 into its component powers of 2. You would wind up with the following:

```
(1 * 256) + (1 * 128) + (0 * 64) + (1 * 32) + (0 * 16) + (0 * 8)
+ (1 * 4) + (1 * 2) + (1 * 1) = 423
```

As you can see by scanning the binary digits in the above equation, the resulting binary number is 110100111. You can prove to yourself that this equals 423 by doing the math!

The computer term given to each digit of a binary number is a **bit** (a contraction of "binary digit"). Eight bits make up a **byte**. Four bits is called a **nibble**, a play on words that shows even old-school computer scientists had a sense of humor.

A computer's limited memory means it can generally deal with numbers up to a certain length. Each register, for example, is usually 32 or 64 bits in length, which is why we speak of 32-bit and 64-bit CPUs.

Therefore, a 32-bit CPU can handle a maximum base-number of 4,294,967,295, which is the base 2 number 11111111111111111111111111111111. That is 32 ones—count them!

A computer can handle numbers larger than the CPU maximum, but the calculations must be split up and managed in a special and longer way, much like the long multiplication you performed in school.

Hexadecimal Numbers

Working with binary numbers can become tedious because writing or typing them can take a long time. For this reason, in computer programming, we often use another number format known as **hexadecimal** or **hex** for short. This is **base 16**.

Of course, there aren't 16 distinct numbers to use for digits; there are only 10. To supplement these, we use the first six letters, **a** through **f**.

They are equivalent to decimal numbers like so:

- a = 10

- b = 11

- c = 12

- d = 13

- e = 14

- f = 15

Here's a base 16 example using the same format as before:

4096	256	16	1
c	0	d	e

Notice first that you can make hexadecimal numbers look like words. That means you can have a little bit of fun. :]

Now the values of each digit refer to powers of 16. In the same way as before, you can convert this number to decimal like so:

```
(12 * 4096) + (0 * 256) + (13 * 16) + (14 * 1) = 49374
```

You translate the letters to their decimal equivalents and then perform the usual calculations.

But why bother with this?

Hexadecimal is useful because each hexadecimal digit can represent precisely four binary digits. The binary number 1111 is equivalent to hexadecimal f. You can simply concatenate the binary digits representing each hexadecimal digit, creating a hexadecimal number shorter than its binary or decimal equivalents.

For example, consider the number c0de from above:

```
c = 1100
0 = 0000
d = 1101
e = 1110

c0de = 1100 0000 1101 1110
```

This is helpful, given how computers use long 32-bit or 64-bit binary numbers. Recall that the largest 32-bit number in decimal is 4,294,967,295. In hexadecimal, it is ffffffff. That's much more compact and clear.

How Code Works

Computers have many constraints, and by themselves, they can only do a small number of things. The power that the computer programmer adds through coding is putting these small things together in the correct order to produce something much bigger.

Coding is much like writing a recipe. You assemble ingredients (the data) and give the computer a step-by-step recipe for using them.

Here's an example:

```
Step 1. Load photo from the hard drive.
Step 2. Resize photo to 400 pixels wide by 300 pixels high.
Step 3. Apply sepia filter to photo.
Step 4. Print photo.
```

This set of steps is what's known as **pseudo-code**. It isn't written in a valid computer programming language but represents the **algorithm** that you want to use. In this case, the algorithm takes a photo, resizes it, applies a filter and then prints it. It's a relatively straightforward algorithm, but it's an algorithm nonetheless!

Swift code is just like this: a step-by-step list of instructions for the computer. These instructions will get more complex as you read this book, but the principle is the same: You are simply telling the computer what to do, one step at a time.

Each programming language is a high-level, pre-defined way of expressing these steps. The compiler knows how to interpret the code you write and convert it into instructions the CPU can execute.

There are many different programming languages, each with its own advantages and disadvantages. Swift is a highly modern language. It incorporates the strengths of many other languages while ironing out some of their weaknesses. In years to come, programmers may look back on Swift as old and crusty, too. But for now, it continues to improve and evolve.

This chapter has briefly covered computer hardware, number representation and code, and how they all work together to create a modern program. That was a lot to cover in one section! Now it's time to learn about the tools you'll use to write in Swift as you follow along with this book.

Playgrounds

The set of tools you use to write software is called a **toolchain**. The part of the toolchain into which you write your code is known as the **Integrated Development Environment** (**IDE**). The most commonly used IDE for Swift is called Xcode, and that's what you'll be using.

Xcode includes a handy document type called a **playground**, which allows you to quickly write and test code without building a complete app. You'll use playgrounds throughout the book to practice coding, so it's essential to understand how they work. That's what you'll learn during the rest of this chapter.

Creating a Playground

To get started with a playground, click **File ▸ New ▸ Playground**. Xcode will present you with a choice of templates:

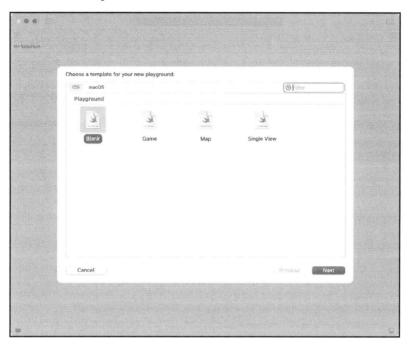

The platform you choose defines which version of the template Xcode will use to create the playground. Currently, your options are **iOS** or **macOS**. Each platform comes with its own environment set up and ready for you to begin playing around with code.

For this book, choose whichever platform you wish. You won't be writing any platform-specific code; instead, you'll be learning the core principles of the Swift language.

Select the **Blank** template and click **Next**. Xcode will now ask you to name the playground and select a location to save it.

The name is merely cosmetic and for your own use; when you create your playgrounds, feel free to choose names that will help you remember what they're about. For example, while working through Chapter 1, "Expressions, Variables & Constants", you may want to name your playground **Chapter1**.

Click **Create** to create and save the playground. Xcode then presents you with the playground, like so:

Even blank playgrounds don't start empty but have some basic starter code to get you going. Don't worry — you'll soon learn what this code means.

Playgrounds Overview

At first glance, a playground may look like a fancy text editor. Well, here's some news for you: It is essentially just that!

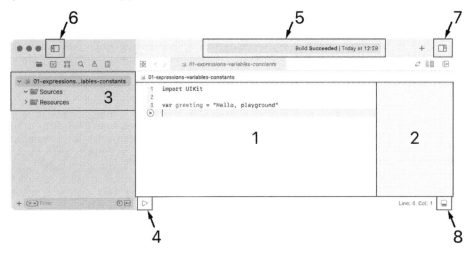

The previous screenshot highlights the first and most important things to know about:

1. **Source editor**: This is the area in which you'll write your Swift code. It's much like a text editor such as Notepad or TextEdit. You'll notice the use of what's known as a monospaced font, meaning all characters are the same width. This even spacing makes the code much easier to read and format.

2. **Results sidebar**: This area shows the results of your code. You'll learn more about how code executes as you read through the book. The results sidebar will be the main place to confirm your code is working as expected.

3. **Resources tree**: This shows the list of resources contained within the playground. Here you'll find a tree of resources for the playground, starting with the main playground file, then additional sources and resources. This allows you to build complex playgrounds that split the sources into multiple files.

4. **Execution control**: This control lets you run the entire playground file or clear state so you can run it again. By default, playgrounds do not execute automatically. You can change this setting to execute with every change by long-pressing it and selecting "Automatically Run".

5. **Activity viewer**: This shows the status of the playground. The screenshot shows that the playground has finished executing and is ready to handle more code in the source editor. When the playground executes, this viewer will indicate this with a spinner.

6. **Left panel control**: This toggles the left panel where the resources tree is. Keep this closed for now.

7. **Right panel control**: This toggles the right panel. Here you'll find information about the source file that's open. You'll usually keep this closed.

8. **Bottom panel control**: This toggles the bottom panel. In here, you'll find output from the running playground. You'll open this later.

You can turn on line numbers on the left side of the source editor by clicking **Xcode ▸ Preferences… ▸ Text Editing ▸ Line Numbers**. Line numbers can be handy when you want to refer to parts of your code.

Playgrounds execute the code in the source editor from top to bottom. The play button floats next to each line as you move the cursor over it and lets you run from the beginning of the file up to and including the line you click. To force a re-execution, you can click on the **Execution control** button twice–once to stop and clear it and again to rerun.

Once the playground execution is finished, Xcode updates the results sidebar to show the results of the corresponding line in the source editor. You'll see how to interpret the results of your code as you work through the examples in this book.

> **Note**: Under certain conditions, Xcode may incorrectly disable line-based execution. In these cases, use the execution control button to run the entire playground.

Getting Started With Swift

Now that you know how computers work and what this "playground" thing is, it's time to start writing some Swift!

You can follow along with your own playground. Simply create one and type in the code as you go!

First up is something that helps you organize your code. Read on!

Code Comments

The Swift compiler generates executable code from your source code. To accomplish this, it uses a detailed set of rules you will learn about in this book. Sometimes these details can obscure the big picture of *why* you wrote your code a certain way or even what problem you are solving. To prevent this, it's good to document what you wrote so that the next human who passes by will be able to make sense of your work. That next human, after all, may be a future you.

Like most other programming languages, Swift allows you to document your code using what are called **comments**. These allow you to write any text directly alongside your code and are ignored by the compiler.

The first way to write a comment is like so:

```
// This is a comment. It is not executed.
```

This is a **single-line comment**.

You could stack these up like so to allow you to write paragraphs:

```
// This is also a comment.
// Over multiple lines.
```

However, there is a better way to write comments which span multiple lines. Like so:

```
/* This is also a comment.
   Over many..
   many...
   many lines. */
```

This is a **multi-line comment**. The start is denoted by /* and the end is denoted by */. Simple!

Swift also allows you to nest comments like so:

```
/* This is a comment.

/* And inside it
is
another comment.
*/

Back to the first.
*/
```

This capability might not seem particularly interesting, but it may be if you have seen other programming languages. Many do not allow you to nest comments like this, as when it sees the first */; it thinks you are closing the first comment. Use code comments where necessary to document your code, explain your reasoning, or simply leave jokes for your colleagues. :]

Printing Out

It's also useful to see the results of what your code is doing. In Swift, you can achieve this through the `print` command.

`print` will output whatever you want to the **debug area** (sometimes referred to as the console).

For example, consider the following code:

```
print("Hello, Swift Apprentice reader!")
```

This statement will output a nice message to the debug area like so:

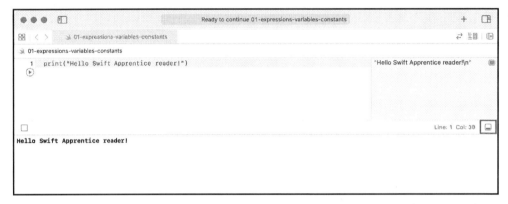

You can hide or show the debug area using the button highlighted in the box in the above screenshot. You can also click **View ▸ Debug Area ▸ Show Debug Area** to do the same thing.

Arithmetic Operations

When you take one or more pieces of data and turn them into another piece of data, this is known as an **operation**.

The simplest way to understand operations is to think about arithmetic. The addition operation takes two numbers and converts them into the sum of the two numbers. The subtraction operation takes two numbers and converts them into the difference between the two numbers.

You'll find simple arithmetic all over your apps; from tallying the number of "likes" on a post, to calculating the correct size and position of a button or a window, numbers are indeed everywhere!

In this section, you'll learn about Swift's various arithmetic operations by considering how they apply to numbers. In later chapters, you see operations for types other than numbers.

Simple Operations

All operations in Swift use a symbol known as the **operator** to denote the type of operation they perform. Consider the four arithmetic operations you learned in your early school days: addition, subtraction, multiplication and division. For these simple operations, Swift uses the following operators:

- Add: +

- Subtract: −

- Multiply: *

- Divide: /

These operators are used like so:

```
2 + 6
10 − 2
2 * 4
24 / 3
```

Each of these lines is an **expression**, meaning each has a value. In these cases, all four expressions have the same value: 8. Notice how the code looks similar to how you would write the operations out on pen and paper. You can enter these straight into your playground.

The line numbers in light blue have not yet run. To run your code, click on the light-blue play button on the last line next to the cursor.

Upon running, the playground removes the blue sidebar from the lines that have run; you can also see the values of these expressions in the right-hand bar, known as the **results sidebar**.

If you want, you can remove the whitespace surrounding the operator:

```
2+6
```

When you make this change, the blue sidebar reappears to indicate which lines need to be rerun. You can run again by clicking the blue arrow or using the keyboard shortcut **Shift-Enter**.

> **Note**: Shift-Enter runs all statements up to the current cursor and advances to the next line. This shortcut makes it easy to advance one line and run the entire playground step-by-step. It's a great shortcut to commit to muscle memory.

Removing the whitespace is all or nothing; you can't mix styles. For example:

```
2+6    // OK
2 + 6 // OK
2 +6  // ERROR
2+ 6  // ERROR
```

The first error will be:

```
Consecutive statements on a line must be separated by ';'
```

And for the second error, you'll see:

```
'+' is not a postfix unary operator
```

You don't need to understand these error messages at the moment. Just be aware that you must have whitespace on both sides of the operator or no whitespace on either side!

It's often easier to read expressions when you have white space on either side.

Decimal Numbers

All of the operations above have used whole numbers, more formally known as **integers**. However, as you will know, not every number is whole.

As an example, consider the following:

```
22 / 7
```

You may be surprised to know this results in the number 3. If you only use integers in your expression, Swift also makes the result an integer. In this case, the result is rounded down to the next integer.

You can tell Swift to use decimal numbers by changing the statement to the following:

```
22.0 / 7.0
```

This time, the result is 3.142857142857143, as expected.

The Remainder Operation

The four operations you've seen so far are easy to understand because you've been doing them for most of your life. Swift also has more complex operations. All of them are standard mathematical operations, just less common. Let's turn to them now.

The first is the **remainder** operation, also called the modulo operation. In division, the denominator goes into the numerator a whole number of times plus a remainder. This remainder is exactly what the remainder operation gives. For example, 10 modulo 3 equals 1 because 3 goes into 10 three times, with a remainder of 1.

In Swift, the remainder operator is the % symbol, and you use it like so:

```
28 % 10
```

In this case, the result equals 8 because 10 goes into 28 twice with a remainder of 8. If you want to compute the same thing using decimal numbers, you do it like so:

```
(28.0).truncatingRemainder(dividingBy: 10.0)
```

This line computes 28 divided by 10 and then **truncates** the result, chopping off any extra decimals and returns the remainder of that. The result is identical to % when there are no decimals.

Shift Operations

The **shift left** and **shift right** operations take the binary form of a decimal number and shift the digits left or right, respectively. Then they return the decimal form of the new binary number.

For example, the decimal number 14 in binary, padded to 8 digits, is `00001110`. Shifting this left by two places results in `00111000`, which is 56 in decimal.

Here's an illustration of what happens during this shift operation:

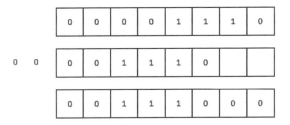

The digits that fill the empty spots on the right become `0`. The digits that fall off the end on the left are lost. Shifting right is the same, but the digits move to the right.

The operators for these two operations are as follows:

- Shift left: <<

- Shift right: >>

These are the first operators you've seen that contain more than one character. Operators can contain any number of characters.

Here's an example that uses both of these operators:

```
1 << 3
32 >> 2
```

Both of these values equal the number 8.

One reason for using shifts is to make multiplying or dividing by powers of two easy. Notice that shifting left by one is the same as multiplying by two, shifting left by two is the same as multiplying by four, and so on.

Likewise, shifting right by one is the same as dividing by two, shifting right by two is the same as dividing by four, and so on.

In the old days, code often used this trick because shifting bits is much simpler for a CPU to do than complex multiplication and division arithmetic. Therefore the code was quicker if it used shifting.

However, CPUs are much faster these days, and compilers can even convert multiplication and division by powers of two into shifts for you. So you'll see shifting only for binary twiddling, which you probably won't see unless you become an embedded systems programmer!

Order of Operations

Of course, it's likely that when you calculate a value, you'll want to use multiple operators. Here's an example of how to do this in Swift:

```
((8000 / (5 * 10)) - 32) >> (29 % 5)
```

Note the use of parentheses, which in Swift serve two purposes: to make it clear to anyone reading the code — including yourself — what you meant, and to disambiguate. For example, consider the following:

```
350 / 5 + 2
```

Does this equal 72 (350 divided by 5, plus 2) or 50 (350 divided by 7)? Those of you who paid attention in school will be screaming, "72!" And you would be right!

Swift uses the same reasoning and achieves this through what's known as **operator precedence**. The division operator (/) has higher precedence than the addition operator (+), so the code executes the division operation first in this example.

If you wanted Swift to do the addition first — that is, to return 50 — then you could use parentheses like so:

```
350 / (5 + 2)
```

The precedence rules follow the same that you learned in math at school. Multiply and divide have the same precedence, higher than add and subtract, which also have the same precedence.

Math Functions

Swift also has a vast range of math functions for you to use when necessary. You never know when you'll need to pull out some trigonometry, especially when you're a pro at Swift and writing games!

> **Note**: Not all of these functions are part of Swift. The operating system provides some. Don't remove the import statement that comes as part of the playground template or Xcode will tell you it can't find these functions.

For example, consider the following:

```
sin(45 * Double.pi / 180)
// 0.7071067811865475

cos(135 * Double.pi / 180)
// -0.7071067811865475
```

These convert an angle from degrees to radians and then compute the sine and cosine, respectively. Notice how both use `Double.pi`, a constant Swift provides us, ready-made with pi to as much precision as possible by the computer. Neat!

Then there's this:

```
(2.0).squareRoot()
// 1.414213562373095
```

This code computes the square root of 2. Did you know that the sine of 45° equals 1 over the square root of 2? Try it out!

Not mentioning these would be a shame:

```
max(5, 10)
// 10

min(-5, -10)
// -10
```

These compute the maximum and minimum of two numbers, respectively.

If you're particularly adventurous, you can even combine these functions like so:

```
max((2.0).squareRoot(), Double.pi / 2)
// 1.570796326794897
```

Naming Data

At its simplest, computer programming is all about manipulating data. Remember, everything you see on your screen can be reduced to numbers you send to the CPU. Sometimes you represent and work with this data as various types of numbers, but other times the data comes in more complex forms such as text, images and collections.

In your Swift code, you can give each piece of data a name you can refer to later. The name carries with it a **type annotation** that denotes what sort of data the name refers to, such as text, numbers, or a date. You'll learn about some basic types in this chapter and encounter many other types throughout this book.

Constants

Take a look at this:

```
let number: Int = 10
```

This code declares a constant called `number`, of type `Int`. Then it sets the value of the constant to the number `10`.

> **Note**: Thinking back to operators, here's another one. The equals sign, =, the **assignment operator**.

The type `Int` can store integers. The way you store decimal numbers is like so:

```
let pi: Double = 3.14159
```

This constant is similar to the `Int` constant, except the name and the types are different. This time, the constant is a `Double`, which can store decimals with high precision.

There's also a type called `Float`, short for floating-point that stores decimals with lower precision than `Double`. In fact, `Double` has about double the precision of `Float`, which is why it's called `Double` in the first place. A `Float` takes up less memory than a `Double`, but generally, memory use for numbers isn't a huge issue and you'll see `Double` used in most places.

Once you've declared a constant, you can't change its data. For example, consider the following code:

```
number = 0
```

This code produces an error:

```
Cannot assign to value: 'number' is a 'let' constant
```

In Xcode, you would see the error represented this way:

```
let number: Int = 10
number = 0 /* error: cannot assign to value: 'number' is a 'let' constant */    ⊙  Cannot assign to value: 'number' is a 'let' constant
```

Constants are useful for values that aren't going to change. For example, if you were modeling an airplane and needed to refer to the total number of seats installed, you could use a constant.

You might even use a constant for something like a person's age. Even though their age will change as their birthday comes, you might only be concerned with their age at this particular instant.

Variables

Often you want to change the data behind a name. For example, if you were keeping track of your bank account balance with deposits and withdrawals, you might use a variable rather than a constant.

If your program's data never changed, it would be rather dull! But as you've seen, changing the data behind a constant is impossible.

When you know you'll need to change some data, use a variable to represent that data instead of a constant. You declare a variable in a similar way, like so:

```
var variableNumber: Int = 42
```

Only the first part of the statement is different: You declare constants using `let`, whereas you declare variables using `var`.

Once you've declared a variable, you're free to change it to whatever you wish, as long as the type remains the same. For example, to change the variable declared above, you could do this:

```
variableNumber = 0
variableNumber = 1_000_000
```

To change a variable, you simply assign it a new value.

Note: In Swift, you can optionally use underscores to make larger numbers more human-readable. The quantity and placement of the underscores is up to you.

Now is a good time to take a closer look at the results sidebar of the playground. When you type the code above into a playground, you'll see that the results sidebar on the right shows the current value of `variableNumber` at each line:

```
var variableNumber: Int = 42     42
variableNumber = 0               0
variableNumber = 1_000_000       1000000
```

The results sidebar will show a relevant result for each line if one exists. In the case of a variable or constant, the result will be the new value, whether you've just declared a constant or declared or reassigned a variable.

Using Meaningful Names

Always try to choose meaningful names for your variables and constants. Good names act as documentation and make your code easy to read. A good name *specifically* describes the role of a variable or constant. Here are some examples of good names:

- `personAge`
- `numberOfPeople`
- `gradePointAverage`

Often a bad name is not descriptive enough. Here are some examples of bad names:

- `a`
- `temp`
- `average`

The key is to ensure that you'll understand what the variable or constant refers to when you reread it later. Don't make the mistake of thinking you have an infallible memory! It's common in computer programming to look back at your code as early as a day or two later and forget what it does. Make it easier by giving your variables and constants intuitive, precise names.

Also, note how the names above are written. In Swift, it is common to **camel case** names. For variables and constants, follow these rules to case your names properly:

- Start with a lowercase letter.
- If the name is made up of multiple words, join them together and start the other words with an uppercase letter.
- If one of these words is an abbreviation, write the entire abbreviation in the same case (e.g.: `sourceURL` and `urlDescription`)

In Swift, you can even use the full range of Unicode characters. For example, you could declare a variable like so:

```
var 🐶🐮: Int = -1
```

That might make you laugh, but use caution with special characters like these. They are harder to type and likely to bring you more pain than amusement.

Special characters like these probably make more sense in *data* that you store rather than in Swift code; you'll learn more about Unicode in Chapter 9, "Strings."

Increment and Decrement

A common operation that you will need is to increment or decrement a variable. In Swift, you achieve it like so:

```
var counter: Int = 0

counter += 1
// counter = 1

counter -= 1
// counter = 0
```

The counter variable begins as 0. The increment sets its value to 1, and then the decrement sets its value back to 0.

These operators are similar to the assignment operator (=), except they also perform an addition or subtraction. They take the current value of the variable, add or subtract the given value and assign the result to the variable.

In other words, the code above is shorthand for the following:

```
var counter: Int = 0
counter = counter + 1
counter = counter - 1
```

Similarly, the *= and /= operators do the equivalent for multiplication and division, respectively:

```
counter = 10

counter *= 3  // same as counter = counter * 3
// counter = 30

counter /= 2  // same as counter = counter / 2
// counter = 15
```

Mini-exercises

If you haven't been following along with the code in Xcode, now's the time to create a new playground and try some exercises to test yourself!

1. Declare a constant of type Int called myAge and set it to your age.

2. Declare a variable of type Double called averageAge. Initially, set it to your own age. Then, set it to the average of your age and the age of 30.

3. Create a constant called testNumber and initialize it with whatever integer you want. Next, create another constant called evenOdd and set it equal to testNumber modulo 2. Now change testNumber to various numbers. What do you notice about evenOdd?

4. Create a variable called answer and initialize it with the value 0. Increment it by 1. Add 10 to it. Multiply it by 10. Then, shift it to the right by 3. After all of these operations, what's the answer?

Challenges

Before moving on, here are some challenges to test your knowledge of variables and constants. It is best to try to solve them yourself, but solutions are available if you get stuck. These came with the download or are available at the printed book's source code link listed in the introduction.

Challenge 1: Variables

Declare a constant Int called myAge and set it equal to your age. Also, declare an Int variable called dogs and set it equal to the number of dogs you own. Then imagine you bought a new puppy and increment the dogs variable by one.

Challenge 2: Make it Compile

Given the following code:

```
age: Int = 16
print(age)
age = 30
print(age)
```

Modify the first line so that it compiles. Did you use var or let?

Challenge 3: Compute the Answer

Consider the following code:

```
let x: Int = 46
let y: Int = 10
```

Work out what answer equals when you add the following lines of code:

```
// 1
let answer1: Int = (x * 100) + y
// 2
let answer2: Int = (x * 100) + (y * 100)
// 3
let answer3: Int = (x * 100) + (y / 10)
```

Challenge 4: Add Parentheses

Add as many parentheses to the following calculation, ensuring that it doesn't change the result of the calculation.

```
8 - 4 * 2 + 6 / 3 * 4
```

Challenge 5: Average Rating

Declare three constants called rating1, rating2 and rating3 of type Double and assign each a value. Calculate the average of the three and store the result in a constant named averageRating.

Challenge 6: Electrical Power

The power of an electrical appliance is calculated by multiplying the voltage by the current. Declare a constant named voltage of type Double and assign it a value. Then declare a constant called current of type Double and assign it a value. Finally, calculate the power of the electrical appliance you've just created, storing it in a constant called power of type Double.

Challenge 7: Electrical Resistance

The resistance of such an appliance can then be calculated (in a long-winded way) as the power divided by the current squared. Calculate the resistance and store it in a constant called resistance of type Double.

Challenge 8: Random Integer

You can create a random integer number using the function `arc4random()`. This function picks a number anywhere between 0 and 4294967295. You can use the modulo operator to truncate this random number to whatever range you want. Declare a constant `randomNumber` and assign it a random number generated with `arc4random()`. Then calculate a constant called `diceRoll` and use the random number you just found to create a random number between 1 and 6. (**Hint**: You must include the line `import Foundation` to access `arc4random()`. If this method of creating a random number seems primitive, you are right! There is an easier, more expressive way to generate random numbers you will learn about in Chapter 4, "Advanced Control Flow".)

Challenge 9: Quadratic Equations

A quadratic equation has the form `a·x² + b·x + c = 0`. The values of x which satisfy this are solved by using the equation `x = (-b ± sqrt(b² - 4·a·c)) / (2·a)`. Declare three constants named `a`, `b` and `c` of type `Double`. Then calculate the two values for x using the equation above (noting that the ± means plus or minus — so one value of x for each). Store the results in constants called `root1` and `root2` of type `Double`.

Key Points

- Computers, at their most fundamental level, perform simple mathematics.

- A programming language allows you to write code, which the compiler converts into instructions that the CPU can execute.

- Computers operate on numbers in base 2 form, otherwise known as binary.

- The IDE you use to write Swift code is named Xcode.

- By providing immediate feedback about how code is executing, playgrounds allow you to write and test Swift code quickly and efficiently.

- Code comments are denoted by a line starting with // or multiple lines bookended with /* and */.

- You use comments to document your code.

- You can use `print` to output information to the debug area.

- The arithmetic operators are:

```
Add: +
Subtract: -
Multiply: *
Divide: /
Remainder: %
```

- Swift makes many functions `min()`, `max()`, `squareRoot()`, `sin()` and `cos()`. You will learn many more throughout this book.

- Constants and variables give names to data.

- Once you've declared a constant, you can't change its data, but you can change a variable's data at any time.

- Always give variables and constants meaningful names to save yourself and your colleagues headaches later.

- Operators to perform arithmetic and then assign back to the variable:

```
Add and assign: +=
Subtract and assign: -=
Multiply and assign: *=
Divide and assign: /=
```

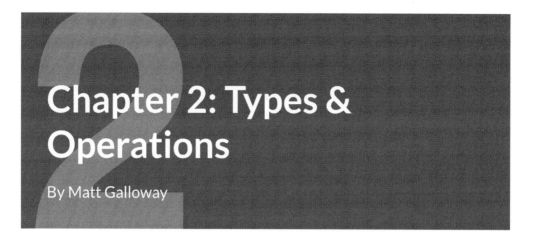

Chapter 2: Types & Operations

By Matt Galloway

Now that you know how to perform basic operations and manipulate data using these operations, it's time to learn more about **types**. Formally, a **type** describes a set of values and the operations you can perform on them. In this chapter, you'll learn about handling different types, including strings that allow you to represent text. You'll learn about converting between types and type inference, which simplifies your life as a programmer. Finally, you'll learn about tuple types, which allow you to group values of any type together.

Type Conversion

Sometimes you'll have data in one format and need to convert it to another. The naïve way to attempt this would be like so:

```
var integer: Int = 100
var decimal: Double = 12.5
integer = decimal
```

Swift will complain if you try to do this and spit out an error on the third line:

```
Cannot assign value of type 'Double' to type 'Int'
```

Some programming languages aren't as strict and will perform conversions like this silently. Experience shows this kind of silent, automatic conversion is a source of software bugs and often hurts performance. Swift disallows you from assigning a value of one type to another and avoids these issues.

Remember, computers rely on us programmers to tell them what to do. In Swift, that includes being explicit about type conversions. If you want the conversion to happen, you have to say so!

Instead of simply assigning, you need to say that you want to convert the type explicitly. You do it like so:

```
integer = Int(decimal)
```

The assignment on the third line now tells Swift unequivocally that you want to convert from the original type, Double, to the new type, Int.

> **Note**: In this case, assigning the decimal value to the integer results in a loss of precision: The integer variable ends up with the value 12 instead of 12.5. This danger of loss is why it's important to be explicit. Swift wants to ensure you know what you're doing and that you may lose data by performing the type conversion.

Operators With Mixed Types

So far, you've only seen operators acting independently on integers or doubles. But what if you have an integer that you want to multiply by a double?

You might think you could do it like this:

```
let hourlyRate: Double = 19.5
let hoursWorked: Int = 10
let totalCost: Double = hourlyRate * hoursWorked
```

If you try that, you'll get an error on the final line:

```
Binary operator '*' cannot be applied to operands of type
'Double' and 'Int'
```

This error is because, in Swift, you can't apply the * operator to mixed types. This rule also applies to the other arithmetic operators. It may seem surprising at first, but Swift is being rather helpful.

Swift forces you to be explicit about what you mean when you want an Int multiplied by a Double because the result can be only *one* type. Do you want the result to be an Int, converting the Double to an Int before performing the multiplication? Or do you want the result to be a Double, converting the Int to a Double before performing the multiplication?

In this example, you want the result to be a Double. You don't want an Int because, in that case, Swift would convert the hourlyRate constant into an Int to perform the multiplication, rounding it down to 19 and losing the precision of the Double.

You need to tell Swift you want it to consider the hoursWorked constant to be a Double, like so:

```
let totalCost: Double = hourlyRate * Double(hoursWorked)
```

Now, each of the operands will be a Double when Swift multiplies them, so totalCost is a Double as well.

Type Inference

Every variable or constant you've seen in this book so far includes a type annotation. You may be asking yourself why you need to bother writing the : Int and : Double since the right-hand side of the assignment *is already* an Int or a Double. It's redundant, to be sure; your crazy-clever brain can see this without too much work.

It turns out the Swift compiler can deduce this as well. It doesn't need you to tell it the type all the time — it can figure it out on its own. This is done through a process called **type inference**. Not all programming languages have this, but Swift does, and it's a key component of Swift's power as a language.

You can simply drop the type in most places where you see one.

For example, consider the following constant declaration:

```
let typeInferredInt = 42
```

Sometimes it's useful to check the inferred type of a variable or constant. You can do this in a playground by holding down the **Option** key and clicking on the variable or constant's name. Xcode will display a popover like this:

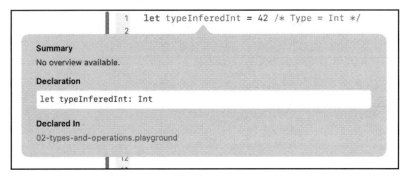

Xcode tells you the inferred type by giving you the declaration you would have used without type inference. In this case, the type is Int.

It works for other types, too:

```
let typeInferredDouble = 3.14159
```

Option-clicking on this reveals the following:

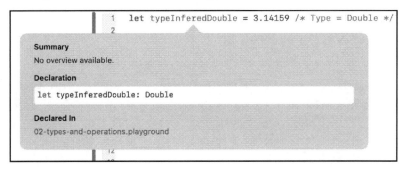

You can see from this that type inference isn't magic. Swift is simply doing what your brain does very easily. Programming languages that don't use type inference can often feel verbose because you must specify the often obvious type each time you declare a variable or constant.

> **Note**: In later chapters, you'll learn about more complex types where sometimes Swift can't infer the type. That's a pretty rare case, though, and you'll see type inference used for most of the code examples in this book — except in cases where we want to highlight the type for you.

Sometimes you want to define a constant or variable and ensure it's a certain type, even though what you're assigning to it is a different type. You saw earlier how you could convert from one type to another. For example, consider the following:

```
let wantADouble = 3
```

Here, Swift infers the type of `wantADouble` as `Int`. But what if you wanted `Double` instead?

The first thing you could do is the following:

```
let actuallyDouble = Double(3)
```

This is like you saw before with type conversion.

Another option would be to not use type inference at all and do the following:

```
let actuallyDouble: Double = 3
```

There is a third option, like so:

```
let actuallyDouble = 3 as Double
```

This uses a new keyword you haven't seen before, `as`. It also performs a type conversion, and you'll see it again later in this book.

> **Note**: Literal values like 3 don't have a type, and it's only when using them in an expression or assigning them to a constant or variable that Swift infers a type for them.
>
> A literal number value that doesn't contain a decimal point can be used as an Int as well as a Double. This is why you're allowed to assign the value 3 to constant actuallyDouble.
>
> Literal number values that *do* contain a decimal point cannot be integers. This means we could have avoided this entire discussion had we started with:
>
> ```
> let wantADouble = 3.0
> ```
>
> Sorry! :]

Mini-exercises

1. Create a constant called age1 and set it equal to 42. Create a constant called age2 and set it equal to 21. Check using Option-click that the type for both has been inferred correctly as Int.

2. Create a constant called avg1 and set it equal to the average of age1 and age2 using the naïve operation (age1 + age2) / 2. Use Option-click to check the type and check the result of avg1. Why is it wrong?

3. Correct the mistake in the above exercise by converting age1 and age2 to type Double in the formula. Use Option-click to check the type and check the result of avg1. Why is it now correct?

Strings

Numbers are essential in programming, but they aren't the only type of data you need to work within your apps. Text is also an extremely common data type used to represent things like people's names, addresses, or even the words of a book. All of these are examples of text that an app might need to handle.

Most computer programming languages store text in a data type called a **string**. This chapter introduces you to strings, first by giving background on strings and then showing you how to use them in Swift.

How Computers Represent Strings

Computers think of strings as a collection of individual **characters**. In Chapter 1, "Expressions, Variables & Constants", you learned that numbers are the language of CPUs, and all code, in whatever programming language, can be reduced to raw numbers. Strings are no different!

That may sound very strange. How can characters be numbers? At its base, a computer needs to translate a character into the computer's language, and it does so by assigning each character a different number. This forms a two-way mapping from characters to numbers called a **character set**.

When you press a character key on your keyboard, you are actually communicating the number of the character to the computer. Your word processor application converts that number into a picture of the character or glyph, which gets presented to you.

Unicode

In isolation, a computer can choose whatever character set mapping it likes. If the computer wants the letter **a** to equal the number 10, then so be it. But when computers start talking to each other, they need to use a common character set.

If two computers used different character sets, they would think the strings contained different characters when one computer transferred a string to the other.

There have been several standards over the years, but the most modern standard is **Unicode**, which defines the character set mapping that almost all computers use today.

> **Note**: You can read more about Unicode at its official website, http://unicode.org/.

As an example, consider the word **cafe**. The Unicode standard tells us that the letters of this word should be mapped to numbers like so:

c	a	f	e
99	97	102	101

The number associated with each character is called a **code point**. So in the example above, **c** uses code point 99, **a** uses code point 97, and so on.

Of course, Unicode is not just for the simple Latin characters used in English, such as **c**, **a**, **f** and **e**. It also lets you map characters from languages around the world. The word **cafe**, as you're probably aware, is derived from French, in which it's written as **café**. Unicode maps these characters like so:

c	a	f	é
99	97	102	233

And here's an example using Chinese characters (this, according to Google translate, means "Computer Programming"):

电	脑	编	程
30005	33041	32534	31243

You've probably heard of emojis, which are small pictures you can use in your text. These pictures are, in fact, just normal characters and are also mapped by Unicode. For example:

💩	😀
128169	128512

This is only two characters. The code points for these are very large numbers, but each is still only a single code point. The computer considers these as no different than any other two characters.

> **Note**: The word "emoji" comes from Japanese, where "e" means picture and "moji" means character.

Strings in Swift

Like any reasonable programming language, Swift can work directly with characters and strings. It does so through the data types `Character` and `String`. In this section, you'll learn about these data types and how to work with them.

Characters and Strings

The `Character` data type can store a single character. For example:

```
let characterA: Character = "a"
```

This stores the character **a**. It can hold any character — even an emoji:

```
let characterDog: Character = "🐶"
```

But this data type is designed to hold only single characters. On the other hand, the `String` data type stores multiple characters. For example:

```
let stringDog: String = "Dog"
```

It's as simple as that! The right-hand side of this expression is known as a **string literal**; it's the Swift syntax for representing a string.

Of course, type inference applies here as well. If you remove the type in the above declaration, then Swift does the right thing and makes the `stringDog` a `String` constant:

```
let stringDog = "Dog" // Inferred to be of type String
```

Note: There's no such thing as a character literal in Swift. A character is simply a string of length one. However, Swift infers the type of any string literal to be `String`, so if you want a `Character` instead, you must make the type explicit.

Concatenation

You can do much more than create simple strings. Sometimes you need to manipulate a string, and one common way to do so is to combine it with another string.

In Swift, you do this in a rather simple way: by using the addition operator. Just as you can add numbers, you can add strings:

```
var message = "Hello" + " my name is "
let name = "Matt"
message += name // "Hello my name is Matt"
```

You need to declare `message` as a variable rather than a constant because you want to modify it. You can add string literals together, as in the first line, and add string variables or constants together, as in the last line.

It's also possible to add characters to a string. However, Swift's strictness with types means you have to be explicit when doing so, just as you have to be when you work with numbers if one is an `Int` and the other is a `Double`.

To add a character to a string, you do this:

```
let exclamationMark: Character = "!"
message += String(exclamationMark) // "Hello my name is Matt!"
```

With this code, you explicitly convert the `Character` to a `String` before adding it to `message`.

Interpolation

You can also build up a string by using **interpolation**, which is a special Swift syntax that lets you build a string in a way that's easy to read:

```
message = "Hello my name is \(name)!" // "Hello my name is Matt!"
```

I'm sure you'll agree that this is much more readable than the previous section's example. It's an extension of the string literal syntax, whereby you replace certain parts of the string with other values. You enclose the value you want to insert in parentheses preceded by a backslash.

This syntax works, in the same way, to build a string from other data types, such as numbers:

```
let oneThird = 1.0 / 3.0
let oneThirdLongString = "One third is \(oneThird) as a
decimal."
```

Here, you use a `Double` in the interpolation. At the end of this code, your `oneThirdLongString` constant will contain the following:

```
One third is 0.3333333333333333 as a decimal.
```

Of course, it would take infinite characters to represent one-third as a decimal because it's a repeating decimal. String interpolation with a `Double` gives you no way to control the precision of the resulting string. This is an unfortunate consequence of using string interpolation: It's simple but offers no ability to customize the output.

Multi-line Strings

Swift has a neat way to express strings that contain multiple lines. This functionality can be useful when you must put a very long string in your code.

You do it like so:

```
let bigString = """
  You can have a string
  that contains multiple
  lines
  by
  doing this.
  """
print(bigString)
```

The three double quotes signify that this is a multiline string. The first and final newlines do not become part of the string. This makes it more flexible as you don't have to have the three double quotes on the same line as the string.

In the case above, it will print the following:

```
You can have a string
that contains multiple
lines
by
doing this.
```

Notice that the two-space margin in the multiline string literal is stripped out of the result. Swift looks at the number of leading spaces on the final three double-quotes line. Using this as a baseline, Swift requires that all lines above it have at least that much space so it can remove it from each line. This rule lets you format your code with pretty indentation without affecting the output.

Mini-exercises

1. Create a string constant called `firstName` and initialize it to your first name. Also, create a string constant called `lastName` and initialize it to your last name.

2. Create a string constant called `fullName` by adding the `firstName` and `lastName` constants together, separated by a space.

3. Using interpolation, create a string constant called `myDetails` that uses the `fullName` constant to create a string introducing yourself. For example, my string would read: `"Hello, my name is Matt Galloway."`.

Tuples

Sometimes data comes in pairs or triplets. An example is a pair of (x, y) coordinates on a 2D grid. Similarly, a set of coordinates on a 3D grid is comprised of an x-value, a y-value and a z-value. In Swift, you can represent such related data in a straightforward way by using a *tuple*.

A tuple is a type that represents data composed of more than one value of any type. You can have as many values in your tuple as you like. For example, you can define a pair of 2D coordinates where each axis value is an integer, like so:

```
let coordinates: (Int, Int) = (2, 3)
```

The type of coordinates is (Int, Int). The types of the values within the tuple, in this case, Int, are separated by commas and surrounded by parentheses. The code for creating the tuple is much the same, with each value separated by commas and surrounded by parentheses.

Type inference can infer tuple types too:

```
let coordinates = (2, 3)
```

You could similarly create a tuple of Double values, like so:

```
let coordinatesDoubles = (2.1, 3.5)
// Inferred to be of type (Double, Double)
```

Or you could mix and match the types comprising the tuple, like so:

```
let coordinatesMixed = (2.1, 3)
// Inferred to be of type (Double, Int)
```

And here's how to access the data inside a tuple:

```
let x1 = coordinates.0
let y1 = coordinates.1
```

You can reference each item by its position in the tuple, starting with zero. So in this example, x1 will equal 2 and y1 will equal 3.

> **Note**: Starting with zero is a common convention in computer programming called **zero indexing**. You'll see this again in Chapter 7, "Arrays, Dictionaries & Sets."

In the previous example, it may not be immediately apparent that the first value, at index 0, is the x-coordinate, and the second value, at index 1, is the y-coordinate. This ambiguity is another demonstration of why it's essential to *always* name your variables in a way that avoids confusion.

Fortunately, Swift allows you to name the individual parts of a tuple, and you can be explicit about what each part represents. For example:

```
let coordinatesNamed = (x: 2, y: 3)
// Inferred to be of type (x: Int, y: Int)
```

Here, the code annotates the values of coordinatesNamed to contain a label for each part of the tuple.

Then, when you need to access each part of the tuple, you can access it by its name:

```
let x2 = coordinatesNamed.x
let y2 = coordinatesNamed.y
```

This code is easier to understand. More often than not, it's helpful to name the components of your tuples.

If you want to access multiple parts of the tuple at the same time, as in the examples above, you can also use a shorthand syntax to make it easier:

```
let coordinates3D = (x: 2, y: 3, z: 1)
let (x3, y3, z3) = coordinates3D
```

This example declares three new constants, x3, y3 and z3, and assigns each part of the tuple to them. The code is equivalent to the following:

```
let coordinates3D = (x: 2, y: 3, z: 1)
let x3 = coordinates3D.x
let y3 = coordinates3D.y
let z3 = coordinates3D.z
```

If you want to ignore a certain element of the tuple, you can replace the corresponding part of the declaration with an underscore. For example, if you were performing a 2D calculation and wanted to ignore the z-coordinate of coordinates3D, you'd write the following:

```
let (x4, y4, _) = coordinates3D
```

This line of code only declares x4 and y4. The _ is special and simply means you're ignoring this part for now.

> **Note**: You'll find that you can use the underscore (also called the wildcard operator) throughout Swift to ignore a value.

Mini-exercises

1. Declare a constant tuple that contains three Int values followed by a Double. Use this to represent a date (month, day, year) followed by an average temperature for that date.

2. Change the tuple to name the constituent components. Give them names related to the data they contain: `month`, `day`, `year` and `averageTemperature`.

3. In one line, read the day and average temperature values into two constants. You'll need to employ the underscore to ignore the month and year.

4. Up until now, you've only seen constant tuples. But you can create variable tuples, too. Change the tuple you created in the exercises above to a variable by using `var` instead of `let`. Now change the average temperature to a new value.

A Whole Lot of Number Types

You've been using `Int` to represent whole numbers. An `Int` is represented with 64 bits on most modern hardware and with 32 bits on older or more resource-constrained systems. Swift provides many more number types that use different amounts of storage. For whole numbers, you can use the explicit **signed** types `Int8`, `Int16`, `Int32`, `Int64`. These types consume 1, 2, 4, and 8 bytes of storage, respectively. Each of these types use 1 bit to represent the sign.

If you are only dealing with non-negative values, there is a set of explicit **unsigned** types that you can use. These include `UInt8`, `UInt16`, `UInt32` and `UInt64`. While you cannot represent negative values with these, the extra 1 bit lets you represent values twice as big as their **signed** counterparts.

Here is a summary of the different integer types and their storage size in bytes. Most of the time, you will just want to use an `Int`.

These become useful if your code interacts with another piece of software that uses one of these more exact sizes or needs to optimize for storage size.

Type	Minimum Value	Maximum Value	Storage size
Int8	-128	127	1
UInt8	0	255	1
Int16	-32768	32767	2
UInt16	0	65535	2
Int32	-2147483648	2147483647	4
UInt32	0	4294967295	4
Int64	-9223372036854775808	9223372036854775807	8
UInt64	0	18446766073709551615	8

You've been using Double to represent fractional numbers. Swift offers a Float type with less range and precision than Double but requires half as much storage. Modern hardware is optimized for Double, so it should be your go-to unless there is good reason to use a Float.

Type	Minimum Value	Maximum Value	Precision	Storage size
Float	1.175494E-38	3.402823E+38	6 digits	4
Double	2.225073e-308	1.797693E+308	15 digits	8

Most of the time, you will just use Int and Double to represent numbers, but you might encounter the other types occasionally.

For example, suppose you need to add an Int16 with a UInt8 and an Int32. You can do that like so:

```
let a: Int16 = 12
let b: UInt8 = 255
let c: Int32 = -100000

let answer = Int(a) + Int(b) + Int(c)   // answer is an Int
```

Type Aliases

A useful feature of Swift is being able to create your own type which is an alias of another type. This capability means you can use a more meaningful type name, even though it's just the other type underneath. This is known as a **type alias**.

It's simple to create a type alias like so:

```
typealias Animal = String
```

This statement creates an alternate name for String called Animal. When the compiler sees this type, it simply treats it as a String. Therefore you could do something like this:

```
let myPet: Animal = "Dog"
```

This feature might not seem useful right now, but sometimes types can become complex and creating an alias for them can give them a more descriptive and explicit name. For example, you might do the following:

```
typealias Coordinates = (Int, Int)
let xy: Coordinates = (2, 4)
```

This code creates a type called `Coordinates`, a tuple containing two `Int`s and then uses it.

As you see more and more Swift, you'll see how type aliases can be very powerful and simplify code.

A Peek Behind the Curtains: Protocols

Even though there are a dozen different numeric types, they are easy to understand and use because they all roughly support the same operations. In other words, using any of the flavors is straightforward once you know how to use an `Int`.

One of Swift's truly great features is that it formalizes the idea of type commonality using what are known as **protocols**. By learning the protocol, you instantly understand how all the types using that protocol work.

In the case of integers, the functionality can be diagrammed like so:

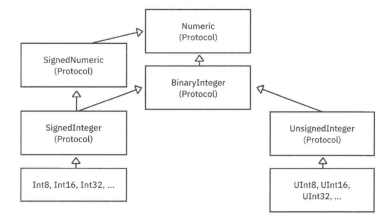

The arrows indicate conformance to (sometimes called *adoption of*) a protocol. While this graph does not show all the protocols that integer types conform to — it gives you insight into how things are organized.

Swift is the first protocol-based language. As you begin to understand the protocols that underlie the types, you can leverage the system in ways not possible with other languages.

By the end of this book, you'll be hooking into existing protocols and even creating new ones of your own.

Challenges

Before moving on, here are some challenges to test your knowledge of types and operations. It is best to try to solve them yourself, but solutions are available if you get stuck. These came with the download or are available at the printed book's source code link listed in the introduction.

Challenge 1: Coordinates

Create a constant called `coordinates` and assign a tuple containing two and three to it.

Challenge 2: Named Coordinate

Create a constant called `namedCoordinate` with a `row` and `column` component.

Challenge 3: Which Are Valid?

Which of the following are valid statements?

```
let character: Character = "Dog"
let character: Character = "🐶"
let string: String = "Dog"
let string: String = "🐶"
```

Challenge 4. Does it Compile?

```
let tuple = (day: 15, month: 8, year: 2015)
let day = tuple.Day
```

Challenge 5: Find the Error

What is wrong with the following code?

```
let name = "Matt"
name += " Galloway"
```

Challenge 6: What is the Type of value?

What is the type of the constant named value?

```
let tuple = (100, 1.5, 10)
let value = tuple.1
```

Challenge 7: What is the Value of month?

What is the value of the constant named month?

```
let tuple = (day: 15, month: 8, year: 2015)
let month = tuple.month
```

Challenge 8: What is the Value of summary?

What is the value of the constant named summary?

```
let number = 10
let multiplier = 5
let summary = "\(number) multiplied by \(multiplier) equals \
(number * multiplier)"
```

Challenge 9: Compute the Value

What is the sum of a and b, minus c?

```
let a = 4
let b: Int32 = 100
let c: UInt8 = 12
```

Challenge 10: Different Precision πs

What is the numeric difference between Double.pi and Float.pi?

Key Points

- Type conversion allows you to convert values of one type into another.

- Type conversion is required when using an operator, such as the basic arithmetic operators (+, −, *, /), with mixed types.

- Type inference allows you to omit the type when Swift already knows it.

- **Unicode** is the standard for mapping characters to numbers.

- A single mapping in Unicode is called a **code point**.

- The Character data type stores single characters, and the String data type stores collections of characters or strings.

- You can combine strings by using the addition operator.

- You can use **string interpolation** to build a string in place.

- You can use tuples to group data into a single data type.

- Tuples can either be unnamed or named. Their elements are accessed with index numbers for unnamed tuples or programmer-given names for named tuples.

- There are many kinds of numeric types with different storage and precision capabilities.

- Type aliases can be used to create a new type that is simply a new name for another type.

- Protocols are how Swift organizes types by describing the operations and properties they share.

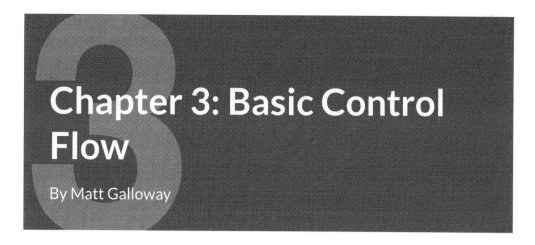

Chapter 3: Basic Control Flow

By Matt Galloway

When writing a computer program, you must tell the computer what to do in different scenarios. For example, a calculator app would need to do one thing if the user taps the addition button and another if the user taps the subtraction button.

In computer programming terms, this concept is known as **control flow**, named so because various methods control the flow of the program. This chapter will teach you how to make decisions and repeat tasks in your programs using syntax to control the flow. You'll also learn about **Booleans**, which represent true and false values, and how you can use these to compare data.

Comparison Operators

You've seen a few types, such as Int, Double and String. Here you'll learn about another type that lets you compare values through the **comparison operators**.

When you perform a comparison, such as looking for the greater of two numbers, the answer is either *true* or *false*. Swift has a data type just for this! It's called a Bool, which is short for Boolean, after a rather clever man named George Boole who invented an entire field of mathematics around the concept of true and false.

Here is how you use a Boolean in Swift:

```
let yes: Bool = true
let no: Bool = false
```

And because of Swift's type inference, you can leave off the type annotation:

```
let yes = true
let no = false
```

A Boolean can only be true or false, denoted by the keywords true and false. In the code above, you use the keywords to set the state of each constant.

Boolean Operators

You commonly use Booleans to compare values. For example, you may have two values and want to know if they're equal: either they are (true), or they aren't (false).

In Swift, you do this using the == operator which is called the **equality operator**:

```
let doesOneEqualTwo = (1 == 2)
```

Swift infers that doesOneEqualTwo is a Bool. Clearly, 1 does not equal 2, so doesOneEqualTwo will be false.

Similarly, you can find out if two values are *not* equal using the != operator:

```
let doesOneNotEqualTwo = (1 != 2)
```

This time, the comparison is true because 1 does not equal 2, so doesOneNotEqualTwo will be true.

The prefix ! operator, also called the **not-operator**, toggles true to false and false to true. Another way to write the above is:

```
let alsoTrue = !(1 == 2)
```

Because 1 does not equal 2, (1 == 2) is false, and then ! flips it to true.

Two more operators let you determine if a value is greater than (>) or less than (<) another value. You'll likely know these from mathematics:

```
let isOneGreaterThanTwo = (1 > 2)
let isOneLessThanTwo = (1 < 2)
```

And it's not rocket science to prove that isOneGreaterThanTwo will equal false and isOneLessThanTwo will equal true.

There's also an operator that lets you test if a value is less than *or* equal to another value: <=. It's a combination of < and == and will return true if the first value is either less than the second value or equal to it.

Similarly, there's an operator that lets you test if a value is greater than or equal to another — you may have guessed that it's >=.

Boolean Logic

Each of the examples above tests just one condition. When George Boole invented the Boolean, he had much more planned for it than these humble beginnings. He invented Boolean logic, which lets you combine multiple conditions to form a result.

One way to combine conditions is by using **AND**. When you AND two Booleans together, the result is another Boolean. If both input Booleans are true, then the result is true. Otherwise, the result is false.

George Boole

In Swift, the operator for Boolean AND is &&, used like so:

```
let and = true && true
```

In this case, and will be true. If either of the values on the right were false, then and would be false.

Another way to combine conditions is by using **OR**. When you OR together two Booleans, the result is true if *either* of the input Booleans is true. Only if *both* input Booleans are false will the result be false.

In Swift, the operator for Boolean OR is | |, used like so:

```
let or = true || false
```

In this case, or will be true. If both values on the right were false, then or would be false. If both were true, then or would still be true.

Swift uses Boolean logic to evaluate multiple conditions. Maybe you want to determine if two conditions are true; in that case, you'd use AND. If you only care whether one of two conditions is true, then you'd use OR.

For example, consider the following code:

```
let andTrue = 1 < 2 && 4 > 3     // true
let andFalse = 1 < 2 && 3 > 4     // false

let orTrue = 1 < 2 || 3 > 4       // true
let orFalse = 1 == 2 || 3 == 4    // false
```

Each of these tests two separate conditions, combining them with either AND or OR.

It's also possible to use Boolean logic to combine more than two comparisons. For example, you can form a complex comparison like so:

```
let andOr = (1 < 2 && 3 > 4) || 1 < 4   // true
```

The parentheses disambiguates the expression. First, Swift evaluates the sub-expression inside the parentheses, and then it evaluates the entire expression, following these steps:

```
1. (1 < 2 && 3 > 4) || 1 < 4
2. (true && false) || true
3. false || true
4. true
```

String Equality

Sometimes you want to determine if two strings are equal. For example, a children's game of naming an animal in a photo would need to determine if the player answered correctly.

In Swift, you can compare strings using the standard equality operator, ==, in the same way you compare numbers. For example:

```
let guess = "dog"
let dogEqualsCat = guess == "cat"
```

Here, dogEqualsCat is a Boolean that, in this case, equals false because "dog" does not equal "cat". Simple!

Just as with numbers, you can compare not just for equality but also to determine if one value is greater than or less than another value. For example:

```
let order = "cat" < "dog"
```

This syntax checks if one string comes before another alphabetically. In this case, order equals true because "cat" comes before "dog".

> **Note**: You will learn more about string equality in Chapter 9, "Strings". Some interesting things crop up when strings contain special characters and capitalization.

Toggling a Bool

A Bool often represents the state of something being "on" or "off". In those cases, it's common to toggle between states. For example, you could use a Bool to represent the state of a light switch in your application and toggle between the states of "on" and "off".

For these situations, Swift provides a handy way to flip a Bool from true to false and back again. Like so:

```
var switchState = true
switchState.toggle() // switchState = false
switchState.toggle() // switchState = true
```

Here, the variable called `switchState` starts as `true`. Then, after one `toggle`, it becomes `false`. After another `toggle`, it's set to `true` again.

> **Note**: The `toggle()` here is a call to a **function**. You'll learn more about these in Chapter 5, "Functions", and how they apply to types in Chapter 13, "Methods".

Mini-Exercises

1. Create a constant called `myAge` and set it to your age. Then, create a constant named `isTeenager` that uses Boolean logic to determine if the age denotes someone in the age range of 13 to 19.

2. Create another constant named `theirAge` and set it to 30. Then, create a constant named `bothTeenagers` that uses Boolean logic to determine if both ages denote teenagers.

3. Create a constant named `reader` and set it to your name as a `String`. Create a constant named `author` and set it to my name, Matt Galloway. Create a constant named `authorIsReader` that uses string equality to determine if `reader` and `author` are equal.

4. Create a constant named `readerBeforeAuthor` which uses string comparison to determine if `reader` comes before `author`.

The if Statement

The first and most common way of controlling the flow of a program is through the use of an **if statement**, which allows the program to do something only *if* a certain condition is true. For example, consider the following:

```
if 2 > 1 {
  print("Yes, 2 is greater than 1.")
}
```

This is a simple `if` statement. If the condition is true, the statement will execute the code between the braces. The statement won't execute the code between the braces if the condition is false. It's as simple as that!

At the heart of the `if` statement is the **condition**. The condition is the thing being checked, and then the code in the braces either runs or doesn't. Therefore, an `if` statement is a form of **conditional statement**. You'll see that term crop up again in this chapter.

You can extend an `if` statement to provide code to run if the condition is false. This is known as the **else clause**. Here's an example:

```
let animal = "Zebra"

if animal == "Cat" || animal == "Dog" {
  print("Animal is a house pet.")
} else {
  print("Animal is not a house pet.")
}
```

Here, if `animal` equals either `"Cat"` or `"Dog"`, the statement will run the first code block. If `animal` does not equal either `"Cat"` or `"Dog"`, then the statement will run the block inside the `else` part of the `if` statement, printing the following to the debug area:

```
Animal is not a house pet.
```

But you can go even further than that with `if` statements. Sometimes you want to check one condition, then another. This is where **else-if** comes into play, nesting another `if` statement in the `else` clause of a previous `if` statement.

You can use it like so:

```
let hourOfDay = 12
var timeOfDay: String

if hourOfDay < 6 {
  timeOfDay = "Early morning"
} else if hourOfDay < 12 {
  timeOfDay = "Morning"
} else if hourOfDay < 17 {
  timeOfDay = "Afternoon"
} else if hourOfDay < 20 {
  timeOfDay = "Evening"
} else if hourOfDay < 24 {
  timeOfDay = "Late evening"
} else {
  timeOfDay = "INVALID HOUR!"
}
print(timeOfDay)
```

These nested `if` statements test multiple conditions one by one until a true condition is found. Only the code associated with that *first* true condition is executed, regardless of whether subsequent `else-if` conditions are also true. In other words, the order of your conditions matters!

You can add an `else` clause at the end to handle the case where none of the conditions are true. This `else` clause is optional if you don't need it; here, you *do* need it to ensure that `timeOfDay` has a valid value by the time you print it out.

In the example above, the `if` statement takes a number representing an hour of the day and converts it to a string representing the part of the day to which the hour belongs. Working with a 24-hour clock, the statements are checked in order, one at a time:

- The first check is to see if the hour is less than 6. If so, that means it's early morning.

- If the hour is not less than 6, the statement continues to the first `else-if`, where it checks the hour to see if it's less than 12.

- Then, as conditions prove false, the statement checks the hour to see if it's less than 17, then less than 20, then less than 24.

- The last part of the statement executes if the hour is not in the range of values.

- Finally, after all the conditions have been checked, the code prints the value of `timeOfDay` to the console.

Since the `hourOfDay` constant is 12 in the example, the code will print the following:

```
Afternoon
```

Notice that even though both the `hourOfDay < 20` and `hourOfDay < 24` conditions are also true, the statement only executes the first block whose condition is true; in this case, the block with the `hourOfDay < 17` condition.

Short-Circuiting

An important fact about `if` statements is what happens when there are multiple Boolean conditions separated by ANDs (&&) or ORs (||).

Consider the following code:

```
if 1 > 2 && name == "Matt Galloway" {
  // ...
}
```

The first condition of the if statement, 1 > 2 is false. Therefore the whole expression can never be true.

So Swift will not even bother to check the second part of the expression, namely the check of name. Similarly, consider the following code:

```
if 1 < 2 || name == "Matt Galloway" {
  // ...
}
```

Since 1 < 2 is true, the whole expression must be true no matter the value of name. Therefore, once again, the check of name is not executed. This short-circuiting behavior will come in handy when dealing with more complex conditions.

Constant and Variable Scope

if statements introduce a new concept **scope**, which controls the visibility and lifetime of constants and variables through the use of braces. Imagine you want to calculate the fee to charge your client. Here's the deal you've made:

You earn $25 for every hour up to 40 hours and $50 for every hour after that.

Using Swift, you can calculate your fee in this way:

```
var hoursWorked = 45

var price = 0
if hoursWorked > 40 {
  let hoursOver40 = hoursWorked - 40   // hoursOver40 = 5
  price += hoursOver40 * 50            // price = 250
  hoursWorked -= hoursOver40           // hoursWorked = 40
}
price += hoursWorked * 25              // price = 1250

print(price)
```

This code takes the number of hours and checks if it's over 40. If so, the code calculates the number of hours over 40, multiplies that by $50 and then adds the result to the price. The code then subtracts the number of hours over 40 from the hours worked. It multiplies the remaining hours worked by $25 and adds that to the total price.

In the example above, the result is as follows:

```
1250
```

The interesting thing here is the code inside the `if` statement. There is a declaration of a new constant, `hoursOver40`, to store the number of hours over 40. Clearly, you can use it inside the `if` statement. But what happens if you try to use it after the `print` statement, for example?

```
...

print(price)
print(hoursOver40)
```

This would result in the following error:

This error informs you that you're only allowed to use the `hoursOver40` constant within the scope it was created. In this case, the `if` statement introduced a new scope, so you can no longer use the constant when that scope finishes.

However, each scope can use variables and constants from its parent scope. In the example above, the scope inside the `if` statement uses the `price` and `hoursWorked` variables from the parent scope.

The Ternary Conditional Operator

Now I want to introduce a new operator, one you didn't see in Chapter 2, "Types & Operations". It's called the **ternary conditional operator** and it's related to `if` statements.

If you wanted to determine the minimum and maximum of two variables, you could use `if` statements like so:

```
let a = 5
let b = 10

let min: Int
if a < b {
  min = a
} else {
  min = b
}

let max: Int
if a > b {
  max = a
} else {
  max = b
}
```

You know how this works by now, but it's a lot of code. Wouldn't it be nice if you could shrink this to just a couple of lines? Well, you can, thanks to the ternary conditional operator!

The ternary conditional operator takes a condition and returns one of two values, depending on whether the condition is true or false. The syntax is as follows:

```
(<CONDITION>) ? <TRUE VALUE> : <FALSE VALUE>
```

You can use this operator to rewrite your long code block above like so:

```
let a = 5
let b = 10

let min = a < b ? a : b
let max = a > b ? a : b
```

In the first example, the condition is a < b. If this is true, the result assigned back to min will be the value of a; if it's false, the result will be the value of b.

I'm sure you'll agree that it's much simpler! This is a useful operator that you'll find yourself using regularly. Whether it's better to use the ternary conditional operator or an `if` and `else` block in a particular case comes down to what is easier to read and what you prefer.

> **Note**: Because finding the greater or smaller of two numbers is such a common operation, the Swift standard library provides two functions for this purpose: max and min. If you were paying attention earlier in the book, then you'll recall you've already seen these.

Mini-Exercises

1. Create a constant named myAge and initialize it with your age. Write an if statement to print out Teenager if your age is between 13 and 19 and Not a teenager if your age is not between 13 and 19.

2. Create a constant named answer and use a ternary condition to set it equal to the result you print out for the same cases in the above exercise. Then print out answer.

Loops

Loops are Swift's way of executing code multiple times. In this section, you'll learn about one type of loop: the **while loop**. If you know another programming language, you'll find the concepts and maybe even the syntax familiar.

While Loops

A while loop repeats a code block while a condition is true. You create a while loop this way:

```
while <CONDITION> {
   <LOOP CODE>
}
```

The loop checks the condition before every iteration. If the condition is true, then the loop executes and moves on to another iteration. If the condition is false, then the loop stops. Like if statements, while loops introduce a scope.

The simplest while loop takes this form:

```
while true { }
```

This `while` loop never ends because the condition is always `true`. Of course, you would never write such a `while` loop because your program would spin forever! This situation is known as an **infinite loop**, and while it might not cause your program to crash, it will likely cause your computer to freeze.

Here's a more useful example of a `while` loop:

```
var sum = 1

while sum < 1000 {
  sum = sum + (sum + 1)
}
```

This code calculates a mathematical sequence to the point where the value of `sum` is greater than `1000`.

The loop executes as follows:

- **Before iteration 1:** sum = 1, loop condition = true

- **Before iteration 2:** sum = 3, loop condition = true

- **Before iteration 3:** sum = 7, loop condition = true

- **Before iteration 4:** sum = 15, loop condition = true

- **Before iteration 5:** sum = 31, loop condition = true

- **Before iteration 6:** sum = 63, loop condition = true

- **Before iteration 7:** sum = 127, loop condition = true

- **Before iteration 8:** sum = 255, loop condition = true

- **Before iteration 9:** sum = 511, loop condition = true

- **Before iteration 10:** sum = 1023, loop condition = false

Before the tenth iteration, the `sum` variable is `1023`, and therefore the loop condition of `sum < 1000` becomes false. At this point, the loop stops.

repeat-while Loops

A variant of the `while` loop is called the **repeat-while loop**. It differs from the `while` loop in that the condition is evaluated *at the end* of the loop rather than at the beginning. You construct a `repeat-while` loop like this:

```
repeat {
   <LOOP CODE>
} while <CONDITION>
```

Here's the example from the last section, but using a `repeat-while` loop:

```
sum = 1

repeat {
   sum = sum + (sum + 1)
} while sum < 1000
```

In this example, the outcome is the same as before. However, that isn't always the case — you might get a different result with a different condition.

Consider the following `while` loop:

```
sum = 1

while sum < 1 {
   sum = sum + (sum + 1)
}
```

Consider the corresponding `repeat-while` loop, which uses the same condition:

```
sum = 1

repeat {
   sum = sum + (sum + 1)
} while sum < 1
```

In the case of the regular `while` loop, the condition `sum < 1` is `false` right from the start. That means the body of the loop won't be reached! The value of `sum` will equal 1 because the loop won't execute any iterations.

In the case of the `repeat-while` loop, `sum` will equal 3 because the loop executes once.

Breaking Out of a Loop

Sometimes you want to break out of a loop early. You can do this using the break statement, which immediately stops the loop's execution and continues on to the code after the loop.

For example, consider the following code:

```
sum = 1

while true {
  sum = sum + (sum + 1)
  if sum >= 1000 {
    break
  }
}
```

Here, the loop condition is true, so the loop normally iterates forever. However, the break means the while loop will exit once the sum is greater than or equal to 1000.

You've seen how to write the same loop in different ways, demonstrating that there are often many ways to achieve the same result in computer programming.

You should choose the method that's easiest to read and conveys your intent in the best way possible. This skill is one you'll internalize with enough time and practice.

Mini-Exercises

1. Create a variable named counter and set it equal to 0. Create a while loop with the condition counter < 10, which prints out counter is X (where X is replaced with counter value) and then increments counter by 1.

2. Create a variable named counter and set it equal to 0. Create another variable named roll and set it equal to 0. Create a repeat-while loop. Inside the loop, set roll equal to Int.random(in: 1...6), which means to pick a random number between 1 and 6. Then increment counter by 1. Finally, print After X rolls, roll is Y where X is the value of counter and Y is the value of roll. Set the loop condition so the loop finishes when the first 1 is rolled.

Challenges

Before moving on, here are some challenges to test your knowledge of basic control flow. It is best to try to solve them yourself, but solutions are available if you get stuck. These came with the download or are available at the printed book's source code link listed in the introduction.

Challenge 1: Find the Error

What's wrong with the following code?

```
let firstName = "Matt"

if firstName == "Matt" {
  let lastName = "Galloway"
} else if firstName == "Ray" {
  let lastName = "Wenderlich"
}
let fullName = firstName + " " + lastName
```

Challenge 2: Boolean Challenge

In each of the following statements, what is the value of the Boolean answer constant?

```
let answer = true && true
let answer = false || false
let answer = (true && 1 != 2) || (4 > 3 && 100 < 1)
let answer = ((10 / 2) > 3) && ((10 % 2) == 0)
```

Challenge 3: Snakes and Ladders

Imagine you're playing a game of snakes & ladders that goes from position 1 to position 20. On it, there are ladders at positions 3 and 7, which take you to 15 and 12, respectively. Then there are snakes at positions 11 and 17, which take you to 2 and 9, respectively.

Create a constant called currentPosition, which you can set to whatever position between 1 and 20 you like. Then create a constant called diceRoll, which you can set to whatever roll of the dice you want. Finally, calculate the final position considering the ladders and snakes, calling it nextPosition.

Challenge 4: Number of Days in a Month

Given a month (represented with a String in all lowercase) and the current year (represented with an Int), calculate the number of days in the month. Remember that because of leap years, February has 29 days when the year is a multiple of 4 but not a multiple of 100. February also has 29 days when the year is a multiple of 400.

Challenge 5: Next Power of Two

Given a number, determine the next power of two greater than or equal to that number.

Challenge 6: Triangular Number

Given a number, print the triangular number of that depth. You can get a refresher on triangular numbers here: https://en.wikipedia.org/wiki/Triangular_number

Challenge 7: Fibonacci

Calculate the nth Fibonacci number. Remember that Fibonacci numbers start their sequence with 1 and 1, and then subsequent numbers in the sequence are equal to the previous two values added together. You can get a refresher here: https://en.wikipedia.org/wiki/Fibonacci_number

Challenge 8: Make a Loop

Use a loop to print out the multiplication or times table up to 12 of a given factor.

Challenge 9: Dice Roll Table

Print a table showing the number of combinations to create each number from 2 to 12, given two six-sided dice rolls. You should not use a formula but compute the number of combinations exhaustively by considering each possible dice roll.

Key Points

- You use the Boolean data type `Bool` to represent true and false.

- The comparison operators, all of which return a Boolean, are:

Name	Operator
Equal	==
Not Equal	!=
Less than	<
Greater than	>
Less than or equal	<=
Greater than or equal	>=

- You can use Boolean logic (&& and ||) to combine comparison conditions.

- You use `if` statements to make simple decisions based on a condition.

- You use `else` and `else-if` within an `if` statement to extend the decision-making beyond a single condition.

- Short-circuiting ensures that only the minimal required parts of a Boolean expression are evaluated.

- You can use the ternary operator (a ? b : c) instead of a simple `if` statement.

- Variables and constants belong to a scope beyond which you cannot use them. A scope inherits variables and constants from its parent.

- `while` loops allow you to perform a particular task zero or more times until a condition is met.

- `repeat-while` loops always execute the loop at least once.

- The `break` statement lets you break out of a loop.

Chapter 4: Advanced Control Flow

By Matt Galloway

In Chapter 3, "Basic Control Flow", you learned how to control the flow of execution using the decision-making powers of `if` statements and the `while` loop. In this chapter, you'll continue to learn how to control the flow of execution. You'll learn about another loop known as the `for` loop.

Loops may not sound very interesting, but they're very common in computer programs. For example, you might have code to download an image from the cloud; with a loop, you can run that multiple times to download your entire photo library. Or, if you have a game with multiple computer-controlled characters, you might need a loop to go through each one and make sure it knows what to do next.

You'll also learn about `switch` statements, which are particularly powerful in Swift. They let you inspect a value and decide what to do based on that value, and they're incredibly powerful when used with some advanced Swift features such as pattern matching.

Countable Ranges

Before you dive into the `for` loop statement, you need to know about the **Countable Range** data types that let you represent a sequence of countable integers. Let's look at two types of ranges.

First, there's **countable closed range**, which you represent like so:

```
let closedRange = 0...5
```

The three dots (`...`) indicate that this range is closed, which means the range goes from 0 to 5 inclusive. That's the numbers (`0, 1, 2, 3, 4, 5`).

Second, there's **countable half-open range**, which you represent like so:

```
let halfOpenRange = 0..<5
```

Here, you replace the three dots with two dots and a less-than sign (`..<`). Half-open means the range goes from 0 up to, but not including, 5. That's the numbers (`0, 1, 2, 3, 4`).

Both open and half-open ranges must always be increasing. In other words, the second number must always be greater than or equal to the first. Countable ranges are commonly used in both `for` loops and `switch` statements, which means that throughout the rest of the chapter, you'll use ranges as well!

A Random Interlude

A common need in programming is to be able to generate random numbers. And Swift provides the functionality built into the language, which is pretty handy!

As an example, imagine an application that needs to simulate rolling a die. You may want to do something until the code rolls a six. Now that you know about `while` loops, you can do that with the `random` feature. You could do that like so:

```
while Int.random(in: 1...6) != 6 {
    print("Not a six")
}
```

Note: The `random(in:)` here is a call to a **function**. You'll see more about these in Chapter 5, "Functions", and how they apply to types in Chapter 13, "Methods".

For Loops

In Chapter 3, "Basic Control Flow", you looked at while loops. Now that you know about ranges, it's time to look at another type of loop: the **for loop**. This is probably the most common loop you'll see, and you'll use it to run code a certain number of times.

You construct a for loop like this:

```
for <CONSTANT> in <COUNTABLE RANGE> {
  <LOOP CODE>
}
```

The loop begins with the for keyword, followed by a name given to the loop constant (more on that shortly), followed by in, followed by the range to loop through. Here's an example:

```
let count = 10
var sum = 0
for i in 1...count {
  sum += i
}
```

The for loop iterates through the range 1 to count in the code above. During the first iteration, i will equal the first element in the range: 1. Each time through the loop, i will increment until it's equal to count; the loop will execute one final time and then finish.

> **Note:** If you'd used a half-open range, i would equal count – 1 during the last iteration.

Inside the loop, you add i to the sum variable; it runs 10 times to calculate the sequence 1 + 2 + 3 + 4 + 5 + ... up to 10.

Here are the values of the constant i and variable sum for each iteration:

- **Start of iteration 1:** i = 1, sum = 0

- **Start of iteration 2:** i = 2, sum = 1

- **Start of iteration 3:** i = 3, sum = 3

- **Start of iteration 4:** i = 4, sum = 6

- **Start of iteration 5:** `i = 5`, `sum = 10`

- **Start of iteration 6:** `i = 6`, `sum = 15`

- **Start of iteration 7:** `i = 7`, `sum = 21`

- **Start of iteration 8:** `i = 8`, `sum = 28`

- **Start of iteration 9:** `i = 9`, `sum = 36`

- **Start of iteration 10:** `i = 10`, `sum = 45`

- **After iteration 10:** `sum = 55`

In terms of scope, the `i` constant is only visible inside the scope of the `for` loop, which means it's not available outside of the loop.

> **Note**: If you're mathematically astute, you might notice that this example computes **triangle numbers**. Here's a quick explanation: http://bbc.in/1O89TGP

Xcode's playground gives you a handy way to visualize such an iteration. Look at the `sum += i` line in the results pane. You will notice a box on the right. Click on it:

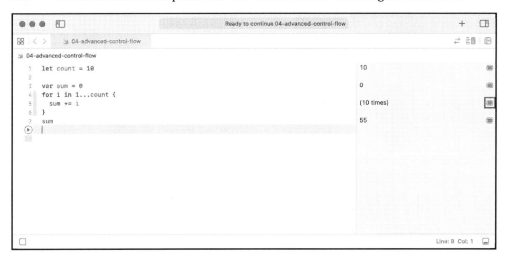

Xcode will display a graph underneath the line within the playground code editor:

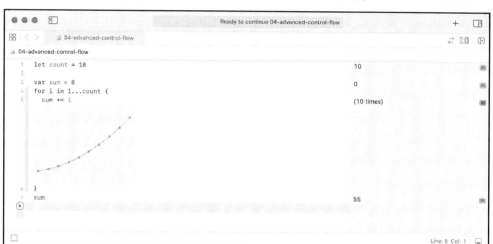

This graph lets you visualize the sum variable as the loop iterates.

Finally, sometimes you only want to loop a fixed number of times, but you don't need to track the loop counter at all.

In that case, you can employ the underscore to indicate you're ignoring it, like so:

```
sum = 1
var lastSum = 0

for _ in 0..<count {
  let temp = sum
  sum = sum + lastSum
  lastSum = temp
}
```

This code doesn't require a loop constant; the loop simply needs to run a certain number of times. In this case, the range is 0 up to, but not including, count and is half-open. This approach is the usual way of writing loops that run a fixed number of times.

It's also possible to perform the iteration only under certain conditions. For example, imagine you wanted to compute a sum similar to that of triangle numbers but only for odd numbers:

```
sum = 0
for i in 1...count where i % 2 == 1 {
  sum += i
}
```

The previous loop has a where clause in the for loop statement. The loop still runs through all values in the range 1 to count, but it will only execute the loop's code block when the where condition is true; in this case, when i is odd.

Continue and Labeled Statements

Sometimes you'd like to skip a loop iteration for a particular case without breaking out of the loop entirely. You can do this with the continue statement, which immediately ends the current iteration of the loop and starts the next iteration.

> **Note**: In many cases, you can use the simpler where clause you just learned about. The continue statement gives you a higher level of control, letting you execute part of a loop before you skip to the next iteration.

Take the example of an eight-by-eight grid, where each cell holds a row value multiplied by the column. It looks much like a multiplication table, doesn't it?

	0	1	2	3	4	5	6	7
0	0	0	0	0	0	0	0	0
1	0	1	2	3	4	5	6	7
2	0	2	4	6	8	10	12	14
3	0	3	6	9	12	15	18	21
4	0	4	8	12	16	20	24	28
5	0	5	10	15	20	25	30	35
6	0	6	12	18	24	30	36	42
7	0	7	14	21	28	35	42	49

Let's say you wanted to calculate the sum of all cells but exclude all even rows, as shown below:

	0	1	2	3	4	5	6	7
0								
1	0	1	2	3	4	5	6	7
2								
3	0	3	6	9	12	15	18	21
4								
5	0	5	10	15	20	25	30	35
6								
7	0	7	14	21	28	35	42	49

Using a for loop, you can achieve this as follows:

```
sum = 0

for row in 0..<8 {
  if row % 2 == 0 {
    continue
  }

  for column in 0..<8 {
    sum += row * column
  }
}
```

When the row modulo 2 equals 0, the row is even. In this case, continue makes the for loop skip to the next row. Just like break, continue works with both for loops and while loops.

Now consider how you could calculate the sum of all cells, excluding those where the column is greater than or equal to the row.

To illustrate, you should sum the following cells:

	0	1	2	3	4	5	6	7
0								
1	0							
2	0	2						
3	0	3	6					
4	0	4	8	12				
5	0	5	10	15	20			
6	0	6	12	18	24	30		
7	0	7	14	21	28	35	42	

Using a `for` loop, you can achieve this as follows:

```
sum = 0

rowLoop: for row in 0..<8 {
  columnLoop: for column in 0..<8 {
    if row == column {
      continue rowLoop
    }
    sum += row * column
  }
}
```

The previous code block uses **labeled statements**, labeling the two loops as `rowLoop` and `columnLoop`, respectively. When the row equals the column inside the inner `columnLoop`, the outer `rowLoop` will continue.

You can use labeled statements like these with `break` to break out of a specific loop. Normally, `break` and `continue` work on the innermost loop, so you need to use labeled statements to act on the outer loop.

Mini-Exercises

1. Create a constant named `range` and set it equal to a range starting at 1 and ending with 10 inclusive. Write a `for` loop that iterates over this range and prints the square of each number.

2. Write a `for` loop to iterate over the same range as in the exercise above and print the square root of each number. You'll need to type convert your loop constant to a `Double` type to use the standard square root function. The `sqrt()` function that calculates square roots is not available to your playground unless you also import the library where it is defined. If the compiler complains about the `sqrt`, add `import Foundation` somewhere near the beginning of your playground file.

3. Above, you saw a `for` loop that iterated over only the even rows like so:

```
sum = 0
for row in 0..<8 {
  if row % 2 == 0 {
    continue
  }
  for column in 0..<8 {
    sum += row * column
  }
}
```

Change this to use a `where` clause on the first `for` loop to skip even rows instead of using `continue`. Confirm that the sum is still 448, as in the initial example.

Switch Statements

You can also control flow via the `switch` statement. It executes different code depending on the value of a variable or constant. Here's a `switch` statement that acts on an integer:

```
let number = 10

switch number {
case 0:
  print("Zero")
default:
  print("Non-zero")
}
```

In this example, the code will print the following:

```
Non-zero
```

The purpose of this `switch` statement is to determine whether or not a number is zero. It will get more complex — I promise!

To handle a specific case, you use `case` followed by the value you want to check for, which in this case is `0`. Then, you use `default` to signify what should happen for all other values. Unlike an `if` statement that can omit the `else`, a `switch` statement must have some code to execute for *every possible value* of the thing you're checking.

Here's another example:

```swift
switch number {
case 10:
  print("It's ten!")
default:
  break
}
```

This time you check for 10, in which case, you print a message. Nothing should happen for other values. You use the `break` statement when you want nothing to happen for a case. Writing `break` tells Swift that you *meant* to not write any code here and that nothing should happen. Cases can never be empty, so you *must* write some code, even if it's just a `break`!

Of course, `switch` statements also work with data types other than integers. They work with any data type!

Here's an example of switching on a string:

```swift
let string = "Dog"

switch string {
case "Cat", "Dog":
  print("Animal is a house pet.")
default:
  print("Animal is not a house pet.")
}
```

This code will print the following:

```
Animal is a house pet.
```

In this example, you provide two values for the case, meaning that if the value is equal to either "Cat" or "Dog", then the statement will execute the case.

Advanced switch Statements

You can also give your switch statements more than one case. In Chapter 3, "Basic Control Flow", you saw an if statement that used multiple else clauses to convert an hour of the day to a string describing that part of the day.

You could rewrite that more succinctly with a switch statement, like so:

```
let hourOfDay = 12
var timeOfDay: String

switch hourOfDay {
case 0, 1, 2, 3, 4, 5:
  timeOfDay = "Early morning"
case 6, 7, 8, 9, 10, 11:
  timeOfDay = "Morning"
case 12, 13, 14, 15, 16:
  timeOfDay = "Afternoon"
case 17, 18, 19:
  timeOfDay = "Evening"
case 20, 21, 22, 23:
  timeOfDay = "Late evening"
default:
  timeOfDay = "INVALID HOUR!"
}

print(timeOfDay)
```

This code will print the following:

```
Afternoon
```

Remember ranges?

Well, you can use ranges to simplify this `switch` statement. You can rewrite the above code using ranges:

```
switch hourOfDay {
case 0...5:
  timeOfDay = "Early morning"
case 6...11:
  timeOfDay = "Morning"
case 12...16:
  timeOfDay = "Afternoon"
case 17...19:
  timeOfDay = "Evening"
case 20..<24:
  timeOfDay = "Late evening"
default:
  timeOfDay = "INVALID HOUR!"
}
```

This code is more concise than writing out each value individually for all cases.

When there are multiple cases, the statement will execute the first one that matches. You'll probably agree that this is more concise and clear than using an `if` statement for this example.

It's slightly more precise because the `if` statement method didn't address negative numbers, which here are correctly deemed invalid.

It's also possible to match a case to a condition based on a property of the value. As you learned in Chapter 2, "Types & Operations," you can use the modulo operator to determine if an integer is even or odd.

Consider this code that uses the constant `number` you defined as `10` above:

```
switch number {
case let x where x % 2 == 0:
  print("Even")
default:
  print("Odd")
}
```

This code will print the following:

```
Even
```

This `switch` statement uses the `let-where` syntax, meaning the case will match only when a certain condition is true. The `let` part binds a value to a name, while the `where` part provides a Boolean condition that must be true for the case to match.

In this example, you've designed the case to match if the value is even — in other words, if the value modulo 2 equals 0.

The method by which you can match values based on conditions is known as **pattern matching**.

In the previous example, the binding introduced an unnecessary constant x; it's merely another name for `number`.

You can use `number` in the `where` clause and replace the binding with an underscore to ignore it.

```
switch number {
case _ where number % 2 == 0:
  print("Even")
default:
  print("Odd")
}
```

Partial Matching

Another way you can use `switch` statements with matching to great effect is as follows:

```
let coordinates = (x: 3, y: 2, z: 5)

switch coordinates {
case (0, 0, 0): // 1
  print("Origin")
case (_, 0, 0): // 2
  print("On the x-axis.")
case (0, _, 0): // 3
  print("On the y-axis.")
case (0, 0, _): // 4
  print("On the z-axis.")
default:        // 5
  print("Somewhere in space")
}
```

This `switch` statement makes use of **partial matching**. Here's what each case does, in order:

1. Matches precisely where the value is (`0, 0, 0`). This value is the origin of 3D space.

2. Matches y=0, z=0 and any value of x. This match means the coordinate is on the x-axis.

3. Matches x=0, z=0 and any value of y. This match means the coordinate is on the y-axis.

4. Matches x=0, y=0 and any value of z. This match means the coordinate is on the z-axis.

5. Matches all other coordinates.

You're using the underscore to mean that you don't care about the value. If you don't want to ignore the value, you can bind it and use it in your `switch` statement.

Here's an example of how to do this:

```
switch coordinates {
case (0, 0, 0):
  print("Origin")
case (let x, 0, 0):
  print("On the x-axis at x = \(x)")
case (0, let y, 0):
  print("On the y-axis at y = \(y)")
case (0, 0, let z):
  print("On the z-axis at z = \(z)")
case let (x, y, z):
  print("Somewhere in space at x = \(x), y = \(y), z = \(z)")
}
```

Here, the axis cases use the `let` syntax to pull out the pertinent values. The code then prints the values using string interpolation to build the string.

Notice how you don't need a default in this `switch` statement. This is because the final case is essentially the default; it matches anything because there are no constraints on any part of the tuple. When the `switch` statement exhausts all possible values with its cases, no default is necessary.

Also, notice how you could use a single `let` to bind all values of the tuple: `let (x, y, z)` is the same as (`let x, let y, let z`).

Finally, you can use the same `let-where` syntax you saw earlier to match more complex cases. For example:

```
switch coordinates {
case let (x, y, _) where y == x:
  print("Along the y = x line.")
case let (x, y, _) where y == x * x:
  print("Along the y = x^2 line.")
default:
  break
}
```

Here, you match the "y equals x" and "y equals x squared" lines.

And those are the basics of `switch` statements!

Mini-Exercises

1. Write a switch statement that takes an age as an integer and prints out the life stage related to that age. You can make up the life stages or use these categorizations: 0-2 years, Infant; 3-12 years, Child; 13-19 years, Teenager; 20-39, Adult; 40-60, Middle-aged; 61+, Elderly.

2. Write a `switch` statement that takes a tuple containing a string and an integer. The string is a name, and the integer is an age. Use the same cases you used in the previous exercise and `let` syntax to print out the name followed by the life stage. For example, for myself, it would print out `"Matt is an adult"`.

Challenges

Before moving on, here are some challenges to test your knowledge of advanced control flow. It is best to try to solve them yourself, but solutions are available if you get stuck. These came with the download or are available at the printed book's source code link listed in the introduction.

Challenge 1: How Many Times

In the following for loop, what will be the value of sum, and how many iterations will happen?

```
var sum = 0
for i in 0...5 {
   sum += i
}
```

Challenge 2: Count the Letter

In the while loop below, how many instances of "a" will there be in aLotOfAs? Hint: aLotOfAs.count tells you how many characters are in the string aLotOfAs.

```
var aLotOfAs = ""
while aLotOfAs.count < 10 {
   aLotOfAs += "a"
}
```

Challenge 3: What Will Print

Consider the following `switch` statement:

```
switch coordinates {
case let (x, y, z) where x == y && y == z:
  print("x = y = z")
case (_, _, 0):
  print("On the x/y plane")
case (_, 0, _):
  print("On the x/z plane")
case (0, _, _):
  print("On the y/z plane")
default:
  print("Nothing special")
}
```

What will this code print when `coordinates` is each of the following?

```
let coordinates = (1, 5, 0)
let coordinates = (2, 2, 2)
let coordinates = (3, 0, 1)
let coordinates = (3, 2, 5)
let coordinates = (0, 2, 4)
```

Challenge 4: Closed Range Size

A closed range can never be empty. Why?

Challenge 5: The Final Countdown

Print a countdown from 10 to 0. (Note: do not use the `reversed()` method, which will be introduced later.)

Challenge 6: Print a Sequence

Print 0.0, 0.1, 0.2, 0.3, 0.4, 0.5, 0.6, 0.7, 0.8, 0.9, 1.0. (Note: do not use the `stride(from:by:to:)` function, which will be introduced later.)

Key Points

- You can use **countable ranges** to create a sequence of integers, incrementing to move from one value to the next.

- **Closed ranges** include both the start and end values.

- **Half-open ranges** include the start value and stop one before the end value.

- **For loops** allow you to iterate over a range.

- The **continue** statement lets you finish the current loop iteration and begin the next iteration.

- **Labeled statements** let you use break and continue on an outer loop.

- You use **switch** statements to decide which code to run depending on the value of a variable or constant.

- The power of a switch statement comes from leveraging **pattern matching** to compare values using complex rules.

Chapter 5: Functions

By Matt Galloway

Functions are a core part of many programming languages. Simply put, a function lets you define a block of code that performs a task. Then, whenever your app needs to execute that task, you can run the function instead of copying and pasting the same code everywhere.

In this chapter, you'll learn how to write your own functions and see firsthand how Swift makes them easy to use.

Function Basics

Imagine you have an app that frequently needs to print your name. You can write a function to do this:

```
func printMyName() {
    print("My name is Matt Galloway.")
}
```

The code above is known as a **function declaration**. You define a function using the `func` keyword. After that comes the name of the function, followed by parentheses. You'll learn more about the need for these parentheses in the next section.

After the parentheses comes an opening brace, followed by the code you want to run in the function, followed by a closing brace. With your function defined, you can use it like so:

```
printMyName()
```

This prints out the following:

```
My name is Matt Galloway.
```

If you suspect that you've already used a function in previous chapters, you're correct! `print`, which prints the text you give to the console, is indeed a function. In the next section, you'll learn how to pass data to a function and get data back when it finishes.

Function Parameters

In the previous example, the function simply prints out a message. That's great, but sometimes you want to **parameterize** your function, which lets it perform differently depending on the data passed into it via its **parameters**.

As an example, consider the following function:

```
func printMultipleOfFive(value: Int) {
    print("\(value) * 5 = \(value * 5)")
}

printMultipleOfFive(value: 10)
```

Here, you can see the definition of one parameter inside the parentheses after the function name, named `value` and of type `Int`. In any function, the parentheses contain what's known as the **parameter list**. These parentheses are required both when declaring and invoking the function, even if the parameter list is empty. This function will print out any given multiple of five. In the example, you call the function with an **argument** of 10, so the function prints the following:

```
10 * 5 = 50
```

Note: Take care not to confuse the terms "parameter" and "argument". A function declares its **parameters** in its parameter list. When you call a function, you provide values as **arguments** for the functions' parameters.

You can take this one step further and make the function more general. With two parameters, the function can print out a multiple of any two values.

```
func printMultipleOf(multiplier: Int, andValue: Int) {
  print("\(multiplier) * \(andValue) = \(multiplier *
andValue)")
}

printMultipleOf(multiplier: 4, andValue: 2)
```

There are now two parameters inside the parentheses after the function name: one named `multiplier` and the other named `andValue`, both of type `Int`.

Notice that you need to apply the labels in the parameter list to the arguments when you call a function. In the example above, you need to put `multiplier:` before the multiplier and `andValue:` before the value to be multiplied.

In Swift, you should try to make your function calls read like sentences. In the example above, you would read the last line of code like this:

Print multiple of multiplier 4 and value 2

You can make this even clearer by giving a parameter a different **external name**. For example, you can change the name of the andValue parameter:

```
func printMultipleOf(multiplier: Int, and value: Int) {
    print("\(multiplier) * \(value) = \(multiplier * value)")
}

printMultipleOf(multiplier: 4, and: 2)
```

You assign a different external name by writing it in front of the parameter name. In this example, the parameter's internal name is now value while the external name (the argument label) in the function call is now and. You can read the new call as:

Print multiple of multiplier 4 and 2

The following diagram explains where the external and internal names come from in the function declaration:

The idea is to allow a function call to be readable in a sentence-like manner but still have an expressive name within the function itself. You could have written the above function like so:

```
func printMultipleOf(multiplier: Int, and: Int)
```

This would have the same effect as the function call of being a nice readable sentence. However, now the parameter inside the function is also called and. Having such a generically named parameter in a function with a long body could be confusing.

If you want to have no external name at all, then you can employ the underscore _, as you've seen in previous chapters:

```
func printMultipleOf(_ multiplier: Int, and value: Int) {
    print("\(multiplier) * \(value) = \(multiplier * value)")
}

printMultipleOf(4, and: 2)
```

This change makes it even more readable at the call site. The function call now reads like so:

> *Print multiple of 4 and 2*

You could, if you so wished, take this even further and use _ for all parameters, like so:

```
func printMultipleOf(_ multiplier: Int, _ value: Int) {
    print("\(multiplier) * \(value) = \(multiplier * value)")
}

printMultipleOf(4, 2)
```

In this example, all parameters have no external name. But this illustrates that you should use the underscore wisely. Here, your expression is still understandable, but more complex functions that take many parameters can become confusing and unwieldy with no external parameter names. Imagine if a function took five parameters!

You can also give default values to parameters:

```
func printMultipleOf(_ multiplier: Int, _ value: Int = 1) {
    print("\(multiplier) * \(value) = \(multiplier * value)")
}

printMultipleOf(4)
```

The difference is the = 1 after the second parameter, which means that if no value is provided for the second parameter, it defaults to 1.

Therefore, the code above prints the following:

```
4 * 1 = 4
```

It can be useful to have a default value when you expect a parameter to be one particular value most of the time, and it will simplify your code when you call the function.

Return Values

So far, all the functions you've seen have performed a simple task: printing something out. Functions can also return a value, and the caller of the function can assign the return value to a variable or constant or use it directly in an expression.

With a return value, you can use a function to transform data. You simply take in data through parameters, perform computations and return the result.

Here's how you define a function that returns a value:

```
func multiply(_ number: Int, by multiplier: Int) -> Int {
  return number * multiplier
}

let result = multiply(4, by: 2)
```

To declare that a function returns a value, you add a -> followed by the type of the return value after the set of parentheses and before the opening brace. In this example, the function returns an Int.

Inside the function, you use a return statement to return the value. In this example, you return the product of the two parameters. It's also possible to return multiple values through the use of tuples:

```
func multiplyAndDivide(_ number: Int, by factor: Int)
                  -> (product: Int, quotient: Int) {
  return (number * factor, number / factor)
}

let results = multiplyAndDivide(4, by: 2)
let product = results.product              // 8
let quotient = results.quotient            // 2
```

This function returns *both* the product and quotient of the two parameters: It returns a tuple containing two Int values with appropriate member value names.

The ability to return multiple values through tuples is one of the many things that makes it a pleasure to work with Swift. And it's a handy feature, as you'll see shortly.

You can make both of these functions simpler by removing the return, like so:

```
func multiply(_ number: Int, by multiplier: Int) -> Int {
  number * multiplier
}

func multiplyAndDivide(_ number: Int, by factor: Int)
```

```
                    -> (product: Int, quotient: Int) {
  (number * factor, number / factor)
}
```

You can do this because the function is a **single statement**. If the function had more lines of code, you wouldn't be able to do this. The idea behind this feature is that in such simple functions, it's so obvious, and the return gets in the way of readability.

You need the return for functions with multiple statements because you might make the function return from many different places.

Advanced Parameter Handling

Function parameters are constants, which means they can't be modified.

To illustrate this point, consider the following code:

```
func incrementAndPrint(_ value: Int) {
  value += 1
  print(value)
}
```

This results in an error:

```
func incrementAndPrint(_ value: Int) {
  value += 1       ⊗  Left side of mutating operator isn't mutable: 'value' is a 'let' constant
  print(value)
}
```

The parameter value is the equivalent of a constant declared with let. Therefore, when the function attempts to increment it, the compiler emits an error.

It is important to note that Swift copies the value before passing it to the function, a behavior known as **pass-by-value**.

> **Note**: Pass-by-value and making copies is the standard behavior for all types you've seen so far in this book. You'll see another way things get passed into functions in Chapter 14, "Classes," when you learn about reference types.

Ideally, a function doesn't alter its parameters. When it does, you need to think extra hard about how the value might change to avoid incorrect assumptions that might introduce bugs into your code. By default, the compiler prevents you from making these changes.

Sometimes you *do* want to let a function change a parameter directly, a behavior known as **copy-in copy-out** or **call by value result**. You do it like so:

```
func incrementAndPrint(_ value: inout Int) {
    value += 1
    print(value)
}
```

inout before the parameter type indicates that this parameter should be copied in, that local copy used within the function, and copied back out when the function returns. You need to tweak the function call slightly to complete this example. Add an ampersand (&) before the argument, which makes it clear at the call site that you are using copy-in copy-out:

```
var value = 5
incrementAndPrint(&value)
print(value)
```

Now the function can change the value however it wishes.

This example will print the following:

```
6

6
```

The function increments value and keeps its modified data after the function finishes. The value goes *in* to the function and comes back *out* again, thus the keyword inout.

> **Note**: Under certain conditions, the compiler can simplify copy-in copy-out to what is called *pass-by-reference*. The argument value isn't copied into the parameter. Instead, the parameter will hold a reference to the memory of the original value. This optimization satisfies all requirements of copy-in copy-out while removing the need for copies.

Overloading

Did you notice how you used the same name for several different functions in the previous examples?

```
func printMultipleOf(multiplier: Int, andValue: Int)
func printMultipleOf(multiplier: Int, and value: Int)
func printMultipleOf(_ multiplier: Int, and value: Int)
func printMultipleOf(_ multiplier: Int, _ value: Int)
```

This is called **overloading** and lets you define similar functions using a single name.

However, the compiler must still be able to tell the difference between these functions. Whenever you call a function, it should always be clear which function you're calling.

This is usually achieved through a difference in the parameter list:

• A different number of parameters.

• Different parameter types.

• Different external parameter names, such as the case with `printMultipleOf`.

You can also overload a function name based on a different return type, like so:

```
func getValue() -> Int {
  31
}

func getValue() -> String {
  "Matt Galloway"
}
```

Here, there are two functions called `getValue()`, which return different types: one an `Int` and the other a `String`.

Using these is a little more complicated. Consider the following:

```
let value = getValue()
```

How does Swift know which `getValue()` to call? The answer is, it doesn't. And the compiler will present the following error:

```
let value = getValue()          ⊗  Ambiguous use of 'getValue()'
```

There's no way of knowing which one to call, and it's a chicken-and-egg situation. It's unknown what type value is, so Swift doesn't know which getValue() to call or the return type of getValue().

To fix this, you can declare what type you want value to be, like so:

```
let valueInt: Int = getValue()
let valueString: String = getValue()
```

This will correctly call the Int version of getValue() in the first instance and the String version of getValue() in the second instance.

It's worth noting that overloading should be used with care. Only use overloading for functions that are related and similar in behavior.

When only the return type is overloaded, as in the above example, you lose type inference, which is not recommended.

Mini-Exercises

1. Write a function named printFullName that takes two strings called firstName and lastName. The function should print out the full name defined as firstName + " " + lastName. Use it to print out your own full name.

2. Change the declaration of printFullName to have no external name for either parameter.

3. Write a function named calculateFullName that returns the full name as a string. Use it to store your own full name in a constant.

4. Change calculateFullName to return a tuple containing both the full name and the length of the name. You can find a string's length by using the count property. Use this function to determine the length of your own full name.

Functions as Variables

This may come as a surprise, but functions in Swift are simply another data type. You can assign them to variables and constants like any other type, such as an Int or a String.

To see how this works, consider the following function:

```
func add(_ a: Int, _ b: Int) -> Int {
  a + b
}
```

This function takes two parameters and returns the sum of their values.

You can assign this function to a variable like so:

```
var function = add
```

Here, the variable's name is `function`. The compiler infers the type as `(Int, Int) -> Int` from the `add` function you assign to it.

Notice how the function type `(Int, Int) -> Int` is written the same way you write the parameter list and return type in a function declaration.

Here, the `function` variable is a function type that takes two `Int` parameters and returns an `Int`.

Now you can use the `function` variable in just the same way you'd use `add`, like so:

```
function(4, 2)
```

This returns 6.

Now consider the following code:

```
func subtract(_ a: Int, _ b: Int) -> Int {
  a - b
}
```

Here, you declare another function that takes two `Int` parameters and returns an `Int`. You can set the `function` variable from before to your new `subtract` function **only** because the parameter list and return type of `subtract` is compatible with the type of the `function` variable.

```
function = subtract
function(4, 2)
```

This time, the call to `function` returns 2.

The fact that you can assign functions to variables is handy because it means you can pass functions to other functions. Here's an example of this in action:

```
func printResult(_ function: (Int, Int) -> Int, _ a: Int, _ b:
Int) {
  let result = function(a, b)
  print(result)
}
printResult(add, 4, 2)
```

printResult takes three parameters:

1. function is a function type that takes two Int parameters and returns an Int, declared like so: (Int, Int) -> Int.

2. a is of type Int.

3. b is of type Int.

printResult calls the passed-in function, passing into it the two Int parameters. Then it prints the result to the console:

```
6
```

It's extremely useful to be able to pass functions to other functions, and it can help you write reusable code. Not only can you pass data around to manipulate, but passing functions as parameters means you can be flexible about what code executes.

The Land of No Return

Some functions are never, ever intended to return control to the caller. For example, think about a function designed to halt an application. Perhaps this sounds strange, so let me explain: if an application is about to work with corrupt data, it's often best to crash rather than continue into an unknown and potentially dangerous state. The function fatalError("reason to terminate") is an example of a function like this. It prints the reason for the fatal error and then halts execution to prevent further damage.

Another example of a non-returning function is one that handles an event loop. An event loop is at the heart of every modern application that takes input from the user and displays things on a screen. The event loop services requests coming from the user then passes these events to the application code, which in turn causes the information to be displayed on the screen. The loop then cycles back and services the next event.

These event loops are often started in an application by calling a function known never to return.

Swift will complain to the compiler that a function is known never to return, like so:

```
func noReturn() -> Never {

}
```

Notice the special return type Never, indicating that this function will never return.

If you wrote this code, the compiler would present the following error:

```
func noReturn() -> Never {

}
          ⊗ Global function with uninhabited return        ⊗
            type 'Never' is missing call to another
            never-returning function on all paths
```

This is a long-winded way of saying that the function doesn't call another "no return" function before it returns itself. When it reaches the end, the function returns to the place from which it was called, breaching the contract of the Never return type.

A crude but honest implementation of a function that wouldn't return would be as follows:

```
func infiniteLoop() -> Never {
  while true {
  }
}
```

Why bother with this special return type? It's useful because by the compiler knowing that the function won't ever return, it can make certain optimizations when generating the code to call the function. Essentially, the code that calls the function doesn't need to bother doing anything after the function call because it knows that it will never end before the application is terminated.

Writing Good Functions

Functions let you solve many problems. The best do *one simple task*, making them easier to mix, match, and model into more complex behaviors.

Make functions that are easy to use and understand! Give them well-defined inputs that produce the same output every time. You'll find it's easier to reason about and test good, clean, simple functions in isolation.

Commenting Your Functions

All good software developers document their code. :] Documenting your functions is essential to making sure that when you return to the code later or share it with other people, it can be understood without having to trawl through the code.

Fortunately, Swift has a straightforward tool called **DocC** to document functions that integrates well with Xcode's code completion and other features. Let's take a look at how you can document a function:

```
/// Calculates the average of three values
/// - Parameters:
///    - a: The first value.
///    - b: The second value.
///    - c: The third value.
/// - Returns: The average of the three values.
func calculateAverage(of a: Double, and b: Double, and c:
Double) -> Double {
  let total = a + b + c
  let average = total / 3
  return average
}

calculateAverage(of: 1, and: 3, and: 5)
```

Instead of the usual double-/, you use triple-/. Then the first line is the description of what the function does. Following that is a list of the parameters and, finally, a description of the return value.

If you forget the format of a documentation comment, in Xcode put your cursor on the same line as the function and press **Command-Option-/** or choose "Editor ▸ Structure ▸ Add Documentation". The Xcode editor will insert a comment template for you that you can then fill out.

When you create this kind of code documentation, you will find that the comment changes the font in Xcode from the usual monospace font. Neat right? Well, yes, but there's more.

First, Xcode shows your documentation when code completion comes up, like so:

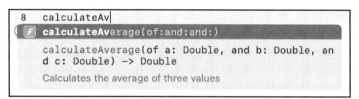

Also, you can hold the **Option** key and click on the function name, and Xcode shows your documentation in a handy popover, like so:

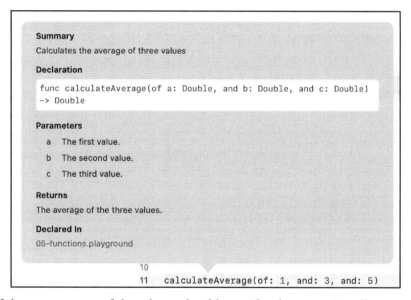

Both of these are very useful, and you should consider documenting all your functions, especially those that are frequently used, overloaded, or complicated. Future you will thank you later. :]

Challenges

Before moving on, here are some challenges to test your knowledge of functions. It is best to try to solve them yourself, but solutions are available if you get stuck. These came with the download or are available at the printed book's source code link listed in the introduction.

Challenge 1: Looping with Stride Functions

In Chapter 4, "Advanced Control Flow", you wrote some for loops with countable ranges. Countable ranges are limited in that they must always be increasing by one. The Swift stride(from:to:by:) and stride(from:through:by:) functions let you loop much more flexibly.

For example, if you wanted to loop from 10 to 20 by 4's you can write:

```
for index in stride(from: 10, to: 22, by: 4) {
  print(index)
}
// prints 10, 14, 18

for index in stride(from: 10, through: 22, by: 4) {
  print(index)
}
// prints 10, 14, 18, and 22
```

- What is the difference between the two stride function overloads?

- Write a loop that goes from 10.0 to (and including) 9.0, decrementing by 0.1.

Chapter 5: Functions   131

Challenge 2: It's Prime Time

When I'm acquainting myself with a programming language, one of the first things I do is write a function to determine whether or not a number is prime. That's your second challenge.

First, write the following function:

```
func isNumberDivisible(_ number: Int, by divisor: Int) -> Bool
```

You'll use this to determine if one number is divisible by another. It should return `true` when `number` is divisible by `divisor`.

Hint: You can use the modulo (%) operator to help you out here.

Next, write the main function:

```
func isPrime(_ number: Int) -> Bool
```

This should return `true` if the `number` is prime and `false` otherwise. A number is prime if it's only divisible by 1 and itself. You should loop through the numbers from 1 to the number and find the number's divisors. If it has any divisors other than 1 and itself, then the number isn't prime. You'll need to use the `isNumberDivisible(_:by:)` function you wrote earlier.

Use this function to check the following cases:

```
isPrime(6)      // false
isPrime(13)     // true
isPrime(8893)   // true
```

Hint 1: Numbers less than 0 should not be considered prime. Check for this case at the start of the function and return early if the number is less than 0.

Hint 2: Use a `for` loop to find divisors. If you start at 2 and end before the number itself, then as soon as you find a divisor, you can return `false`.

Hint 3: If you want to get *really* clever, you can simply loop from 2 until you reach the square root of `number` rather than going all the way up to `number` itself. I'll leave it as an exercise for you to figure out why. It may help to think of the number 16, whose square root is 4. The divisors of 16 are 1, 2, 4, 8 and 16.

Challenge 3: Recursive Functions

In this challenge, you will see what happens when a function calls *itself*, a behavior called **recursion**. This may sound unusual, but it can be quite useful.

You will write a function that computes a value from the **Fibonacci sequence**. Any value in the sequence is the sum of the previous two values. The sequence is defined such that the first two values equal 1. That is, fibonacci(1) = 1 and fibonacci(2) = 1.

Write your function using the following declaration:

```
func fibonacci(_ number: Int) -> Int
```

Then, verify you've written the function correctly by executing it with the following numbers:

```
fibonacci(1)  // = 1
fibonacci(2)  // = 1
fibonacci(3)  // = 2
fibonacci(4)  // = 3
fibonacci(5)  // = 5
fibonacci(10) // = 55
```

Hint 1: For values of number less than 1, you should return 0.

Hint 2: To start the sequence, hard-code a return value of 1 when number equals 1 or 2.

Hint 3: For any other value, you'll need to return the sum of calling fibonacci with number − 1 and number − 2.

Key Points

- You use a **function** to define a task that you can execute as many times as you like without writing the code multiple times.

- Functions are defined with zero or more **parameters** and optionally a return value.

- You can add an external name to a function parameter to change the label you use in a function call, or you can use an underscore to denote no label.

- Parameters are passed as constants, unless you mark them as inout, in which case they are copied-in and copied-out.

- Functions can have the same name with different parameters. This is called **overloading**.

- Functions can have a special Never return type to inform Swift that this function will never exit.

- You can assign functions to variables and pass them to other functions.

- Strive to create functions that are clearly named and have one job with repeatable inputs and outputs.

- Function documentation can be created by prefixing the function with a comment section using ///.

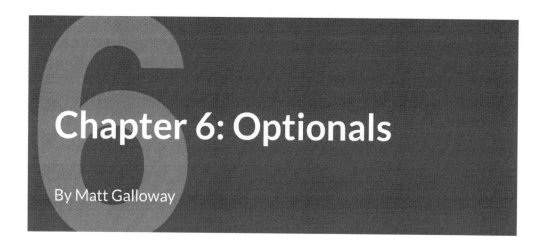

Chapter 6: Optionals

By Matt Galloway

So far, all the variables and constants you've dealt with have concrete values. When you had a string variable, like var name, it had a string value associated with it, like "Matt Galloway". It could have been an empty string, like "", but there was a value to which you could refer.

That's one of the built-in safety features of Swift: If the type says Int or String, then there's an actual integer or string there, guaranteed.

This chapter will introduce you to the concept of **optionals**, a special Swift type that can represent a value and the absence of that value. By the end of this chapter, you'll know why you need optionals and how to use them safely.

Introducing nil

Sometimes, it's necessary to represent the absence of a value. Imagine a scenario where you need to refer to a person's identifying information; you want to store the person's name, age and occupation. Name and age are both things that must have a value — everyone has them. But not everyone is employed, so the absence of a value for occupation is something you need to handle.

Without knowing about optionals, this is how you might represent the person's name, age and occupation:

```
var name = "Matt Galloway"
var age = 30
var occupation = "Software Developer & Author"
```

But what if I become unemployed? Maybe I've won the lottery and want to give up work altogether (I wish!). This is when it would be useful to be able to refer to the absence of a value.

Why couldn't you just use an empty string? You *could*, but optionals are a much better solution. Read on to see why.

Sentinel Values

A value representing a special condition, such as the absence of a value, is known as a **sentinel value** or a special value. That's what your empty string would be in the previous example.

Let's look at another example. Say your code requests something from a server, and you use a variable to store any returned error code:

```
var errorCode = 0
```

You represent the lack of an error with a zero in the success case. That means 0 is a sentinel value.

This arrangement works like the empty string for occupation, but it's potentially confusing for the programmer because it arbitrarily steals a value. 0 might be a valid error code — or could be in the future if the server changed how it responded. Either way, you can't be completely confident that the server didn't return an error without consulting the documentation about special values.

In these two examples, it would be much better if a special *type* could represent the absence of a value. It would then be explicit when a value exists and when one doesn't. The compiler could check for you.

nil is the name given to the absence of a value, and you're about to see how Swift incorporates this concept into the language in a rather elegant way.

Some other programming languages simply embrace sentinel values. Some, like Objective-C, have the concept of `nil`, but it is merely a synonym for zero (a sentinel value).

Swift introduces a new type, **Optional**, that handles the possibility that a value could be `nil`. It removes the ambiguity introduced by using sentinel values. If you're handling a non-optional type, you're guaranteed to have a value and don't need to worry about a sentinel value with special meaning. Similarly, if you use an optional type, you know you must handle the `nil` case.

Introducing Optionals

Optionals are Swift's solution to the problem of representing both a value and the absence of a value. An optional can hold either a value *or* `nil`.

Think of an optional as a box: it either contains exactly one value or is empty. When it doesn't contain a value, it's said to contain `nil`. The box itself always exists; it's always there for you to open and look inside.

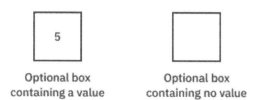

Optional box
containing a value

Optional box
containing no value

On the other hand, a string or an integer doesn't have this box around it. Instead, there's always a value, such as `"hello"` or 42. Remember, non-optional types are guaranteed to have an actual value.

Note: Those who've studied physics may be thinking about Schroedinger's cat right now. Optionals are a little bit like that, except it's not a matter of life and death!

You declare a variable of an optional type by using the following syntax:

```
var errorCode: Int?
```

The only difference between this and a standard declaration is the question mark at the end of the type. In this case, errorCode is an "optional Int". This means the variable is like a box containing either an Int or nil.

> **Note:** You can add a question mark after any type to create an optional type. This optional type is said to *wrap* the regular non-optional type. For example, optional type String? wraps type String. In other words: an optional box of type String? holds either a String or nil.
>
> Also, note how an optional type must be made explicit using a type annotation (here : Int?). Optional types can never be inferred from initialization values, as those values are of a regular, non-optional type, or nil, which can be used with any optional type.

Setting the value is simple. You can either set it to an Int, like so:

```
errorCode = 100
```

Or you can set it to nil, like so:

```
errorCode = nil
```

This diagram may help you visualize what's happening:

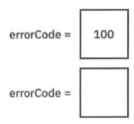

The optional box always exists. When you assign 100 to the variable, you're filling the box with the value. When you assign nil to the variable, you're emptying the box.

Take a few minutes to think about this concept. The box analogy will be a big help as you go through the rest of the chapter and use optionals.

Mini-Exercises

1. Make an optional String called myFavoriteSong. If you have a favorite song, set it to a string representing that song. If you have more than one favorite song or no favorite, set the optional to nil.

2. Create a constant called parsedInt and set it equal to Int("10"), which tries to parse the string 10 and convert it to an Int. Check the type of parsedInt using Option-Click. Why is it an optional?

3. Change the string being parsed in the above exercise to a non-integer (try dog, for example). What does parsedInt equal now?

Unwrapping Optionals

It's all well and good that optionals exist, but you may be wondering how you can look inside the box and manipulate the value it contains.

Take a look at what happens when you print out the value of an optional:

```
var result: Int? = 30
print(result)
```

This prints the following:

```
Optional(30)
```

> **Note:** You will also see a warning on this line which says, "Expression implicitly coerced from 'Int?' to Any". This is because Swift warns that you're using an optional in place of the Any type as it's something that usually means you did something wrong. You can change the code to print(result as Any) to silence the warning.

That isn't really what you wanted, although it makes sense if you think about it. Your code has printed the box, and the result says, "result is an optional that contains the value 30".

To see how an optional type is different from a non-optional type, see what happens if you try to use `result` as if it were a normal integer:

```
print(result + 1)
```

This code triggers an error:

```
Value of optional type 'Int?' must be unwrapped to a value of
type 'Int'
```

It doesn't work because you're trying to add an integer to a box — not to the value inside the box but to the box itself, which doesn't make sense.

Force Unwrapping

The error message indicates the solution: It tells you that the optional `must` be unwrapped. You need to unwrap the value from its box. It's like Christmas!

Let's see how that works. Consider the following declarations:

```
var authorName: String? = "Matt Galloway"
var authorAge: Int? = 30
```

There are two different methods you can use to unwrap these optionals. The first is known as **force unwrapping**, and you perform it like so:

```
var unwrappedAuthorName = authorName!
print("Author is \(unwrappedAuthorName)")
```

This code prints:

```
Author is Matt Galloway
```

Great! That's what you'd expect.

The exclamation mark after the variable name tells the compiler that you want to look inside the box and take out the value. The result is a value of the wrapped type. This means unwrappedAuthorName is of type `String`, not `String?`.

The word "force" and the exclamation mark ! probably convey a sense of danger to you, and they should.

You should use force unwrapping sparingly. To see why consider what happens when the optional doesn't contain a value:

```
authorName = nil
print("Author is \(authorName!)")
```

This code produces the following error that you will see in your console:

```
Fatal error: Unexpectedly found nil while unwrapping an Optional
value
```

The error occurs because the variable contains no value when you try to unwrap it. What's worse is that you get this error at runtime rather than compile-time – which means you'd only notice the error if you happened to execute this code with some invalid input.

Worse yet, if this code were inside an app, the runtime error would cause the app to crash!

How can you play it safe?

To stop the runtime error here, you could wrap the code that unwraps the optional in a check, like so:

```
if authorName != nil {
    print("Author is \(authorName!)")
} else {
    print("No author.")
}
```

The if statement checks if the optional contains nil. If it doesn't, it contains a value you can unwrap.

The code is now safe, but it's still not perfect. If you rely on this technique, you'll have to remember to check for nil every time you want to unwrap an optional. That will become tedious, and one day you'll forget and again end up with the possibility of a runtime error.

Back to the drawing board, then!

Optional Binding

Swift includes a feature known as **optional binding**, which lets you safely access the value inside an optional. You use it like so:

```
if let unwrappedAuthorName = authorName {
  print("Author is \(unwrappedAuthorName)")
} else {
  print("No author.")
}
```

You'll immediately notice that there are no exclamation marks here. This optional binding gets rid of the optional type. If the optional contains a value, this value is unwrapped and stored in, or *bound to*, the constant unwrappedAuthorName. The if statement then executes the first block of code, within which you can safely use unwrappedAuthorName, as it's a regular non-optional String.

If the optional doesn't contain a value, then the if statement executes the else block. In that case, the unwrappedAuthorName variable doesn't even exist.

You can see how optional binding is much safer than force unwrapping, and you should use it whenever an optional might be nil. Force unwrapping is only appropriate when an optional *is guaranteed* to contain a value.

Because naming things is so hard, it's common practice to give the unwrapped constant the same name as the optional (thereby *shadowing* that optional):

```
if let authorName = authorName {
  print("Author is \(authorName)")
} else {
  print("No author.")
}
```

You can even unwrap multiple values at the same time, like so:

```
if let authorName = authorName,
   let authorAge = authorAge {
  print("The author is \(authorName) who is \(authorAge) years
old.")
} else {
  print("No author or no age.")
}
```

This code unwraps two values. It will only execute the if part of the statement when both optionals contain a value.

You can combine unwrapping multiple optionals with additional Boolean checks. For example:

```
if let authorName = authorName,
   let authorAge = authorAge,
   authorAge >= 40 {
   print("The author is \(authorName) who is \(authorAge) years
old.")
} else {
   print("No author or no age or age less than 40.")
}
```

Here, you unwrap name and age and check that age is greater than or equal to 40. The expression in the if statement will only be true if name is non-nil, *and* age is non-nil, *and* age is greater than or equal to 40.

Now you know how to safely look inside an optional and extract its value if one exists.

Shorthand

You will have noticed in the examples above that you can end up repeating yourself a lot when using optional binding. Take the following example:

```
if let authorName = authorName {
   print("The author is \(authorName)")
}
```

It might seem quite strange to write authorName twice there. Well, Swift has an answer to that. You can use a shorthand form of optional binding in cases where you don't want to change the variable's name. The above example can be rewritten as:

```
if let authorName {
   print("The author is \(authorName)")
}
```

You can, of course, also unwrap multiple optionals at the same time with this syntax, like so:

```
if let authorName, let authorAge {
   print("The author is \(authorName) who is \(authorAge) years
old.")
}
```

You will find this comes in handy and saves some extra typing. It's very common to need to simply check if a variable is non-nil and, if so, do some logic.

Mini-Exercises

1. Using your `myFavoriteSong` variable from earlier, use optional binding to check if it contains a value. If it does, print out the value. If it doesn't, print `"I don't have a favorite song."`

2. Change `myFavoriteSong` to the opposite of what it is now. If it's `nil`, set it to a string; if it's a string, set it to `nil`. Observe how your printed result changes.

Introducing guard

Sometimes you want to check a condition and only continue executing a function if the condition is true, such as when you use optionals. Imagine a function that fetches some data from the network. That fetch might fail if the network is down. The usual way to encapsulate this behavior is using an optional, which has a value if the fetch succeeds, and `nil` otherwise.

Swift has a useful and powerful feature to help in situations like this: the **guard statement**. Let's take a look at it with this contrived example for now:

```
func guardMyCastle(name: String?) {
  guard let castleName = name else {
    print("No castle!")
    return
  }

  // At this point, `castleName` is a non-optional String

  print("Your castle called \(castleName) was guarded!")
}
```

The guard statement comprises `guard` followed by a condition that can include both Boolean expressions and optional bindings, followed by `else`, followed by a block of code. The block of code covered by the `else` will execute if the condition is *false*. The block of code that executes if the condition is false *must* return. If you accidentally forget, the compiler will stop you — this is the guard statement's true beauty.

You may hear programmers talking about the "happy path" through a function; this is the path you'd expect to happen most of the time. Any other path followed would be due to an error or another reason why the function should return earlier than expected.

Guard statements ensure the happy path remains on the left-hand side of the code; this is usually a good thing as it makes code more readable and understandable. Also, because the guard statement must return in the false case, the Swift compiler knows that if the condition was true, anything checked in the guard statement's condition *must* be true for the remainder of the function.

You could simply use an if-let binding and return when it's nil. However, when you use guard, you are explicitly saying that this must return if the statement in the guard is false. Thus the compiler can make sure that you have added a return. The compiler is providing some excellent safety for you!

Let's see guard in a more "real world" example. Consider the following function:

```swift
func calculateNumberOfSides(shape: String) -> Int? {
    switch shape {
    case "Triangle":
        return 3
    case "Square":
        return 4
    case "Rectangle":
        return 4
    case "Pentagon":
        return 5
    case "Hexagon":
        return 6
    default:
        return nil
    }
}
```

This function takes a shape name and returns the number of sides the shape has. If the shape isn't known, or you pass something that isn't a shape, it returns nil.

You could use this function like so:

```swift
func maybePrintSides(shape: String) {
    let sides = calculateNumberOfSides(shape: shape)

    if let sides = sides {
        print("A \(shape) has \(sides) sides.")
    } else {
        print("I don't know the number of sides for \(shape).")
    }
}
```

There's nothing wrong with this, and it would work.

However, the same logic could be written with a guard statement like so:

```
func maybePrintSides(shape: String) {
  guard let sides = calculateNumberOfSides(shape: shape) else {
    print("I don't know the number of sides for \(shape).")
    return
  }

  print("A \(shape) has \(sides) sides.")
}
```

When your functions get more complex, guard comes into its own. You may have multiple guards at the top of the function that set up the initial conditions correctly. You'll see it used extensively in Swift code.

Nil Coalescing

There's a rather handy alternative way to unwrap an optional. You use it when you want to get a value out of the optional *no matter what* — and in the case of nil, you'll use a default value. This operation is called **nil coalescing**. Here's how it works:

```
var optionalInt: Int? = 10
var mustHaveResult = optionalInt ?? 0
```

The nil coalescing happens on the second line, with the double question mark (??), known as the **nil coalescing operator**. This line means mustHaveResult will equal either the value inside optionalInt or 0 if optionalInt contains nil. In this example, mustHaveResult contains the concrete Int value of 10.

The previous code is equivalent to the following:

```
var optionalInt: Int? = 10
var mustHaveResult: Int
if let unwrapped = optionalInt {
  mustHaveResult = unwrapped
} else {
  mustHaveResult = 0
}
```

Set the optionalInt to nil, like so:

```
optionalInt = nil
mustHaveResult = optionalInt ?? 0
```

Now mustHaveResult equals 0.

Challenges

Before moving on, here are some challenges to test your knowledge of optionals. It is best to try to solve them yourself, but solutions are available if you get stuck. These came with the download or are available at the printed book's source code link listed in the introduction.

Challenge 1: You Be the Compiler

Which of the following are valid statements?

```
var name: String? = "Ray"
var age: Int = nil
let distance: Float = 26.7
var middleName: String? = nil
```

Challenge 2: Divide and Conquer

First, create a function that returns the number of times an integer can be divided by another integer without a remainder. The function should return `nil` if the division doesn't produce a whole number. Name the function `divideIfWhole`.

Then, write code that tries to unwrap the optional result of the function. There should be two cases: upon success, print `"Yep, it divides \(answer) times"`, and upon failure, print `"Not divisible :["`.

Finally, test your function:

1. Divide 10 by 2. This should print `"Yep, it divides 5 times."`

2. Divide 10 by 3. This should print `"Not divisible :[."`

Hint 1: Use the following as the start of the function signature:

```
func divideIfWhole(_ value: Int, by divisor: Int)
```

You'll need to add the return type, which will be an optional!

Hint 2: You can use the modulo operator (%) to determine if a value is divisible by another; recall that this operation returns the remainder from the division of two numbers. For example, `10 % 2 = 0` means that 10 is divisible by 2 with no remainder, whereas `10 % 3 = 1` means that 10 is divisible by 3 with a remainder of 1.

Challenge 3: Refactor and Reduce

The code you wrote in the last challenge used `if` statements. In this challenge, refactor that code to use `nil` coalescing instead. This time, make it print "It divides X times" in all cases, but if the division doesn't result in a whole number, then X should be 0.

Challenge 4: Nested Optionals

Consider the following nested optional — it corresponds to a number inside a box inside a box inside a box.

```
let number: Int??? = 10
```

If you print number you get the following:

```
print(number)
// Optional(Optional(Optional(10)))

print(number!)
// Optional(Optional(10))
```

Do the following:

1. Fully force unwrap and print `number`.

2. Optionally bind and print `number` with `if let`.

3. Write a function `printNumber(_ number: Int???)` that uses `guard` to print the number only if it is bound.

Key Points

- `nil` represents the absence of a value.

- Non-optional variables and constants are never `nil`.

- **Optional** variables and constants are like boxes that can contain a value *or* be empty (`nil`).

- To work with the value inside an optional, you must first unwrap it from the optional.

- The safest way to unwrap an optional's value is by using **optional binding** or **nil coalescing**. Use **forced unwrapping** only when appropriate, as it could produce a runtime error.

- You can `guard let` to bind an optional. If the binding fails, the compiler forces you to exit the current function (or halt execution). This construction guarantees that your program never executes with an uninitialized value.

Section II: Collection Types

So far, you've mostly seen data in the form of single elements. Although tuples can have multiple pieces of data, you have to specify the size upfront; a tuple with three strings is a completely different type from a tuple with two strings, and converting between them isn't trivial. In this section, you'll learn about **collection types** in Swift. Collections are flexible "containers" that let you store any number of values together.

There are several collection types in Swift, but three important ones are arrays, dictionaries and sets. You'll learn to apply custom operations and loop over collection types. Finally, you'll revisit strings, which are collections of characters.

All the collection types share similar interfaces but have very different use cases. As you read through these chapters, keep the differences in mind, and you'll begin to develop a feel for which type you should use when.

Chapter 7: Arrays, Dictionaries & Sets

By Eli Ganim

As discussed in the introduction to this section, collections are flexible "containers" that let you store any number of values together. Before discussing these collections, you need to understand the concept of *mutable* vs. *immutable* collections.

As part of exploring the differences between the collection types, you'll also consider performance: how quickly the collections can perform certain operations, such as adding or searching through it.

The usual way to talk about performance is with **big-O notation**. If you're unfamiliar with it, start reading the chapter for a brief introduction.

Big-O notation is a way to describe **running time**, or how long an operation takes to complete. The idea is that the exact time an operation takes isn't as important; the relative difference in scale matters.

Imagine you have a list of names in some random order, and you must look up the first name on the list. It doesn't matter whether the list has a single name or a million names — glancing at the first name always takes the same time. That's an example of a **constant time** operation, or **O(1)** in big-O notation.

Now say you have to find a particular name on the list. You need to scan the list and look at every name until you either find a match or reach the end. Again, we're not concerned with the exact amount of time this takes, just the relative time compared to other operations.

To figure out the running time, think in terms of units of work. You need to look at every name, so consider there to be one "unit" of work per name. If you had 100 names, that's 100 units of work. What if you double the number of names to 200? How does that change the amount of work?

The answer is it *also* doubles the amount of work. Similarly, if you quadruple the number of names, that quadruples the amount of work.

This increase in work is an example of a **linear time** operation, or **O(N)** in big-O notation. The input size is the variable N, which means the amount of time the process takes is also N. There's a direct, linear relationship between the input size (the number of names in the list) and the time it will take to search for one name.

You can see why constant time operations use the number one in $O(1)$. They're just a single unit of work, no matter what!

You can read more about big-O notation by searching the Web. You'll only need constant and linear time in this book, but there are other such **time complexities** out there.

Big-O notation is essential when dealing with collection types because collections can store vast amounts of data. You need to be aware of running times when you add, delete or edit values.

For example, if collection type A has constant-time searching and collection type B has linear-time searching, which you choose to use will depend on how much searching you're planning to do.

Mutable Versus Immutable Collections

Like the previous types you've read about, such as `Int` or `String`, when you create a collection, you must declare it as either a constant or a variable.

If the collection doesn't need to change after you've created it, you should make it immutable by declaring it as a constant with `let`. Alternatively, if you need to add, remove or update values in the collection, you should create a mutable collection by declaring it as a variable with `var`.

Arrays

Arrays are the most common collection type you'll run into in Swift. Arrays are typed, just like regular variables and constants, and store multiple values like a simple list.

Before you create your first array, consider in detail what an array is and why you might want to use one.

What Is an Array?

An array is an ordered collection of values of the same type. The elements in the array are **zero-indexed**, which means the index of the first element is 0, the index of the second element is 1, and so on. Knowing this, you can determine that the last element's index is the number of values in the array minus one.

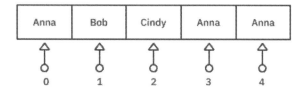

There are five elements in this array, at indices 0–4.

All values are of type String, so you can't add non-string types to an array that holds strings. Notice that the same value can appear multiple times.

When Are Arrays Useful?

Arrays are useful when storing your items in a particular order. You may want the elements sorted, or you may need to fetch elements by index without iterating through the entire array.

For example, if you were storing high-score data, then the order would matter. You would want the highest score to come first in the list (i.e., at index 0) with the next-highest score after that, and so on.

Creating Arrays

The easiest way to create an array is using an **array literal**. This approach concisely provides array values as a list of values separated by commas and surrounded by square brackets.

```
let evenNumbers = [2, 4, 6, 8]
```

Since the array literal only contains integers, Swift infers the type of `evenNumbers` to be an array of `Int` values. This type is written as `[Int]`. The type inside the square brackets defines the type of values the array can store, which the compiler will enforce when adding elements to the array. If you try to add a string, for example, the compiler will return a type error, and your code won't compile.

You can create an empty using the empty array literal `[]`. Because the compiler isn't able to infer a type from this, you need to use a type annotation to make the type explicit:

```
var subscribers: [String] = []
```

It's also possible to create an array with all of its values set to a default value:

```
let allZeros = Array(repeating: 0, count: 5) // [0, 0, 0, 0, 0]
```

It's good practice to declare arrays that aren't going to change as constants. For example, consider this array:

```
let vowels = ["A", "E", "I", "O", "U"]
```

`vowels` is an array of strings whose values can't be changed. But that's fine since the list of vowels doesn't tend to change very often!

Accessing Elements

Being able to create arrays is useless unless you know how to fetch values from an array. In this section, you'll learn several ways to access an array's elements.

Using Properties and Methods

Imagine creating a game of cards, and you want to store the players' names in an array. The list will need to change as players join or leave the game, so you need to declare a mutable array:

```
var players = ["Alice", "Bob", "Cindy", "Dan"]
```

In this example, `players` is a mutable array because you assigned it to a variable.

Before the game starts, you need to make sure there are enough players. You can use the `isEmpty` *property* to check if there's at least one player:

```
print(players.isEmpty)
// > false
```

Note: You'll learn about properties in Chapter 12, "Properties". For now, think of them as variables that are built into values. To access a property, place a dot after the name of the constant or variable that holds the value and follow it with the name of the property you want to access.

The array isn't empty, but you need at least two players to start a game. You can get the number of players using the `count` property:

```
if players.count < 2 {
  print("We need at least two players!")
} else {
  print("Let's start!")
}
// > Let's start!
```

It's time to start the game! You decide that the order of play is by the order of names in the array. How would you get the first player's name?

Arrays provide the `first` property to fetch the first object of an array:

```
var currentPlayer = players.first
```

Printing the value of `currentPlayer` reveals something interesting:

```
print(currentPlayer as Any)
// > Optional("Alice")
```

The property `first` returns an *optional* because if the array were empty, the `first` element would be missing and thus `nil`. The `print()` method realizes `currentPlayer` is optional and generates a warning. To suppress the warning, add `as Any` to the type to be printed.

Similarly, arrays have a `last` property that returns the last value in an array or `nil` if the array is empty:

```
print(players.last as Any)
// > Optional("Dan")
```

Another way to get values from an array is by calling `min()`. This *method* returns the element with the lowest *value* in the array — not the lowest index!

If the array contained strings, then it would return the string that's the lowest in alphabetical order, which in this case is `"Alice"`:

```
currentPlayer = players.min()
print(currentPlayer as Any)
// > Optional("Alice")
```

> **Note**: You'll learn about methods in Chapter 13, "Methods". For now, think of them as functions that are built into values. To call a method, place a dot after the name of the constant or variable that holds the value and follow it with the name of the method you want to call. Like functions, don't forget to include the parameter list in parenthesis, even if it's empty, to call the method.

Obviously, `first` and `min()` will not always return the same value. For example:

```
print([2, 3, 1].first as Any)
// > Optional(2)
print([2, 3, 1].min() as Any)
// > Optional(1)
```

As you might have guessed, arrays also have a `max()` method.

> **Note**: The `first` and `last` properties and the `min()` and `max()` methods aren't unique to arrays. Every collection type has these properties and methods, in addition to many others. You'll learn more about this behavior when you read about protocols in Chapter 17, "Protocols".

Now that you know how to get the first player, you'll announce who that player is:

```
if let currentPlayer {
    print("\(currentPlayer) will start")
}
// > Alice will start
```

You use `if let` to unwrap the optional you got back from `min()`; otherwise, the statement would print `Optional("Alice") will start`, which is not what you want.

These properties and methods are helpful if you want to get the first, last, minimum or maximum elements. But what if the element you want can't be obtained with one of these properties or methods?

Using Subscripting

The most convenient way to access elements in an array is by using the subscript syntax. This syntax lets you access any value directly by using its index inside square brackets:

```
var firstPlayer = players[0]
print("First player is \(firstPlayer)")
// > First player is "Alice"
```

Because arrays are zero-indexed, you use index 0 to fetch the first object. You can use a greater index to get the next elements in the array, but if you try to access an index beyond the array's size, you'll get a runtime error.

```
var player = players[4]
// > fatal error: Index out of range
```

You receive this error because `players` contains only four strings. Index 4 represents the fifth element, but there *is* no fifth element in this array.

When you use subscripts, you don't have to worry about optionals since trying to access a non-existing index doesn't return `nil`; it simply causes a runtime error.

Using Countable Ranges to Make an ArraySlice

You can use the subscript syntax with countable ranges to fetch more than a single value from an array. For example, if you'd like to get the next two players, you could do this:

```
let upcomingPlayersSlice = players[1...2]
print(upcomingPlayersSlice[1], upcomingPlayersSlice[2])
// > "Bob Cindy\n"
```

The constant `upcomingPlayersSlice` is an `ArraySlice` of the original array. The reason for this type difference is to make clear that `upcomingPlayersSlice` shares storage with `players`.

The range you used is `1...2`, representing the second and third items in the array. You can use an index here if the start value is smaller than or equal to the end value and within the array's bounds.

It is also easy to make a brand-new, zero-indexed `Array` from an `ArraySlice` like so:

```
let upcomingPlayersArray = Array(players[1...2])
print(upcomingPlayersArray[0], upcomingPlayersArray[1])
// > "Bob Cindy\n"
```

Checking for an Element

You can check if there's at least one occurrence of a specific element in an array by using `contains(_:)`, which returns `true` if it finds the element in the array, and `false` otherwise.

You can use this strategy to write a function that checks if a given player is in the game:

```
func isEliminated(player: String) -> Bool {
  !players.contains(player)
}
```

Now you can use this function any time you need to check if a player has been eliminated:

```
print(isEliminated(player: "Bob"))
// > false
```

You could even test for the existence of an element in a specific range using an `ArraySlice`:

```
players[1...3].contains("Bob") // true
```

Now that you can get data *out* of your arrays, it's time to look at mutable arrays and how to change their values.

Modifying Arrays

You can make changes to mutable arrays, such as adding and removing elements, updating existing values, and moving elements around into a different order. In this section, you'll see how to work with the array to match up what's going on with your game.

Appending Elements

If new players want to join the game, they must sign up and add their names to the array. Eli is the first player to join the existing four players. You can add Eli to the end of the array using the append(_:) method:

```
players.append("Eli")
```

If you try to append anything other than a string, the compiler will show an error. Remember, arrays can only store values of the same type. Also, append(_:) only works with mutable arrays.

The next player to join the game is Gina. You can append her to the game another way by using the += operator:

```
players += ["Gina"]
```

The right-hand side of this expression is an array with a single element: the string "Gina". By using +=, you're appending the elements of that array to players.

Now the array looks like this:

```
print(players)
// > ["Alice", "Bob", "Cindy", "Dan", "Eli", "Gina"]
```

Here, you added a single element to the array, but you can see how easy it would be to append *multiple* items using the += operator by adding more names after Gina's.

Inserting Elements

An unwritten rule of this card game is that the players' names have to be in alphabetical order. This list is missing a player that starts with the letter F. Luckily, Frank has just arrived. You want to add him to the list between Eli and Gina. To do that, you can use the insert(_:at:) method:

```
players.insert("Frank", at: 5)
```

The at argument defines where you want to add the element. Remember that the array is zero-indexed, so index 5 is Gina's index, causing her to move up as Frank takes her place.

Removing Elements

During the game, the other players caught Cindy and Gina cheating. They should be removed from the game! You know that Gina is last in `players`, so you can remove her easily with the `removeLast()` method:

```
var removedPlayer = players.removeLast()
print("\(removedPlayer) was removed")
// > Gina was removed
```

This method does two things: It removes the last element and then returns it, in case you need to print it or store it somewhere else — like in an array of cheaters!

To remove Cindy from the game, you need to know the exact index where her name is stored. Looking at the list of players, you see that she's third, so her index is 2.

```
removedPlayer = players.remove(at: 2)
print("\(removedPlayer) was removed")
// > Cindy was removed
```

But how would you get the index of an element if you didn't already know it? There's a method for that! `firstIndex(of:)` returns the *first index* of the element because the array might contain multiple copies of the same value. If the method doesn't find the element, it returns `nil`.

Mini-Exercise

Use `firstIndex(of:)` to determine the position of the element `"Dan"` in `players`.

Updating Elements

Frank has decided everyone should call him Franklin from now on. You could remove the value `"Frank"` from the array and then add `"Franklin"`, but that's too much work for a simple task. Instead, you should use the subscript syntax to update the name.

```
print(players)
// > ["Alice", "Bob", "Dan", "Eli", "Frank"]
players[4] = "Franklin"
print(players)
// > ["Alice", "Bob", "Dan", "Eli", "Franklin"]
```

Be careful not to use an index beyond the array's bounds, or your program will halt.

As the game continues, some players are eliminated, and new ones come to replace them. You can also use subscripting with ranges to update multiple values in a single line of code:

```
players[0...1] = ["Donna", "Craig", "Brian", "Anna"]
print(players)
// > ["Donna", "Craig", "Brian", "Anna", "Dan", "Eli",
"Franklin"]
```

This code replaces the first two players, Alice and Bob, with the four players in the new player's array. As you can see, the size of the range doesn't have to be equal to the size of the array that holds the values you're adding.

Moving Elements

Take a look at this mess! The `players` array contains names that start with A to F, but they aren't in the correct order, which violates the rules of the game.

You can try to fix this situation by moving values one by one to their correct positions:

```
let playerAnna = players.remove(at: 3)
players.insert(playerAnna, at: 0)
print(players)
// > ["Anna", "Donna", "Craig", "Brian", "Dan", "Eli",
"Franklin"]
```

...or by swapping elements, by using `swapAt(_:_:)`:

```
players.swapAt(1, 3)
print(players)
// > ["Anna", "Brian", "Craig", "Donna", "Dan", "Eli",
"Franklin"]
```

This works for a few elements, but to sort the entire array, you should use `sort()`:

```
players.sort()
print(players)
// > ["Anna", "Brian", "Craig", "Dan", "Donna", "Eli",
"Franklin"]
```

If you'd like to leave the original array untouched and return a sorted *copy* instead, use `sorted()` instead of `sort()`.

Iterating Through an Array

It's getting late, so the players decide to stop for the night and continue tomorrow. In the meantime, you'll keep their scores in a separate array. You'll investigate a better approach for this when you learn about dictionaries, but for now, you can continue to use arrays:

```
let scores = [2, 2, 8, 6, 1, 2, 1]
```

Before the players leave, you want to print the names of those still in the game. You can do this using the for-in loop you read about in Chapter 4, "Advanced Control Flow":

```
for player in players {
  print(player)
}
// > Anna
// > Brian
// > Craig
// > Dan
// > Donna
// > Eli
// > Franklin
```

This code iterates over all the elements of players, from index 0 to players.count − 1 and prints their values. In the first iteration, player is equal to the first element of the array; in the second iteration, it's equal to the second element of the array; and so on, until the loop has printed all the elements in the array.

If you need the index of each element, you can iterate over the return value of the array's enumerated() method, which returns tuples with each element's index and value:

```
for (index, player) in players.enumerated() {
  print("\(index + 1). \(player)")
}
// > 1. Anna
// > 2. Brian
// > 3. Craig
// > 4. Dan
// > 5. Donna
// > 6. Eli
// > 7. Franklin
```

Now you can use the technique you've just learned to write a function that takes an array of integers as its input and returns the sum of its elements:

```
func sumOfElements(in array: [Int]) -> Int {
  var sum = 0
  for number in array {
    sum += number
  }
  return sum
}
```

You could use this function to calculate the sum of the players' scores:

```
print(sumOfElements(in: scores))
// > 22
```

Mini-Exercise

Write a for-in loop that prints the players' names and scores.

Running Time for Array Operations

Arrays are stored as a contiguous block in memory. That means if you have ten elements in an array, the ten values are all stored one next to the other. With that in mind, here's the performance cost of various array operations:

Accessing elements: The cost of fetching an element is cheap, meaning it happens in a fixed or constant time. Sometimes this is written $O(1)$. Since all the values are sequential, it's easy to use *random access* and fetch a value at a particular index; all the compiler needs to know is where the array starts and what index you want to fetch.

Inserting elements: The complexity of adding an element depends on the position in which you add the new element:

• If you add to the beginning of the array, Swift requires time proportional to the size of the array because it has to shift all elements over by one to make room. This complexity is called linear time and is sometimes written $O(n)$.

• Likewise, if you add to the middle of the array, all values from that index on need to be shifted over. Doing so will require n/2 operations; therefore, the running time is still linear with the size of the array or $O(n)$.

- If you add to the end of the array using append and there's room, it will take $O(1)$. If there isn't room, Swift will need to make space somewhere else and copy the entire array before adding the new element, which will take $O(n)$. The average case is $O(1)$ because arrays are not full most of the time.

Deleting elements: Deleting an element leaves a gap where the removed element was. All elements in the array must be sequential, so this gap needs to be closed by shifting elements forward.

The complexity is similar to inserting elements: If you remove an element from the end, it's an $O(1)$ operation. Otherwise, the complexity is $O(n)$.

Searching for an element: If the element you're searching for is the first element in the array, the search will end after a single operation. If the element doesn't exist, you need to perform N operations until you realize that the element is not found. On average, searching for an element will take n/2 operations; therefore, searching has a complexity of $O(n)$.

As you learn about dictionaries and sets, you'll see how their performance characteristics differ from arrays. That could hint at which collection type to use for your particular case.

Dictionaries

A dictionary is an unordered collection of pairs, where each pair comprises a **key** and a **value**.

As shown in the diagram below, keys are unique. The same key can't appear twice in a dictionary, but different keys may point to the same value. All keys must be of the same type, and all values must be of the same type.

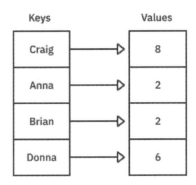

Dictionaries are useful when you want to look up values through an identifier. For example, the table of contents of this book maps chapter names to their page numbers, making it easy to skip to the chapter you want to read.

How is this different from an array? With an array, you can only fetch a value by its index, which has to be an integer, and all indexes have to be sequential. In a dictionary, the keys can be of any type and in no particular order.

Creating Dictionaries

The easiest way to create a dictionary is by using a **dictionary literal**. This is a list of key-value pairs separated by commas, enclosed in square brackets.

For your card game from earlier, instead of using the two arrays to map players to their scores, you can use a dictionary literal:

```
var namesAndScores = ["Anna": 2, "Brian": 2, "Craig": 8,
"Donna": 6]
print(namesAndScores)
// > ["Craig": 8, "Anna": 2, "Donna": 6, "Brian": 2]
```

The compiler infers the dictionary type in this example as [String: Int]. This means namesAndScores is a dictionary with strings as keys and integers as values.

When you print the dictionary, you see no particular order to the pairs. Remember that, unlike arrays, dictionaries are unordered! The empty dictionary literal looks like this: [:]. You can use that to empty an existing dictionary like so:

```
namesAndScores = [:]
```

...or create a new dictionary, like so:

```
var pairs: [String: Int] = [:]
```

The type annotation is required here, as the compiler can't infer the type of the dictionary from the empty dictionary literal.

After you create a dictionary, you can define its capacity:

```
pairs.reserveCapacity(20)
```

Calling `pairs.reserveCapacity(_:)` is an easy way to improve performance when you know how much data the dictionary needs to store. You can add items to the dictionary, and no expensive memory reallocations will occur as long the count remains below the dictionary's capacity.

Accessing Values

As with arrays, there are several ways to access dictionary values.

Using Subscripting

Dictionaries support subscripting to access values. Unlike arrays, you don't access a value by its index but rather by its key. For example, if you want to get Anna's score, you would type:

```
namesAndScores = ["Anna": 2, "Brian": 2, "Craig": 8, "Donna": 6]
// Restore the values

print(namesAndScores["Anna"]!) // 2
```

Notice that the return type is an optional. The dictionary will check if there's a pair with the key Anna, and if there is, return its value. If the dictionary doesn't find the key, it will return `nil`.

```
namesAndScores["Greg"] // nil
```

With arrays, out-of-bounds subscript access causes a runtime error, but dictionaries are different since their results are wrapped in an optional. Subscript access using optionals is powerful. You can find out if a specific player is in the game without iterating over all the keys, as you must do when using an array.

Using Properties and Methods

Dictionaries, like arrays, conform to Swift's `Collection` protocol. Because of that, they share many of the same properties. For example, both arrays and dictionaries have `isEmpty` and `count` properties:

```
namesAndScores.isEmpty  //  false
namesAndScores.count    //  4
```

Note: If you want to know whether a collection has elements, it is always better to use the `isEmpty` property than to compare `count` to zero. Although arrays and dictionaries compute `count` in constant time, not every collection is guaranteed to do so. For example, `count` on a `String` needs to loop through all of its characters. `isEmpty`, by contrast, always runs in constant time, no matter how many values there are for every collection type.

Modifying Dictionaries

It's easy enough to create dictionaries and access their contents — but what about modifying them?

Adding Pairs

Bob wants to join the game.

BOB

Take a look at his details before you let him join:

```
var bobData = [
  "name": "Bob",
  "profession": "Card Player",
  "country": "USA"
]
```

This dictionary is of type [`String: String`], and it's mutable because it's assigned to a variable. Imagine you received more information about Bob, and you wanted to add it to the dictionary. This is how you'd do it:

```
bobData.updateValue("CA", forKey: "state")
```

There's even a shorter way to add pairs, using subscripting:

```
bobData["city"] = "San Francisco"
```

Bob's a professional card player. So far, he sounds like an excellent addition to your roster.

Mini-Exercise

Write a function that prints a given player's city and state.

Updating Values

It appears that in the past, Bob was caught cheating when playing cards. He's not just a professional — he's a card shark! He asks you to change his name and profession so no one will recognize him.

Because Bob seems eager to change his ways, you agree. First, you change his name from Bob to Bobby:

```
bobData.updateValue("Bobby", forKey: "name") // Bob
```

You saw this method above when you read about adding pairs. Why does it return the string Bob? updateValue(_:forKey:) replaces the value of the given key with the new value and returns the old value. If the key doesn't exist, this method will add a new pair and return nil.

As with adding, you can do this with less code by using subscripting:

```
bobData["profession"] = "Mailman"
```

Like updateValue(_:forKey:), this code updates the value for this key or, if the key doesn't exist, creates a new pair.

Removing Pairs

Bob — er, sorry — *Bobby*, still doesn't feel safe, and he wants you to remove all information about his whereabouts:

```
bobData.removeValue(forKey: "state")
```

This method will remove the key `state` and its associated value from the dictionary. As you might expect, there's a shorter way to do this using subscripting:

```
bobData["city"] = nil
```

Assigning `nil` as a key's associated value removes the pair from the dictionary.

> **Note**: If you're using a dictionary that has values that are optional types, `dictionary[key]` = `nil` still removes the key completely. If you want to keep the key and set the value to `nil`, you must use the `updateValue` method.

Iterating Through Dictionaries

The `for-in` loop also works when you want to iterate over a dictionary. But since the items in a dictionary are pairs, you can use a tuple:

```
for (player, score) in namesAndScores {
  print("\(player) - \(score)")
}
// > Craig - 8
// > Anna - 2
// > Donna - 6
// > Brian - 2
```

It's also possible to iterate over just the keys:

```
for player in namesAndScores.keys {
  print("\(player), ", terminator: "") // no newline
}
print("") // print one final newline
// > Craig, Anna, Donna, Brian,
```

You can iterate over just the values in the same manner with the `values` property of the dictionary.

Running Time for Dictionary Operations

To examine how dictionaries work, you need to understand what **hashing** is and how it works. Hashing is the process of transforming a value — String, Int, Double, Bool, etc. — to a numeric value, known as the *hash value*. This value can then be used to quickly look up the values in a *hash table*.

Swift dictionaries have a type requirement for keys. Keys must be **Hashable**, or you will get a compiler error.

Fortunately, in Swift, all basic types are already Hashable and have a hash value. This value must be deterministic — meaning that a given value must *always* return the same hash value. No matter how many times you calculate the hash value for some string, it will always give the same value. However, you should never save a hash value because it will be different each time you run your program.

Here's the performance of various dictionary operations. This extraordinary performance hinges on having a good hashing function that avoids value collisions.

All operations below degenerate to linear time $O(n)$ performance if you have a poor hashing function. Fortunately, the built-in types have great, general-purpose Hashable implementations.

Accessing elements: Getting the value for a key is a constant time operation, or $O(1)$.

Inserting elements: To insert an element, the dictionary needs to calculate the key's hash value and then store data based on that hash. These are all $O(1)$ operations.

Deleting elements: Again, the dictionary needs to calculate the hash value to know exactly where to find and remove the element. This is also an $O(1)$ operation.

Searching for an element: As mentioned above, accessing an element has constant running time, so the complexity for searching is also $O(1)$.

While these running times compare favorably to arrays, remember that you lose order information when using dictionaries.

Sets

A set is an unordered collection of unique values of the same type. This can be extremely useful when you want to ensure that an item doesn't appear more than once in your collection and when the order of your items isn't important.

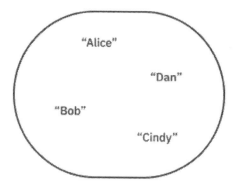

There are four strings in the Set illustration above. Notice that there's no order for the elements.

Creating Sets

You can declare a set explicitly by writing Set followed by the type inside angle brackets:

```
let setOne: Set<Int> = [1]
```

Set Literals

Sets don't have their own literals. You use **array literals** to create a set with initial values. Consider this example:

```
let someArray = [1, 2, 3, 1]
```

This is an array. How do you use array literals to create a set? Like this:

```
var explicitSet: Set<Int> = [1, 2, 3, 1]
```

You have to explicitly declare the variable as a Set. However, you can let the compiler infer the element type like so:

```
var someSet = Set([1, 2, 3, 1])
```

To see the most important features of a set in action, print the set you just created:

```
print(someSet)
// > [2, 3, 1] but the order is not defined
```

First, you can see there's no specific ordering. Second, although you created the set with two instances of the value 1, that value only appears once. Remember, a set's values must be unique.

Accessing Elements

You can use contains(_:) to check for the existence of a specific element:

```
print(someSet.contains(1))
// > true
print(someSet.contains(4))
// > false
```

You can also use the first and last properties, which return one of the elements in the set. However, you won't know which item you'll get because sets are unordered.

Adding and Removing Elements

You can use insert(_:) to add elements to a set. If the element already exists, the method does nothing.

```
someSet.insert(5)
```

You can remove the element from the set like this:

```
let removedElement = someSet.remove(1)
print(removedElement!)
// > 1
```

remove(_:) returns the removed element if it's in the set or nil otherwise.

Running Time for Set Operations

Sets have a very similar implementation to dictionaries, and they also require the elements to be hashable. The running time of all the operations is identical to those of dictionaries.

Challenges

Before moving on, here are some challenges to test your knowledge of arrays, dictionaries and sets. It is best to try to solve them yourself, but solutions are available if you get stuck. These came with the download or are available at the printed book's source code link listed in the introduction.

Challenge 1: Which Is Valid

Which of the following are valid statements?

```
1. let array1 = [Int]()
2. let array2 = []
3. let array3: [String] = []
```

For the next five statements, `array4` has been declared as:

```
let array4 = [1, 2, 3]
```

```
4. print(array4[0])
5. print(array4[5])
6. array4[1...2]
7. array4[0] = 4
8. array4.append(4)
```

For the final five statements, `array5` has been declared as:

```
var array5 = [1, 2, 3]
```

```
9.  array5[0] = array5[1]
10. array5[0...1] = [4, 5]
11. array5[0] = "Six"
12. array5 += 6
13. for item in array5 { print(item) }
```

Challenge 2: Remove the First Number

Write a function that removes the first occurrence of a given integer from an array of integers. This is the signature of the function:

```
func removingOnce(_ item: Int, from array: [Int]) -> [Int]
```

Challenge 3: Remove the Numbers

Write a function that removes all occurrences of a given integer from an array of integers. This is the signature of the function:

```
func removing(_ item: Int, from array: [Int]) -> [Int]
```

Challenge 4: Reverse an Array

Arrays have a reversed() method that returns an array holding the same elements as the original array in reverse order. Write a function that does the same thing without using reversed(). This is the signature of the function:

```
func reversed(_ array: [Int]) -> [Int]
```

Challenge 5: Return the Middle

Write a function that returns the middle element of an array. When the array size is even, return the first of the two middle elements.

```
func middle(_ array: [Int]) -> Int?
```

Challenge 6: Find the Minimum and Maximum

Write a function that calculates the minimum and maximum values in an array of integers. Calculate these values yourself; don't use the methods min and max. Return nil if the given array is empty.

This is the signature of the function:

```
func minMax(of numbers: [Int]) -> (min: Int, max: Int)?
```

Challenge 7: Which Is Valid

Which of the following are valid statements?

```
1. let dict1: [Int, Int] = [:]
2. let dict2 = [:]
3. let dict3: [Int: Int] = [:]
```

For the next four statements, use the following dictionary:

```
let dict4 = ["One": 1, "Two": 2, "Three": 3]
```

```
4. dict4[1]
5. dict4["One"]
6. dict4["Zero"] = 0
7. dict4[0] = "Zero"
```

For the next three statements, use the following dictionary:

```
var dict5 = ["NY": "New York", "CA": "California"]
```

```
8.  dict5["NY"]
9.  dict5["WA"] = "Washington"
10. dict5["CA"] = nil
```

Challenge 8: Long Names

Given a dictionary with two-letter state codes as keys, and the full state names as values, write a function that prints all the states with names longer than eight characters. For example, for the dictionary ["NY": "New York", "CA": "California"], the output would be California.

Challenge 9: Merge Dictionaries

Write a function that combines two dictionaries into one. If a certain key appears in both dictionaries, ignore the pair from the first dictionary. This is the function's signature:

```
func merging(_ dict1: [String: String], with dict2: [String:
String]) -> [String: String]
```

Challenge 10: Count the Characters

Declare a function `occurrencesOfCharacters` that calculates which characters occur in a string, as well as how often each of these characters occur. Return the result as a dictionary. This is the function signature:

```
func occurrencesOfCharacters(in text: String) -> [Character:
Int]
```

Hint: `String` is a collection of characters that you can iterate over with a for statement.Bonus: To make your code shorter, dictionaries have a special subscript operator that lets you add a default value if it is not found in the dictionary. For example, `dictionary["a", default: 0]` creates a 0 entry for the character "a" if it is not found instead of just returning `nil`.

Challenge 11: Unique Values

Write a function that returns `true` if all of the values of a dictionary are unique. Use a set to test uniqueness. This is the function signature:

```
func isInvertible(_ dictionary: [String: Int]) -> Bool
```

Challenge 12: Removing Keys and Setting Values to nil

Given the dictionary:

```
var nameTitleLookup: [String: String?] = ["Mary": "Engineer",
"Patrick": "Intern", "Ray": "Hacker"]
```

Set the value of the key `"Patrick"` to `nil` and completely remove the key and value for `"Ray"`.

Key Points

Sets:

- Are unordered collections of unique values of the same type.

- Are most useful when you need to know whether something is included in the collection or not.

Dictionaries:

- Are unordered collections of key-value pairs.

- The **keys** are all of the same type, and the **values** are all of the same type.

- Use **subscripting** to get values and to add, update or remove pairs.

- If a key is not in a dictionary, lookup returns `nil`.

- The key of a dictionary must be a type that conforms to the **Hashable** protocol.

- Basic Swift types such as `String`, `Int`, `Double` are `Hashable` out of the box.

Arrays:

- Are ordered collections of values of the same type.

- Use **subscripting**, or one of the many properties and methods, to access and update elements.

- Be wary of accessing an index that's out of bounds – doing so halts your program.

Chapter 8: Collection Iteration With Closures

By Matt Galloway

Earlier, you learned about functions. But Swift has another object you can use to break up code into reusable chunks: a **closure**. They become instrumental when dealing with collections.

A closure is simply a function with no name; you can assign it to a variable and pass it around like any other value. This chapter shows you how convenient and valuable closures can be.

Closure Basics

Closures are so named because they can "close over" the variables and constants within the closure's scope. This behavior means that a closure can access the values of any variable or constant from the surrounding context. Variables and constants used within the closure body are said to have been **captured** by the closure.

You may ask, "If closures are functions without names, how do you use them?" To use a closure, you must assign it to a variable or constant.

Here's a declaration of a variable that can hold a closure:

```
var multiplyClosure: (Int, Int) -> Int
```

`multiplyClosure` takes two `Int` values and returns an `Int`. Notice that this is the same as a variable declaration for a function. That's because a closure is simply a function without a name, and the type of a closure is a function type.

For the declaration to compile in a playground, you need to provide an initial definition like so:

```
var multiplyClosure = { (a: Int, b: Int) -> Int in
  return a * b
}
```

This code looks similar to a function declaration, but there's a subtle difference. There's the same parameter list, -> symbol and return type. But with closures, these elements appear inside braces, and there is an `in` keyword after the return type.

With your closure variable defined, you can use it just as if it were a function, like so:

```
let result = multiplyClosure(4, 2)
```

As you'd expect, `result` equals 8. Again, though, there's a subtle difference.

Notice how the closure has no external names for the parameters. You can't set them like you can with functions.

Shorthand Syntax

There are many ways to shorten the syntax of a closure. First, just like normal functions, if the closure consists of a single return statement, you can leave out the `return` keyword like so:

```
multiplyClosure = { (a: Int, b: Int) -> Int in
  a * b
}
```

Next, you can use Swift's type inference to shorten the syntax even more by removing the type information:

```
multiplyClosure = { (a, b) in
  a * b
}
```

Remember, you already declared `multiplyClosure` as a closure taking two `Int`s and returning an `Int`, so you can let Swift infer these types for you.

And finally, you can even omit the parameter list if you want. Swift lets you refer to each parameter by number, starting at zero, like so:

```
multiplyClosure = {
  $0 * $1
}
```

The parameter list, return type and `in` keyword are all gone, and your new closure declaration is much shorter than the original. Numbered parameters like this should only be used when the closure is short and sweet, like the one above.

If the parameter list is longer, it can be confusing to remember what each numbered parameter refers to. In these cases, you should use the named syntax.

Consider the following code:

```
func operateOnNumbers(_ a: Int, _ b: Int,
                      operation: (Int, Int) -> Int) -> Int {
  let result = operation(a, b)
  print(result)
  return result
}
```

This example declares a function named operateOnNumbers, which takes Int values as its first two parameters. The third parameter is named operation and is of a function type. operateOnNumbers itself returns an Int.

You can then use operateOnNumbers with a closure like so:

```
let addClosure = { (a: Int, b: Int) in
  a + b
}
operateOnNumbers(4, 2, operation: addClosure)
```

Remember, closures are simply functions without names. So you shouldn't be surprised to learn that you can also pass in a function as the third parameter of operateOnNumbers, like so:

```
func addFunction(_ a: Int, _ b: Int) -> Int {
  a + b
}
operateOnNumbers(4, 2, operation: addFunction)
```

operateOnNumbers is called the same way, whether the operation is a function or a closure.

The power of the closure syntax comes in handy again. You can define the closure inline with the operateOnNumbers function call like this:

```
operateOnNumbers(4, 2, operation: { (a: Int, b: Int) -> Int in
  return a + b
})
```

There's no need to define the closure and assign it to a local variable or constant. You can declare the closure right where you pass it into the function as a parameter!

But recall that you can simplify the closure syntax to remove a lot of the boilerplate code. You can therefore reduce the above to the following:

```
operateOnNumbers(4, 2, operation: { $0 + $1 })
```

You can even go a step further. The + operator is just a function that takes two arguments and returns one result so that you can write:

```
operateOnNumbers(4, 2, operation: +)
```

There's one more way to simplify the syntax, but it can only be done when the closure is the final parameter passed to a function. In this case, you can move the closure outside of the function call:

```
operateOnNumbers(4, 2) {
  $0 + $1
}
```

This code may look strange, but it's the same as the previous code snippet, except you've removed the operation label and pulled the braces outside the function call parameter list. This form is called **trailing closure syntax**.

Multiple Trailing Closures Syntax

If a function has multiple closures for inputs, you can call it in a special shorthand way. Suppose you have this function:

```
func sequenced(first: ()->Void, second: ()->Void) {
  first()
  second()
}
```

Swift lets you call it like so:

```
sequenced {
  print("Hello, ", terminator: "")
} second: {
  print("world.")
}
```

This example prints, "Hello, world."

Note: If you ever need to remember how to call a function with a closure, Xcode can help you. Type in the method's name (or code complete it) and press the return key twice. The code completion function will fill out trailing closure syntax for you.

Closures With no Return Value

Until now, all the closures you've seen have taken one or more parameters and have returned values. But just like functions, closures aren't required to do these things. Here's how you declare a closure that takes no parameters and returns nothing:

```
let voidClosure: () -> Void = {
  print("Swift Apprentice is awesome!")
}
voidClosure()
```

The closure's type is `() -> Void`. The empty parentheses denote there are no parameters. You must declare a return type so Swift knows you're declaring a closure. This is where `Void` comes in handy, and it means exactly what its name suggests: the closure returns nothing.

> **Note**: `Void` is actually just a typealias for `()`. This means you could have written `() -> Void` as `() -> ()`. A function's parameter list, however, must always be surrounded by parentheses, so `Void -> ()` or `Void -> Void` are invalid.

Capturing From the Enclosing Scope

Finally, let's return to the defining characteristic of a closure: it can access the variables and constants within its scope.

> **Note**: Recall that scope defines the range in which an entity (variable, constant, etc.) is accessible. You saw a new scope introduced with `if`-statements. Closures also introduce a new scope and inherit all entities visible to the scope in which it is defined.

For example, take the following closure:

```
var counter = 0
let incrementCounter = {
  counter += 1
}
```

incrementCounter is relatively simple: It increments the counter variable. The counter variable is defined outside of the closure. The closure can access the variable because the closure is defined in the same scope as the variable. The closure is said to **capture** the counter variable. Any changes it makes to the variable are visible both inside and outside the closure.

Let's say you call the closure five times, like so:

```
incrementCounter()
incrementCounter()
incrementCounter()
incrementCounter()
incrementCounter()
```

After these five calls, counter will equal 5.

The fact that closures can be used to capture variables from the enclosing scope can be extremely useful. For example, you could write the following function:

```
func countingClosure() -> () -> Int {
  var counter = 0
  let incrementCounter: () -> Int = {
    counter += 1
    return counter
  }
  return incrementCounter
}
```

This function takes no parameters and returns a closure. The closure it returns takes no parameters and returns an Int.

The closure returned from this function will increment its internal counter each time it is called. Each time you call this function, you get a different counter.

For example, this could be used like so:

```
let counter1 = countingClosure()
let counter2 = countingClosure()

counter1() // 1
counter2() // 1
counter1() // 2
counter1() // 3
counter2() // 2
```

The two counters created by the function are mutually exclusive and count independently. Neat!

Custom Sorting With Closures

Closures come in handy when you start looking deeper at collections. In Chapter 7, "Arrays, Dictionaries & Sets", you used array's `sort` method to sort an array. By specifying a closure, you can customize how things are sorted. You call `sorted()` to get a sorted version of the array as so:

```
let names = ["ZZZZZZ", "BB", "A", "CCCC", "EEEEE"]
names.sorted()
// ["A", "BB", "CCCC", "EEEEE", "ZZZZZZ"]
```

By specifying a custom closure, you can change how the array is sorted. Specify a trailing closure like so:

```
names.sorted {
    $0.count > $1.count
}
// ["ZZZZZZ", "EEEEE", "CCCC", "BB", "A"]
```

Now the array is sorted by the length of the string, with longer strings coming first.

Iterating Over Collections With Closures

In Swift, collections implement convenient features often associated with **functional programming**. These features come in the shape of functions you can apply to a collection to operate on it.

Operations include things like transforming each element or filtering out certain elements.

All of these functions use closures, as you will see now.

The first of these functions lets you loop over the elements in a collection and perform an operation like so:

```
let values = [1, 2, 3, 4, 5, 6]
values.forEach {
    print("\($0): \($0*$0)")
}
```

This loops through each item in the collection printing the value and its square.

Another function allows you to filter out certain elements, like so:

```
var prices = [1.5, 10, 4.99, 2.30, 8.19]

let largePrices = prices.filter {
  $0 > 5
}
```

Here, you create an array of `Double` to represent the prices of items in a shop. You use the `filter` function to filter out prices greater than $5. This function looks like so:

```
func filter(_ isIncluded: (Element) -> Bool) -> [Element]
```

This definition says that `filter` takes a single parameter, a closure (or function) that takes an `Element` and returns a `Bool`. The `filter` function then returns an array of `Elements`. In this context, `Element` refers to the type of items in the array. In the example above, `Doubles`.

The closure's job is to return `true` or `false` depending on whether or not the value should be included. The array returned from `filter` will contain all elements for which the closure returned `true`.

In this example, `largePrices` will contain the following:

```
(10, 8.19)
```

> **Note:** The array returned from `filter` (and all of these functions) is a new array. The original is not modified at all.

If you're only interested in the first element that satisfies a certain condition, you can use `first(where:)`. For example, using a trailing closure:

```
let largePrice = prices.first {
  $0 > 5
}
```

In this case, `largePrice` would be 10.

However, there is more!

Imagine having a sale and wanting to discount all items to 90% of their original price. There's a handy function named `map` that can achieve this:

```
let salePrices = prices.map {
  $0 * 0.9
}
```

The `map` function will take a closure, execute it on each item in the array and return a new array containing each result with the order maintained. In this case, `salePrices` will contain the following:

```
[1.35, 9, 4.491, 2.07, 7.371]
```

The `map` function can also be used to change the type. You can do that like so:

```
let userInput = ["0", "11", "haha", "42"]

let numbers1 = userInput.map {
  Int($0)
}
```

This code takes some strings that the user input and turns them into an array of `Int?`. They must be optional because the conversion from `String` to `Int` might fail.

If you want to filter out the invalid (missing) values, you can use `compactMap` like so:

```
let numbers2 = userInput.compactMap {
  Int($0)
}
```

This form is almost the same as `map` except it creates an array of `Int` and tosses out the missing values that fail to initialize as integers.

There's also a `flatMap` operation which has a similar name to `map` and `compactMap`. However, it does something a little different. Here it is in action:

```
let userInputNested = [["0", "1"], ["a", "b", "c"], ["🐶"]]
let allUserInput = userInputNested.flatMap {
  $0
}
```

You will notice that `allUserInput` is `["0", "1", "a", "b", "c", "🐶"]`.

Swift expects the return value from the closure given to flatMap to be a collection itself. What it does then takes all these collections and concatenates them together. So, in this case, it's done the trick of unwrapping those inner collections. We end up with a collection containing all the items from the first inner collection, then all the items from the second inner collection, and so on.

Another handy function is reduce. This function takes an initial value and a closure that gets called for each element in the array. Each time the closure is called, it gets two inputs: the current value (that starts as the initial value) and an array element. The closure returns what will be the next current value. This process might sound convoluted, but an example will make it clear.

For example, this could be used with the prices array to calculate the total, like so:

```
let sum = prices.reduce(0) {
    $0 + $1
}
```

The initial value representing a running total is 0. The closure gets called for each element and returns the running total plus the current element. The returned value is the new running total. The final result is the total of all the values in the array. In this case, sum will be:

```
26.98
```

Now that you've seen filter, map and reduce, hopefully, you realize how powerful these functions can be, thanks to the syntax of closures. You can perform a complex calculation iterating over a collection in just a few lines of code.

These functions can use any collection type, including dictionaries. Imagine you represent the stock in your shop with a dictionary mapping the price to the number of items at that price. You could use that to calculate the total value of your stock like so:

```
let stock = [1.5: 5, 10: 2, 4.99: 20, 2.30: 5, 8.19: 30]
let stockSum = stock.reduce(0) {
    $0 + $1.key * Double($1.value)
}
```

The second parameter to the reduce function is a named tuple containing the key and value from the dictionary elements. A type conversion of the value is required to perform the calculation.

Here, the result is:

```
384.5
```

There's another form of reduce named reduce(into:_:). You'd use it when the result you're reducing a collection into is an array or dictionary, like so:

```
let farmAnimals = ["🐎": 5, "🐀": 10, "🐑": 50, "🐄": 1]
let allAnimals = farmAnimals.reduce(into: []) {
  (result, this: (key: String, value: Int)) in
  for _ in 0 ..< this.value {
    result.append(this.key)
  }
}
```

It works the same way as the other version, except that you don't return something from the closure. Instead, each iteration gives you a mutable value. This way, only one array in this example is created and appended to, making reduce(into:_:) more efficient.

Should you need to chop up an array, a few more functions can be helpful. The first function is dropFirst, which works like so:

```
let removeFirst = prices.dropFirst()
let removeFirstTwo = prices.dropFirst(2)
```

The dropFirst function takes a single parameter that defaults to 1 and returns an array with the required number of elements removed from the front. The results are as follows:

```
removeFirst = [10, 4.99, 2.30, 8.19]
removeFirstTwo = [4.99, 2.30, 8.19]
```

Like dropFirst, there also exists dropLast, which removes elements from the end of the array. It works like this:

```
let removeLast = prices.dropLast()
let removeLastTwo = prices.dropLast(2)
```

The results of these are as you would expect:

```
removeLast = [1.5, 10, 4.99, 2.30]
removeLastTwo = [1.5, 10, 4.99]
```

You can select just the first or last elements of an array, as shown below:

```
let firstTwo = prices.prefix(2)
let lastTwo = prices.suffix(2)
```

Here, `prefix` returns the required number of elements from the front of the array, and `suffix` returns the required number of elements from the back of the array. The results of this function are:

```
firstTwo = [1.5, 10]
lastTwo = [2.30, 8.19]
```

And finally, you can remove all elements in a collection by using `removeAll()` qualified by a closure, or unconditionally:

```
prices.removeAll() { $0 > 2 } // prices is now [1.5]
prices.removeAll() // prices is now an empty array
```

Lazy Collections

Sometimes you can have a huge or even infinite collection, but you want to be able to access it somehow. A concrete example of this would be all of the prime numbers. That is an infinite set of numbers. So how can you work with that set? Enter the **lazy collection**. Consider that you might want to calculate the first ten prime numbers. To do this imperatively, you might do something like this:

```
func isPrime(_ number: Int) -> Bool {
    if number == 1 { return false }
    if number == 2 || number == 3 { return true }

    for i in 2...Int(Double(number).squareRoot()) {
        if number % i == 0 { return false }
    }

    return true
}

var primes: [Int] = []
var i = 1
while primes.count < 10 {
    if isPrime(i) {
        primes.append(i)
    }
    i += 1
}
primes.forEach { print($0) }
```

This example defines a function that checks whether a number is prime. Then it generates an array of the first ten prime numbers.

> **Note**: The function to calculate if this is a prime could be better! Calculating primes is a deep topic beyond this chapter's scope. If you're curious, I suggest reading about the Sieve of Eratosthenes.

This code works, but functional is better, as you saw earlier in the chapter. The functional way to get the first ten prime numbers would be to have a sequence of *all* the prime numbers and then use prefix() to get the first ten. However, how can you have a sequence of infinite length and get the prefix() of that? That's where you can use the lazy operation to tell Swift to create the collection on-demand when it's needed.

Let's see it in action. You could rewrite the code above instead like this:

```swift
let primes = (1...).lazy
  .filter { isPrime($0) }
  .prefix(10)
primes.forEach { print($0) }
```

Notice that you start with the open-ended collection 1..., which means 1 until, well, infinity (or rather the maximum integer that the Int type can hold!). Then you use lazy to tell Swift that you want this to be a lazy collection. Then you use filter() and prefix() to filter out the primes and choose the first ten.

At that point, the sequence has yet to be generated, and no numbers have been checked to be prime. Only with the second statement, the primes.forEach is the sequence evaluated, and the first ten prime numbers are evaluated and printed. Neat! :]

Lazy collections are instrumental when the collection is huge (even infinite) or expensive to generate. It saves the computation until precisely when it is needed.

That wraps up collection iteration with closures!

Mini-Exercises

1. Create a constant array called names that contains some names as strings. Any names will do — make sure there are more than three. Now use reduce to create a string that is the concatenation of each name in the array.

2. Using the same names array, first filter the array to contain only names longer than four characters and then create the same concatenation of names as in the above exercise. (Hint: You can chain these operations together.)

3. Create a constant dictionary called namesAndAges containing some names as strings mapped to ages as integers. Now use filter to create a dictionary containing only people under the age of 18.

4. Using the same namesAndAges dictionary, filter out the adults (those 18 or older) and then use map to convert to an array containing just the names (i.e., drop the ages).

Challenges

Before moving on, here are some challenges to test your knowledge of collection iterations with closures. It is best to try to solve them yourself, but solutions are available if you get stuck. Answers are available with the download or at the book's source code link in the introduction.

Challenge 1: Repeating Yourself

Your first challenge is to write a function that will run a given closure a given number of times.

Declare the function like so:

```
func repeatTask(times: Int, task: () -> Void)
```

The function should run the task closure, times number of times. Use this function to print "Swift Apprentice is a great book!" 10 times.

Challenge 2: Closure Sums

In this challenge, you will write a function that you can reuse to create different mathematical sums.

Declare the function like so:

```
func mathSum(length: Int, series: (Int) -> Int) -> Int
```

The first parameter, length, defines the number of values to sum. The second parameter, series, is a closure that can be used to generate a series of values. series should have a parameter that is the position of the value in the series and return the value at that position.

mathSum should calculate length number of values, starting at position 1, and return their sum.

Use the function to find the sum of the first 10 square numbers, which equals 385. Then use the function to find the sum of the first 10 Fibonacci numbers, which equals 143. For the Fibonacci numbers, you can use the function you wrote in Chapter 5, "Functions" — or grab it from the solutions if you're unsure your solution is correct.

Challenge 3: Functional Ratings

In this final challenge, you will have a list of app names with associated ratings they've been given. Note — these are all fictional apps! Create the data dictionary like so:

```
let appRatings = [
  "Calendar Pro": [1, 5, 5, 4, 2, 1, 5, 4],
  "The Messenger": [5, 4, 2, 5, 4, 1, 1, 2],
  "Socialise": [2, 1, 2, 2, 1, 2, 4, 2]
]
```

First, create a dictionary called averageRatings that will contain a mapping of app names to average ratings. Use forEach to iterate through the appRatings dictionary, then use reduce to calculate the average rating. Store this rating in the averageRatings dictionary. Finally, use filter and map chained together to get a list of the app names whose average rating is greater than 3.

Key Points

- **Closures** are functions without names. They can be assigned to variables and passed as parameters to functions.

- Closures have **shorthand syntax** that makes them easier to use than other functions.

- A closure can **capture** the variables and constants from its surrounding context.

- A closure can be used to direct how a collection is sorted.

- A handy set of functions exists on collections that you can use to iterate over a collection and transform it. Transforms comprise mapping each element to a new value, filtering out certain values and reducing the collection down to a single value.

- Lazy collections can be used to evaluate a collection only when strictly needed, which means you can efficiently work with large, expensive or potentially infinite collections.

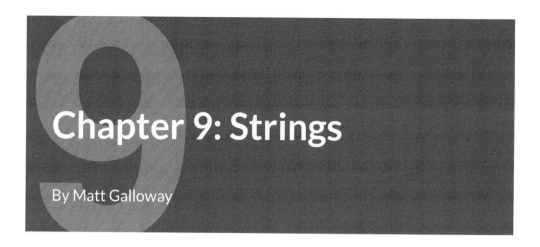

Chapter 9: Strings

By Matt Galloway

So far, you have briefly seen what the type `String` has to offer for representing text. Text is a ubiquitous data type: people's names, addresses and the words of a book. These are examples of text that an app might need to handle. It's worth having a deeper understanding of how `String` works and what it can do.

This chapter deepens your knowledge of strings in general and how strings work in Swift. Swift is one of the few languages that handle Unicode characters correctly while maintaining maximum predictable performance.

Strings as Collections

In Chapter 2, "Types & Operations", you learned what a string is, and what character sets and code points are. To recap, they define the mapping numbers to the character it represents. And now, it's time to look deeper into the String type.

It's pretty easy to conceptualize a string as a collection of characters. Because strings are collections, you can do things like this:

```
let string = "Matt"
for char in string {
  print(char)
}
```

This code will print out every character of Matt individually. Simple, eh?

You can also use other collection operations, such as:

```
let stringLength = string.count
```

This assignment will give you the length of the string.

Now imagine you want to get the fourth character in the string. You may think of doing something like this:

```
let fourthChar = string[3]
```

However, if you did this, you would receive the following error message:

```
'subscript' is unavailable: cannot subscript String with an Int,
see the documentation comment for discussion
```

Why is that? The short answer is that characters do not have a fixed size, so you can't access them like an array. Why not? It's time to take a detour further into how strings work by introducing what a **grapheme cluster** is.

Grapheme Clusters

As you know, a string is made up of a collection of Unicode characters. Until now, you have considered one code point to precisely equal one character and vice versa. However, the term "character" is relatively loose.

It may come as a surprise, but there are two ways to represent some characters. One example is the é in café, an e with an acute accent. You can represent this character with either one or two characters.

The single character to represent this is code point 233. The two-character case is an e on its own, followed by an acute accent **combining character**, a special character that modifies the previous character.

So you can represent the e with an acute accent by either of these means:

é
233

e	´
101	769

The combination of these two characters in the second diagram forms what is known as a **grapheme cluster** defined by the Unicode standard. When you think of a character, you're probably thinking of a grapheme cluster. Grapheme clusters are represented by the Swift type `Character`.

Other examples of combining characters are the special characters used to change the skin color of certain emojis.

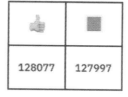

Here, the thumbs-up emoji is followed by a skin tone-combining character. On platforms that support it, including iOS and macOS, the rendered emoji is a single thumbs-up character with the skin tone applied.

Now, look at what this means for strings when they are used as collections. Consider the following code:

```
let cafeNormal = "café"
let cafeCombining = "cafe\u{0301}"

cafeNormal.count      // 4
cafeCombining.count   // 4
```

Both counts equal four because Swift considers a string a collection of grapheme clusters. Also, evaluating the length of a string takes linear time because you need to go through all characters to determine how many grapheme clusters there are. One can not know the character count by looking at how much memory a string takes.

> **Note**: The backslash character, \, is the **escape character**. It is used here followed by a u to indicate that what follows the \u is a Unicode code point in hexadecimal in braces. The acute accent combining character is written using this syntax in the code above. You can use this shorthand to write any Unicode character. I had to use it here for the combining character because I cannot type this character on my keyboard!

However, you can access the underlying Unicode code points in the string via the unicodeScalars **view**. This view is also a collection itself. So, you can do the following:

```
cafeNormal.unicodeScalars.count      // 4
cafeCombining.unicodeScalars.count   // 5
```

In this case, you're seeing the difference in the counts as you'd expect.

You can iterate through this Unicode scalars view like so:

```
for codePoint in cafeCombining.unicodeScalars {
    print(codePoint.value)
}
```

This code will print the following list of numbers, as expected:

```
99
97
102
101
769
```

Indexing Strings

Swift doesn't allow you to get a specific character (err, I mean grapheme cluster) using an integer subscript. While it's certainly possible to write a function to do this, there are good reasons for the standard library not providing it. The first reason is correctness – Characters are variable in size and cannot be accessed using constant offsets. Swift also wants to prevent you from inadvertently writing inefficient, battery-draining string-processing code. You might not see problems with small strings, but performance would be unacceptable with larger strings.

While most other languages sacrifice Unicode correctness and performance with the simplicity of integer indices, Swift uses a special string index type to remove the problem.

In Swift, you must operate on the specific string index type to index into strings. For example, you obtain the index that represents the start of the string like so:

```
let firstIndex = cafeCombining.startIndex
```

If you option-click on firstIndex in a playground, you'll notice that it is of type String.Index and not an integer.

You can then use this value to obtain the Character (grapheme cluster) at that index, like so:

```
let firstChar = cafeCombining[firstIndex]
```

In this case, firstChar will, of course, be **c**. The type of this value is **Character**, a grapheme cluster.

Similarly, you can obtain the last grapheme cluster like so:

```
let lastIndex = cafeCombining.endIndex
let lastChar = cafeCombining[lastIndex]
```

But if you do this, you'll get a fatal error on the console (and an EXC_BAD_INSTRUCTION error in the code):

```
Fatal error: String index is out of bounds
```

This error happens because the endIndex is one past the end of the string. You need to do this to obtain the last character:

```
let lastIndex = cafeCombining.index(before:
cafeCombining.endIndex)
let lastChar = cafeCombining[lastIndex]
```

Here you're obtaining the index just before the end index and then obtaining the character at that index. Alternatively, you could offset from the first character like so:

```
let fourthIndex = cafeCombining.index(cafeCombining.startIndex,
                                      offsetBy: 3)
let fourthChar = cafeCombining[fourthIndex]
```

In this case, fourthChar is é as expected.

But as you know, the é in that case is made up of multiple code points. You can access these code points on the Character type the same way as you can on String through the unicodeScalars view. So you can do this:

```
fourthChar.unicodeScalars.count // 2
fourthChar.unicodeScalars.forEach { codePoint in
  print(codePoint.value)
}
```

This time you're using the forEach function to iterate through the Unicode scalars view. The count is two, and as expected, the loop prints out:

```
101
769
```

Equality With Combining Characters

Combining characters make the equality of strings a little trickier. For example, consider the word **café** written once using the single **é** character, and once using the combining character, like so:

c	a	f	é	
99	97	102	233	

c	a	f	e	´
99	97	102	101	769

These two strings are, of course, logically equal. When printed on-screen, they use the same **glyph** and look the same. But they are represented inside the computer in different ways. Many programming languages would consider these strings to be unequal because those languages work by comparing the code points one by one.

Swift, however, considers these strings to be equal by default. Let's see that in action.

```
let equal = cafeNormal == cafeCombining
```

In this case, equal is true because the two strings are logically the same.

String comparison in Swift uses a technique known as **canonicalization**. Say that three times fast! Before checking equality, Swift canonicalizes both strings, converting them to the same special character representation.

It doesn't matter which way Swift does the canonicalization — using the single character or combining character — as long as both strings get converted to the same style. Once the canonicalization is complete, Swift can compare individual characters to check for equality.

The same canonicalization comes into play when considering how many characters are in a particular string. You saw earlier where café using the single é character and café using the e plus combining accent character had the same length.

Strings as Bi-directional Collections

Sometimes you want to reverse a string. Often this is so you can iterate through it backward. Fortunately, Swift has a rather simple way to do this, through a method called `reversed()` like so:

```
let name = "Matt"
let backwardsName = name.reversed()
```

But what is the type of `backwardsName`? If you said `String`, then you would be wrong. It is a `ReversedCollection<String>`. Changing the type is a smart optimization that Swift makes. Instead of it being a concrete `String`, it is a **reversed collection**. Think of it as a thin wrapper around any collection that allows you to use the collection as if it were the other way around, without incurring additional memory usage.

You can then access every `Character` in the backwards string just as you would any other string, like so:

```
let secondCharIndex =
backwardsName.index(backwardsName.startIndex,
                                   offsetBy: 1)
let secondChar = backwardsName[secondCharIndex] // "t"
```

But what if you want a `String` type? Well, you can do that by initializing a `String` from the reversed collection, like so:

```
let backwardsNameString = String(backwardsName)
```

This code will create a new `String` from the reversed collection. When doing this, you make a fresh (reversed) copy of the original string with its own memory storage. Staying in the reversed collection domain will save memory space, which is fine if you don't need the whole reversed string.

Raw Strings

A **raw string** is useful when you want to avoid special characters or string interpolation. Instead, the complete string as you type it is what becomes the string. To illustrate this, consider the following raw string:

```
let raw1 = #"Raw "No Escaping" \(no interpolation!). Use all the
\ you want!"#
```

```
print(raw1)
```

To denote a raw string, you surround the string with # symbols. This code prints:

```
Raw "No Escaping" \(no interpolation!). Use all the \ you want!
```

If you didn't use the # symbols, this string would try to use interpolation and wouldn't compile because "no interpolation!" is not valid Swift. If you want to include # in your code, you can do that too. You can use any number of # symbols you want as long as the beginning and end match like so:

```
let raw2 = ##"Aren't we "# clever"##
print(raw2)
```

This prints:

```
Aren't we "# clever
```

What if you want to use interpolation with raw strings? Can you do that?

```
let can = "can do that too"
let raw3 = #"Yes we \#(can)!"#
print(raw3)
```

Prints:

```
Yes, we can do that too!
```

There's one more rather fun use of raw strings. You might need to use some ASCII art in your programs from time to time. ASCII art is where you use simple characters to draw out a picture. The problem is that ASCII art often contains the backslash character, \, which is usually the escape character, as you saw earlier. Therefore raw strings are good for ASCII art because otherwise, all the \ would be treated as escapes, and bad things would ensure.

You can try out some ASCII art for yourself:

```
let multiRaw = #"""
   /⎯⎯|         (_)/⎯⎯_¯|
  | (⎯⎯⎯         __| |_| |_
   \⎯⎯ \ \ /\ / / | _| |  _|
    ___) \ V  V /| | | | | |_
   |⎯⎯⎯/ \_/\_/ |_|_|  \__|
   """#
print(multiRaw)
```

Now that looks neat!

The Swift community seems to have thought of everything with raw strings.

Substrings

Another thing you often need to do when manipulating strings is to generate substrings. That is, pull out a part of the string into its own value. Swift can do this using a subscript that takes a range of indices.

For example, consider the following code:

```
let fullName = "Matt Galloway"
let spaceIndex = fullName.firstIndex(of: " ")!
let firstName = fullName[fullName.startIndex..<spaceIndex] //
"Matt"
```

This code finds the index representing the first space (using a force unwrap here because you know one exists). Then it uses a range to find the grapheme clusters between the start index and the index of the space (not including the space).

Now is an excellent time to introduce a new type of range you haven't seen before: the **open-ended range**. This type of range only takes one index and assumes the other is either the start or the end of the collection.

That last line of code can be rewritten by using an open-ended range:

```
let firstName = fullName[..<spaceIndex] // "Matt"
```

This time we omit the `fullName.startIndex`, and Swift will infer that this is what you mean.

Similarly, you can also use a one-sided range to start at a certain index and go to the end of the collection, like so:

```
let lastName = fullName[fullName.index(after: spaceIndex)...]
// "Galloway"
```

There's something interesting to point out with substrings. If you look at their type, you will see they are of type `String.SubSequence` rather than `String`. This `String.SubSequence` is just a `typealias` of `Substring`, which means that `Substring` is the actual type, and `String.SubSequence` is an alias.

Just like with the reversed string, you can force this `Substring` into a `String` by doing the following:

```
let lastNameString = String(lastName)
```

The reason for this extra `Substring` type is a cunning optimization. A `Substring` shares the storage with its parent `String` that it was sliced from. This sharing means that you use no extra memory when you're slicing a string. Then, when you want the substring as a `String`, you explicitly create a new string, and the memory is copied into a new buffer for this new string.

The designers of Swift could have made this copying behavior by default. However, by having the separate type `Substring`, Swift makes it very explicit what is happening. The good news is that `String` and `Substring` share almost all the same capabilities. You might not even realize which type you are using until you return or pass your `Substring` to another function that requires a `String`. In this case, you can explicitly initialize a new `String` from your `Substring`.

Hopefully, it's clear that Swift is opinionated about strings and very deliberate in how it implements them. It is an important bit of knowledge to carry because strings are complex beasts and are used frequently. Getting the API right is important — that's an understatement. :]

Character Properties

You encountered the `Character` type earlier in this chapter. Some rather interesting properties of this type allow you to introspect the character in question and learn about its semantics.

Let's take a look at a few of the properties.

The first is simply finding out if the character belongs to the **ASCII** character set. You can achieve this like so:

```
let singleCharacter: Character = "x"
singleCharacter.isASCII
```

> **Note**: ASCII stands for American Standard Code for Information Interchange. It is a fixed-width 7-bit code for representing strings developed in the 1960s by Bell Labs. Because of its history and importance, the standard 8-bit Unicode encoding (UTF-8) was created as a superset of ASCII. You will learn more about UTF-8 later in this chapter.

In this case, the result is `true` because `"x"` is indeed in the ASCII character set. However, if you did this for something like "🥳", the "party face" emoji, you would get `false`.

Next up is checking if something is whitespace. This can be useful as whitespace often has meaning in things like programming languages.

You can achieve this like so:

```
let space: Character = " "
space.isWhitespace
```

Again, the result here would be `true`.

Next up is checking if something is a hexadecimal digit or not. This check can be useful if you are parsing some text and want to know if something is valid hexadecimal. You can achieve this like so:

```
let hexDigit: Character = "d"
hexDigit.isHexDigit
```

The result is `true`, but if you changed it to check `"s"`, it would be `false`.

Finally, a rather powerful property is being able to convert a character to its numeric value. That might sound simple, say converting the character `"5"` into the number 5. However, it also works on non-Latin characters. For example:

```
let thaiNine: Character = "๙"
thaiNine.wholeNumberValue
```

In this case, the result is 9 because that is the Thai character for the number nine. Neat! :]

These features only scratch the surface of the properties of `Character`. There are too many to go through each one here; however, you can read more in the Swift evolution proposal (https://github.com/apple/swift-evolution/blob/master/proposals/0221-character-properties.md), which added these.

Encoding

So far, you've learned what strings are and explored how to work with them but haven't touched on how strings are stored or encoded.

Strings consist of a collection of Unicode code points. These code points range from the number 0 up to 1114111 (or 0x10FFFF in hexadecimal). This means that the maximum number of bits you need to represent a code point is 21.

However, if you are only ever using low code points, such as if your text contains only Latin characters, you can get away with using only eight bits per code point.

Numeric types in most programming languages come in sizes of addressable, powers-of-2 bits, such as 8-bits, 16-bits and 32-bits. This is because computers are made of billions of transistors, either off or on; they just love powers of two!

When choosing how to store strings, you could store every code point in a 32-bit type, such as UInt32. Your String type would be backed by a [UInt32] (a UInt32 array). Each of these UInt32s is what is known as a **code unit**. However, you would be wasting space because not all those bits are needed, especially if the string uses only low code points.

This choice of how to store strings is known as the string's **encoding**. This particular scheme described above is known as **UTF-32**. However, because it has inefficient memory usage, it is rarely used.

UTF-8

A much more common scheme is called **UTF-8**. This encoding uses 8-bit code units instead. One reason for UTF-8's popularity is that it is fully compatible with the venerable, English-only, 7-bit ASCII encoding. But how do you store code points that need more than eight bits?! Herein lies the magic of the encoding.

If the code point requires up to seven bits, it is represented by simply one code unit and is identical to **ASCII**. But for code points above seven bits, a scheme comes into play that uses up to four **code units** to represent the code point.

Two code units are used for code points of 8 to 11 bits. The first code unit's initial three bits are 110. The remaining five bits are the first five bits of the code point. The second code unit's initial two bits are 10. The remaining six bits are the remaining six bits of the code point.

For example, the code point `0x00BD` represents the ½ character. In binary, this is `10111101` and uses eight bits. In UTF-8, this would comprise two code units of `11000010` and `10111101`.

To illustrate this, consider the following diagram:

Of course, code points higher than 11 bits are also supported. 12- to 16-bit code points use three UTF-8 code units, and 17- to 21-bit code points use four UTF-8 code units, according to the following scheme:

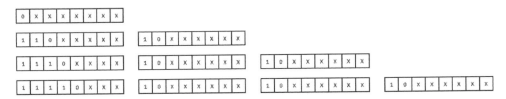

Each **x** is replaced with the bits from the code points.

In Swift, you can access the UTF-8 string encoding through the `utf8` view. For example, consider the following code:

```
let char = "\u{00bd}"
for i in char.utf8 {
  print(i)
}
```

The `utf8` view is a collection, just like the `unicodeScalars` view. Its values are the UTF-8 code units that make up the string. In this case, it's a single character, namely the one that we discussed above.

The above code will print the following:

```
194
189
```

If you pull out your calculator (or have a fantastic mental arithmetic mind), you can validate that these are `11000010` and `10111101`, respectively, as you expected!

Now consider a more complicated example which you'll refer back to later in this section. Take the following string:

+½⇒😶

And iterate through the UTF-8 code units it contains:

```
let characters = "+\u{00bd}\u{21e8}\u{1f643}"
for i in characters.utf8 {
  print("\(i) : \(String(i, radix: 2))")
}
```

This time the print statement will print out both the decimal number and the number in binary. It prints the following, with newlines added to split grapheme clusters:

```
43 : 101011

194 : 11000010
189 : 10111101

226 : 11100010
135 : 10000111
168 : 10101000

240 : 11110000
159 : 10011111
153 : 10011001
131 : 10000011
```

Feel free to verify that these are indeed correct. Notice that the first character used one code unit, the second used two code units, and so on.

UTF-8 is much more compact than UTF-32. For this string, you used 10 bytes to store the 4 code points. In UTF-32, this would be 16 bytes (four bytes per code unit, one code unit per code point, four code points).

There is a downside to UTF-8, though. To handle certain string operations, you need to inspect every byte. For example, if you wanted to jump to the n th code point, you would need to inspect every byte until you have gone past n-1 code points. You cannot simply jump into the buffer because you don't know how far you have to jump.

UTF-16

There is another encoding that is useful to introduce, namely **UTF-16**. Yes, you guessed it. It uses 16-bit code units!

This means that code points that are up to 16 bits use one code unit. But how are code points of 17 to 21 bits represented? These use a scheme known as **surrogate pairs**. These are two UTF-16 code units that, when next to each other, represent a code point from the range above 16 bits.

There is a space within Unicode reserved for these surrogate pair code points. They are split into low and high surrogates. The high surrogates range from 0xD800 to 0xDBFF, and the low surrogates range from 0xDC00 to 0xDFFF.

Perhaps that sounds backward — but the high and low here refer to the bits from the original code point represented by this surrogate.

Take the upside-down face emoji from the string you saw earlier. Its code point is 0x1F643. To find out the surrogate pairs for this code point, you apply the following algorithm:

1. Subtract 0x10000 to give 0xF643, or 0000 1111 0110 0100 0011 in binary.

2. Split these 20 bits into two. This gives you 0000 1111 01 and 10 0100 0011.

3. Take the first and add 0xD800 to it to give 0xD83D. This is your **high surrogate**.

4. Take the second and add 0xDC00 to it to give 0xDE43. This is your **low surrogate**.

So in UTF-16, that upside-down face emoji is represented by the code unit 0xD83D followed by 0xDE43. Neat!

Just as with UTF-8, Swift allows you to access the UTF-16 code units through the utf16 view, like so:

```
for i in characters.utf16 {
  print("\(i) : \(String(i, radix: 2))")
}
```

In this case, the following is printed, again with newlines added to split grapheme clusters:

```
43 : 101011

189 : 10111101
```

```
  8680 : 10000111101000

 55357 : 1101100000111101
 56899 : 1101111001000011
```

As you can see, the only code point that needs to use more than one code unit is the last one, your upside-down face emoji. As expected, the values are correct!

So with UTF-16, your string this time uses 10 bytes (5 code units, 2 bytes per code unit), the same as UTF-8. However, memory usage with UTF-8 and UTF-16 is often different. For example, strings comprised of code points of 7 bits or less will take up twice the space in UTF-16 than in UTF-8.

For a string made up of code points 7 bits or less, the string must be entirely made up of Latin characters in that range. Even the "£" sign is not in this range! So, often, the memory usage of UTF-16 and UTF-8 are comparable.

Swift string views make the `String` type encoding agnostic — Swift is one of the only languages that does this. Internally it uses UTF-8, C-language compatible, `NULL` terminated strings because it hits a sweet spot between memory usage and complexity of operations.

Converting Indexes Between Encoding Views

As you saw earlier, you use indexes to access grapheme clusters in a string. For example, using the same string from above, you can do the following:

```
let arrowIndex = characters.firstIndex(of: "\u{21e8}")!
characters[arrowIndex] // ⇨
```

Here, `arrowIndex` is of type `String.Index` and used to obtain the `Character` at that index.

You can convert this index into the index relating to the start of this grapheme cluster in the `unicodeScalars`, `utf8` and `utf16` views. You do that using the `samePosition(in:)` method on `String.Index`, like so:

```
if let unicodeScalarsIndex = arrowIndex.samePosition(in:
characters.unicodeScalars) {
  characters.unicodeScalars[unicodeScalarsIndex] // 8680
}

if let utf8Index = arrowIndex.samePosition(in: characters.utf8)
{
  characters.utf8[utf8Index] // 226
}
```

```
if let utf16Index = arrowIndex.samePosition(in:
characters.utf16) {
  characters.utf16[utf16Index] // 8680
}
```

unicodeScalarsIndex is of type `String.UnicodeScalarView.Index`. This grapheme cluster is represented by only one code point, so in the `unicodeScalars` view, the scalar returned is the one and only code point. If the `Character` were made up of two code points, such as **e** combined with ´ as you saw earlier, the scalar returned in the code above would be just the "e".

Likewise, `utf8Index` is of type `String.UTF8View.Index`, and the value at that index is the first UTF-8 code unit used to represent this code point. The same goes for the `utf16Index`, which is of type `String.UTF16View.Index`.

Challenges

Before moving on, here are some challenges to test your knowledge of collection iterations with closures. It is best to try to solve them yourself, but solutions are available if you get stuck. Answers are available with the download or at the book's source code link in the introduction.

Challenge 1: Character Count

Write a function that takes a string and prints out the count of each character in the string. For bonus points, print them ordered by the count of each character. For bonus-bonus points, print it as a nice histogram.

Hint: You could use # characters to draw the bars.

Challenge 2: Word Count

Write a function that tells you how many words there are in a string. Do it without splitting the string.

Hint: try iterating through the string yourself.

Challenge 3: Name Formatter

Write a function that takes a string that looks like "Galloway, Matt" and returns one which looks like "Matt Galloway", i.e., the string goes from "<LAST_NAME>, <FIRST_NAME>" to "<FIRST_NAME> <LAST_NAME>".

Challenge 4: Components

A method exists on a string named components(separatedBy:) that will split the string into chunks, which are delimited by the given string, and return an array containing the results.

Your challenge is to implement this yourself.

Hint: There exists a view on String named indices that lets you iterate through all the indices (of type String.Index) in the string. You will need to use this.

Challenge 5: Word Reverser

Write a function that takes a string and returns a version of it with each individual word reversed.

For example, if the string is "My dog is called Rover" then the resulting string would be "yM god si dellac revoR".

Try to do it by iterating through the indices of the string until you find a space and then reversing what was before it. Build up the result string by continually doing that as you iterate through the string.

Hint: You'll need to do a similar thing as you did for Challenge 4 but reverse the word each time. Try to explain to yourself, or the closest unsuspecting family member, why this is better in terms of memory usage than using the function you created in the previous challenge.

Key Points

- Strings are collections of `Character` types.

- A `Character` is **grapheme cluster** and is made up of one or more **code points**.

- A **combining character** is a character that alters the previous character in some way.

- You use special (non-integer) indexes to subscript into the string to a certain grapheme cluster.

- Swift's use of **canonicalization** ensures that the comparison of strings accounts for combining characters.

- Slicing a string yields a substring with the type `Substring`, which shares storage with its parent `String`.

- You can convert from a `Substring` to a `String` by initializing a new `String` and passing the `Substring`.

- Swift `String` has a view called `unicodeScalars`, a collection of the individual Unicode code points that make up the string.

- There are multiple ways to encode a string. UTF-8 and UTF-16 are the most popular.

- The individual parts of an encoding are called **code units**. UTF-8 uses 8-bit code units, and UTF-16 uses 16-bit code units.

- Swift's `String` has views called `utf8` and `utf16`that are collections that allow you to obtain the individual code units in the given encoding.

Chapter 10: Regex

By Ehab Amer

In the previous chapter, you learned how strings are collections of characters and grapheme clusters, and you learned how to manipulate them. You also learned how to find a character inside a string. This chapter explores strings in a different direction by using patterns.

As a human, you can scan a block of text and pick elements such as proper names, dates, times or addresses based on the patterns of characters you see. You don't need to know the exact values in advance to find elements.

What Is a Regular Expression?

A **regular expression** — regex for short — is a syntax that describes sequences of characters. Many modern programming languages, including Swift from Swift 5.7, can interpret regular expressions. In its simplest form, a regular expression looks much like a string. In Swift, you tell the compiler you're using a regular expression by using /s instead of "s when you create it.

```
let searchString = "john"
let searchExpression = /john/
```

The code above defines a regular expression and a String you can use to search some text to find whether it contains "john". Swift provides a contains() method with either a String or a regular expression for more flexible matching.

```
let stringToSearch = "Johnny Appleseed wants to change his name
to John."

stringToSearch.contains(searchString) // false
stringToSearch.contains(searchExpression) // false
```

It might surprise you that .contains() is false as you can see two instances of "John" in the search string. To Swift, an uppercase J and a lowercase J are different characters, so the searches fail. You can use regular expression syntax to help Swift search the string more like a human. Try this expression:

```
let flexibleExpression = /[Jj]ohn/
stringToSearch.contains(flexibleExpression) // true
```

The regular expression above defines a search that begins with either an uppercase or a lowercase J followed by the string "ohn". Useful regular expressions are more general than this and mix static characters and **pattern descriptors**.

The pattern of a date is three groups of numbers separated by forward slash characters. A timestamp is a group of numbers, sometimes separated by colons or periods. Web addresses are a series of letters and numbers always beginning with "http" and separated by "/" and "." and "?". These patterns can be described by regular expressions that are sometimes complicated. But you'll start with something simple and work your way up.

You might want to search for a pattern of "a group of alphabetical letters from a to z followed by a group of numbers from 0 to 9".

One way to represent this in regular expression syntax is `/[a-z]+[0-9]+/`.

This expression will match text including `abcd12345` or `swiftapprentice2023` but won't work on `XYZ567` or `Pennsylvania65000`. The expression only describes lowercase ASCII, not uppercase.

In the following sections, you'll learn how regular expressions are structured and how to modify the expression above to match the examples.

> **Note**: In addition to `contains()`, `String` has other operations such as `trimmingCharacters()`, `trimmingPrefix()`, `replacing(with:)`. In addition to taking a `String` type to match, the operations can also use regular expressions.

Regular Expression Structure

A regular expression mainly consists of two parts:

1. Something to describe which character group you're searching for.

2. A repetition form of that character group.

The example above `[a-z]` describes a single character from a to z. It's followed by + to show it's repeated one or more times. Then the range of digits from 0 to 9 repeats one or more times.

You can see that you concatenate two expressions to form a more complex expression.

Character Representations

Remember that regular expressions are a syntax for defining patterns. Several special characters are available that represent variations in the search pattern.

*   `\d`: Any single character that's a digit. It can replace [0-9].

*   `\w`: Any single character that's part of the ASCII letters or numbers. It can replace [a-zA-Z0-9_].

*   `\s`: Any single character representing whitespace, such as a space or a tab.

You can also express the *inverse* of each set using the uppercased representation.

- \D: Anything that is *not* a digit.

- \W: Anything that is *not* an alphabet character, a digit or an underscore.

- \S: Anything that is *not* whitespace.

Other pattern descriptor symbols give you more control over the matched character.

- [–]: A range of characters or numbers. You don't need to specify the whole alphabet or all digits; you can specify the range you want, like [m–r] or [4–8].

- [ ]: A set of characters to choose from. For example, [AEIOUaeiou] will match vowel characters in uppercase or lowercase.

- |: The *or* operator can do the same as the above vowel example, like A|E|I|O|U| a|e|i|o|u. It's more commonly seen with multicharacter expressions like searching for different endings to words s|ed|ing.

> **Note:** The range [–] representation works with the universal character table. That table has entries for all characters, including accented characters, symbols and emojis. For example, [5–d] is a valid range that includes the digits five through nine, all uppercase letters, the first few lowercase letters, and some math symbols. It's unlikely you'd ever make a range that spans character groupings on purpose.

The magic . character matches *any* character. Be careful using it because it might create matches you don't expect.

Using any of the symbols above matches a single character. If you apply the expression [a–d] to the string abcdefghijk, it'll match each of the four characters a, b, c and d on their own and return four results. If you want a single result with the string abcd, you must have some repetition in the expression.

Repetitions

You have already used the repetition descriptor + for one or more. Multiple types of repetition descriptors exist. They follow the character pattern you want to repeat:

- +: The pattern appears one or more times. The expression [a–z]+ matches one or more lowercase letters in a row.

- ?: The pattern can appear once or not appear. An expression of [a–z]?[0–9]+ matches numbers only or a single lowercase character followed by numbers.

- *: The pattern appears *zero* or more times. An expression of [a–z]*[0–9]+ matches numbers only or one or more lowercase letters followed by numbers.

- {n,} The pattern repeats a minimum *n* times. The + above can also be represented as {1,} and * is the same as {0,}.

- {n,m} The pattern repeats minimum *n* times and a maximum of *m* times.

Mini-Exercise

Now that you've learned to construct regular expressions with different capabilities, how would you adapt /[a–z]+[0–9]+/ from earlier to match all of the example texts abcd12345, swiftapprentice2023, XYZ567, Pennsylvania65000?

Compile Time Checking

What separates Swift regex from other languages (and earlier versions of Swift before 5.7) is its ability to check for correctness at compile time. Consider the following:

```
let lowercaseLetters = /[a-z*/
```

Rather than let this go and fail to match at runtime, the Swift compiler prevents the problem entirely with the error:

```
let lowercaseLetters = /[a-z*/
```

❌ Cannot parse regular expression: expected ']' ❌

You can fix it by adding the missing] character:

```
let lowercaseLetters = /[a-z]*/
```

Wherever it can, the Swift compiler keeps you on the right track by ensuring your regexes are well-formed expressions.

Regular Expression Matches

Regular expression matches can sometimes be surprising. To explore kinds of matching, start with this example:

```
let lettersAndNumbers = /[a-z]+[0-9]+/
```

You saw how to use `.contains()` to see whether a match exists in a string, but it's more powerful to use the method `String.matches(of:)` to find the matched results of the expression within a string. The `.matches(of:)` provides the matched characters and where they appear in the original string using `.range`. You worked with Range types in the previous chapter, "Strings":

```
let testingString1 = "abcdef ABCDEF 12345 abc123 ABC 123 123ABC
123abc abcABC"
for match in testingString1.matches(of: lettersAndNumbers) {
  print(String(match.output))
}
```

The code above will print this output to the console:

```
abc123
```

Now, change the repetition modifier to explore various ways matching works. The ∗ will match each character zero or more times.

```
let possibleLettersAndPossibleNumbers = /[a-z]*[0-9]*/
```

When using `possibleLettersAndPossibleNumbers` with `testingString1`, you might expect that this will give three matches:

- Lowercase letters only `abcdef`.

- Numbers only 12345 and 123.

- Lowercase letters then numbers `abc123`.

However, when you execute this code in the playground, you'll get many more matches.

```
for match in testingString1.matches(of:
possibleLettersAndPossibleNumbers) {
  print(String(match.output)) // 32 times
}
```

How is that possible?

As Swift compares your regular expression to the string, it considers all possibilities. Looking at the expression above, zero or more is possible for each part. Meaning that zero for *both* is a valid option. In other words, this expression can match all possible empty ranges of the string.

Explore matching an empty string using the code below.

```
let emptyString = ""
let matchCount = emptyString.matches(of:
                 possibleLettersAndPossibleNumbers).count //
1
```

The value of `matchCount` isn't zero. An actual match is found within an empty string because the empty string contains a pattern you describe: zero letters followed by zero numbers. This result is called a *zero-length match*.

Avoiding Zero-Length Matches

The regular expression engine starts at a position in the search string and increments along as far as it can while still matching the expression. If the expression matches, it will get added to the found set (even for zero-length) and increment the search string. This repeats until the search string is consumed.

Note: The engine will *never* use the same search position twice to avoid infinite loops.

When you design your expressions, avoid situations where *nothing* is a match.

An expression that doesn't allow zero-length matches would look like this:

```
let fixedPossibleLettersAndPossibleNumbers = /[a-z]+[0-9]*|[a-
z]*[0-9]+/
```

This expression uses the | *or* operator. It describes a pattern of either one or more letters followed by a group of numbers, *or* a group of letters followed by one or more numbers. Either side of the *or* is guaranteed to contain at least one character, a letter or a number. So this expression will never match *nothing*.

```
for match in testingString1.matches(of:
fixedPossibleLettersAndPossibleNumbers) {
    print(String(match.output))
}
```

Running the expression against the sample string will give the following results:

```
abcdef
12345
abc123
123
123
123
abc
abc
```

Although this is better, you're probably expecting four results. The expression matched with eight results instead. Looking at the original string, you'll see the matches in the curly braces: "{abcdef} ABCDEF {12345} {abc123} ABC {123} {123}ABC {123}{abc} {abc}ABC"

Suppose the first four results are the ones you're expecting, but the last four are not.

If you compare the matched strings against your expression, you'll notice that, unfortunately, they match. You want to extract words, not parts of a word, but that's different from what your expression describes.

Result Boundaries

One way to solve this is to specify boundaries that should contain each result. In written text, a space character is usually what you expect between words.

Just as it's easier to use \w instead of [a-zA-Z0-9_], you can specify word boundaries using \b. This special descriptor takes care of the corner cases that crop up because of Unicode.

```
let fixedWithBoundaries = /\b[a-z]+[0-9]*\b|\b[a-z]*[0-9]+\b/
```

This version adds the boundary character \b, known as an anchor, to each side of the two expressions around the *or* operator |.

```
for match in testingString1.matches(of: fixedWithBoundaries) {
  print(String(match.output))
}
```

Now you'll finally see the four results you're expecting:

```
abcdef
12345
abc123
123
```

> **Note**: Regular expressions also understand that lines of text have a beginning and an end. The anchor character ^ will ensure that a match only happens at the beginning of a line, while the anchor $ will only match at the end.

Challenge 1

Create a regular expression that matches any word that contains a sequence of two or more uppercase characters.Examples: 123ABC - ABC123 - ABC - abcABC - ABCabc - abcABC123 - a1b2ABCDEc3d4. It should reject abcA12a3 - abc123.

Test on the sample strings provided above.

Hints: A range expression can contain many range sets. [a-z0-9] can match a lowercase letter or a number. [a-z0-9]+ can match a repetition with a mix of both like a2c456xyz. You can use {2,} two or more.

228 Swift Apprentice: Fundamentals

A Better Way to Write Expressions

So far, you've been writing regular expressions using the standard syntax. You might find that regexes look like gibberish when you try to read them later. Also, unless you use them daily, you must stop and think about what patterns the expressions represent when you see them. Don't worry — it's a common problem. :]

Swift's new Regex type also introduces a friendlier and more readable way to design expressions. Writing expressions in this manner makes it easier to remember what they represent when you return to the code later. This new syntax also makes it possible to leverage code completion to get at pattern descriptors used by your expression. As before, the compiler can provide compile-time diagnostics to help avoid mistakes.

First, add this `import` to the top of your Swift file:

```
import RegexBuilder
```

Using the first regular expression example from earlier, `[a-z]+[0-9]+`, translate it to the new syntax like this:

```
let newlettersAndNumbers = Regex {
    OneOrMore { "a"..."z" }
    OneOrMore { .digit }
}
```

This expression is identical to the compact expression `/[a-z]+\d+/` but written more clearly.

Swift provides several operators and constants to represent the special regular expression commands. Here is the table from earlier in the chapter repeated with the equivalents in RegexBuilder:

- `\d` = `CharacterClass.digit`.

- `\w` = `CharacterClass.word`.

- `\s` = `CharacterClass.whitespace`.

- `\D` = `CharacterClass.digit.inverted`.

- `\W` = `CharacterClass.word.inverted`.

- `\S` = `CharacterClass.whitespace.inverted`.

- `.` = `CharacterClass.any`.

- `\b` = `Anchor.wordBoundary`.

- `[ - ]` = Directly using a range of characters like `"m"..."r"` or `"4"..."8"`.

- `[ ]` = `CharacterClass.anyOf("AEIOUaeiou")`.

- `|` = `ChoiceOf { }` This is more convenient for longer expressions.

- `+` = `OneOrMore { }`.

- `?` = `Optionally { }`.

- `*` = `ZeroOrMore { }`.

- `{n,}` = `Repeat(n...) { }`.

- `{n,m}` = `Repeat(n...m) { }`.

You can represent the expression `\b[a-z]+[0-9]*\b|\b[a-z]*[0-9]+\b` with RegexBuilder like this:

```
let newFixedRegex = Regex {
    Anchor.wordBoundary
    ChoiceOf {
      Regex {
        OneOrMore {
          "a"..."z"
        }
        ZeroOrMore {
          .digit
        }
      }
      Regex {
        ZeroOrMore {
          "a"..."z"
        }
        OneOrMore {
          .digit
        }
      }
    }
    Anchor.wordBoundary
}
```

This time, the `wordBoundary` is present *outside* of the *or* operator `ChoiceOf`. You can control the groupings that fall within the `ChoiceOf` block.

> **Note**: The prefix `CharacterClass` is part of the full name. Usually, in your code, you can use the class names, and the compiler uses type inference to figure out the rest. Instead of `CharacterClass.digit`, you'll likely use `.digit`. If the compiler ever complains that it doesn't know about the `CharacterClass` or any other RegexBuilder commands, check that you have added `import RegexBuilder` to the top of the file.

Challenge 2

Update the expression you created in Challenge 1 to use the new RegexBuilder structure and match expressions that have multiple sequences of uppercase characters. Example `a1b2ABCDEc3d4FGHe5f6g7`

Hint: You can represent the expression `[a-z0-9]` by creating a union between two character classes. E.g., `CharacterClass.digit.union("a"..."z")`.

Refactoring to RegexBuilder

As you complete Challenge 2, you might wonder how this new way is better. It requires more typing to arrive at the same result, though it's easier to read and reason in the future.

Apple recognized there might be many complex regular expressions already in code. So, in Xcode, a refactor option takes any regular expression in your code and converts it to RegexBuilder format. Give it a try.

Place the cursor in any part of a regular expression definition in your code and right-click to reveal the contextual menu. Select Refactor ▸ Convert to Regex Builder.

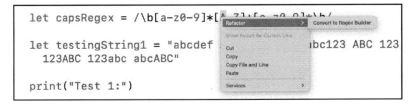

Also, you can refactor from the main Editor menu.

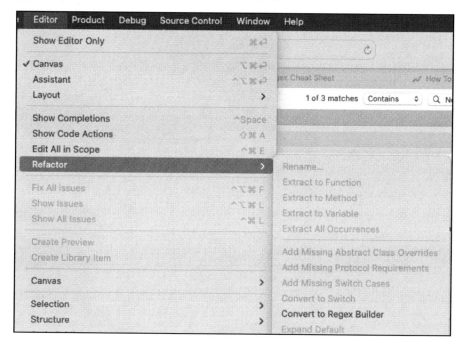

Capturing Results

So far, you've used regular expressions to match a pattern in a larger string. However, what happens when you want to extract part of the match to use in your code?

You might remember from earlier in the chapter that the .matches(of:) output will have the range of the match. So, it would certainly be possible to write some code to use that Range type to traverse the string and pull out the match. Then use some more code to convert the string to a different data type, like an Int. That's a lot of extra work.

Thankfully, regular expressions have something called *Captures* that allows you to assign parts of the result to special variables. With Swift, you can even name the variables in the regular expression and convert the captured value from String to something else you can use in your code.

Using the regular expression syntax, place any descriptors you want to capture from a longer expression by surrounding them in parenthesis (). The expression to capture digits from inside groups of letters would look like: [a-z]+(\d+)[a-z]+.

Or, using RegexBuilder, the expression would look like this:

```
let regexWithCapture = Regex {
  OneOrMore {
    "a"..."z"
  }
  Capture {
    OneOrMore {
      CharacterClass.digit
    }
  }
  OneOrMore {
    "a"..."z"
  }
}
```

When you use a capture, the type of the output changes from `Substring` to a tuple
(`Substring`, `Substring`). Each capture will make the tuple longer to include it. An
expression with two captures will have a tuple of three items, and an expression with
five captures will have a tuple of six. The first item in the tuple is always the full
match of the expression. *(FullMatch, Capture1, Capture2, ...)*

```
let testingString2 = "welc0me to chap7er 10 in sw1ft appren71ce.
" +
    "Th1s chap7er c0vers regu1ar express1ons and regexbu1lder"

for match in testingString2.matches(of: regexWithCapture) {
  print(match.output)
}
```

The printed result of this code is:

```
("elc0me", "0")
("chap7er", "7")
("sw1ft", "1")
("appren71ce", "71")
("h1s", "1")
("chap7er", "7")
("c0vers", "0")
("regu1ar", "1")
("express1ons", "1")
("regexbu1lder", "1")
```

You can also assign the tuple to named variables using a `let` statement with the
output. For the strings above, you might use something like:

```
for match in testingString2.matches(of: regexWithCapture) {
  let (wordMatch, extractedDigit) = match.output
  print("Full Match: \(wordMatch) | Captured value: \
```

```
  (extractedDigit)")
}
```

This code prints:

```
Full Match: elc0me | Captured value: 0
Full Match: chap7er | Captured value: 7
Full Match: sw1ft | Captured value: 1
Full Match: appren71ce | Captured value: 71
Full Match: h1s | Captured value: 1
Full Match: chap7er | Captured value: 7
Full Match: c0vers | Captured value: 0
Full Match: regu1ar | Captured value: 1
Full Match: express1ons | Captured value: 1
Full Match: regexbu1lder | Captured value: 1
```

The digits in the tuple captured from the string are also represented as strings. You can use a `TryCapture` command to manipulate the match with a `transform` closure to change the data type.

```
let regexWithStrongType = Regex {
  OneOrMore {
    "a"..."z"
  }
  TryCapture {
    OneOrMore {
      CharacterClass.digit
    }
  } transform: {foundDigits in
    Int(foundDigits)
  }
  OneOrMore {
    "a"..."z"
  }
}
```

The code above has replaced `Capture` with `TryCapture`. When the `TryCapture` is successful, it passes the matched string into the `transform` closure. The code in the closure converts the matched string into an `Int` type.

Now when you execute code to output the matching tuples, instead of a tuple with two `String` types, you see a `String` type and an `Int` type.

```
("elc0me", 0)
("chap7er", 7)
("sw1ft", 1)
("appren71ce", 71)
("h1s", 1)
("chap7er", 7)
```

```
("c0vers", 0)
("regu1ar", 1)
("express1ons", 1)
("regexbu1lder", 1)
```

You must be aware of something critical when using captures. You won't have multiple captures, even if your capture is inside a repetition. The capture will store the last found value and not all of the other matches.

Consider this example string:

```
let repetition = "123abc456def789ghi"
```

You want to capture the numbers found in the above string, not the letters. Your expression might be:

```
let repeatedCaptures = Regex {
  OneOrMore {
    Capture {
      OneOrMore {
        CharacterClass.digit
      }
    }
    OneOrMore {
      "a"..."z"
    }
  }
}
```

You would expect that the matches will include 123, 456 and 789:

```
for match in repetition.matches(of: repeatedCaptures) {
  print(match.output)
}
```

The output from this code is: ("123abc456def789ghi", "789"). The expression has only *one* capture block. It doesn't matter if it's inside a repetition that iterates only once or a hundred times. The value stored is the one found in the last iteration.

Challenge 3

Change the expression used in the last challenge to capture the text in uppercase. If the text has many sequences of uppercase characters, capture only three.

Key Points

- Regular expressions give you incredible flexibility for matching patterns over simple substring matching.

- Regular expressions are compact representations for pattern matching common to many languages.

- Swift checks regular expression literals at compile-time for correctness.

- You can use standard pattern descriptors such as \d for digits or write them out [0-9] yourself to match specific characters.

- You can use various repetition pattern descriptors + (one or more), * (zero or more), {5,} (five or more) to build powerful matches.

- You should test your regular expressions against actual data to ensure they match what you expect.

- Boundary anchors like ^ (beginning of a line), $ (end of a line) and \b (word) can narrow down the results to words or lines and avoid zero-length matches.

- Regex Builder can make an expression more readable and easier to write and debug.

- You can capture one or more parts of a matched expression.

- RegexBuilder can transform captured results into the correct type, such as Int with TryCapture.

Section III: Building Your Own Types

You can create your own type by combining variables and functions into a new type definition. When you create a new type, you give it a name; thus, these custom types are known as **named types**. Structures are a powerful tool for modeling real-world concepts. You can encapsulate related concepts, properties and methods into a single, cohesive model.

Swift includes four kinds of named types: structures, classes, enumerations and protocols. You'll learn here how other named types use the concepts of methods and properties, how they differ, and where you want to use each.

You'll also learn about protocols & generics, which are types and methods that take as input other types instead of just methods, as well as custom types to build larger and complex things!

Chapter 11: Structures

By Ehab Amer

You've covered some fundamental building blocks of Swift. With variables, conditionals, strings, functions and collections, you're ready to conquer the world! Well, almost.

Most programs that perform complex tasks benefit from higher levels of abstraction. In addition to an Int, String or Array, most programs use new types specific to the domain of the task at hand. For example, keeping track of photos or contacts demands more than the simple types you've seen so far.

This chapter introduces the first **named type–structures**. Structures are types that can store named properties and define actions and behaviors. Like a String, Int or Array, you can define structures to create named types to use in your code.

By the end of this chapter, you'll know how to define and use your own structures.

You'll begin your adventure into custom types with pizza.

Introducing Structures

Imagine you live in a town called Pizzaville. As you might expect, Pizzaville is known for its amazing pizza. You own the most popular (and fastest!) pizza delivery restaurant in Pizzaville — "Swift Pizza".

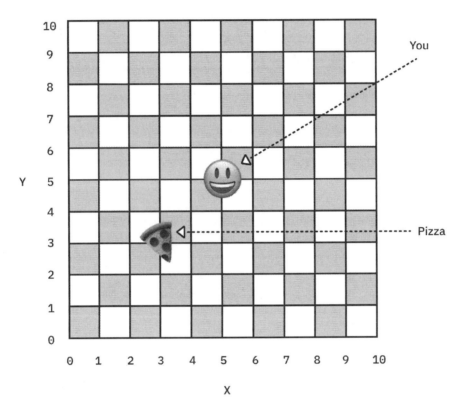

As the owner of a single restaurant, you have a limited delivery area. You want to write a program that calculates if a potential customer is within range for your delivery drivers. The first version of your program might look something like this:

```
let restaurantLocation = (3, 3)
let restaurantRange = 2.5

// Pythagorean Theorem 📐 🎓
func distance(
  from source: (x: Int, y: Int),
  to target: (x: Int, y: Int)
) -> Double {
  let distanceX = Double(source.x - target.x)
```

```
    let distanceY = Double(source.y - target.y)
    return (distanceX * distanceX +
      distanceY * distanceY).squareRoot()
}
```

```
func isInDeliveryRange(location: (x: Int, y: Int)) -> Bool {
  let deliveryDistance = distance(from: location,
                                    to: restaurantLocation)
  return deliveryDistance < restaurantRange
}

isInDeliveryRange(location: (x: 5, y: 5)) // false
```

Simple enough, right? `distance(from:to:)` will calculate how far away you are from your pizza. `isInDeliveryRange(location:)` will return `true` only if you're not too far away.

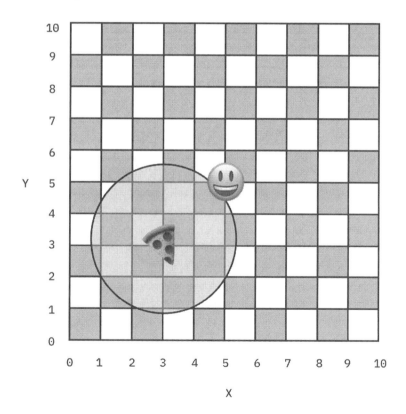

A successful pizza delivery business may eventually expand to include multiple locations, adding a minor twist to the deliverable calculator.

Replace your existing code with the following:

```swift
let restaurantLocation = (3, 3)
let restaurantRange = 2.5

let otherRestaurantLocation = (8, 8)
let otherRestaurantRange = 2.5

// Pythagorean Theorem 📐🎓
func distance
  from source: (x: Int, y: Int),
  to target: (x: Int, y: Int)
) -> Double {
  let distanceX = Double(source.x - target.x)
  let distanceY = Double(source.y - target.y)
  return (distanceX * distanceX +
    distanceY * distanceY).squareRoot()
}

func isInDeliveryRange(location: (x: Int, y: Int)) -> Bool {
  let deliveryDistance =
    distance(from: location, to: restaurantLocation)

  let secondDeliveryDistance =
    distance(from: location, to: otherRestaurantLocation)

  return deliveryDistance < restaurantRange ||
    secondDeliveryDistance < otherRestaurantRange
}

isInDeliveryRange(location: (x: 5, y: 5)) // false
```

`isInDeliveryRange(location:)` checks both locations to see if you can get your pizza from either one.

Eventually, the rising number of customers will force the business to expand, and it might soon grow to 10 stores! Then what? Do you keep updating your function to check against all these sets of coordinates and ranges?

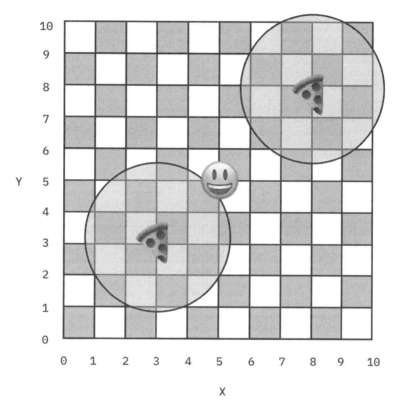

You might briefly consider creating an array of x/y coordinate tuples to keep track of your pizza restaurants, but that would be both difficult to read and maintain. Fortunately, Swift has additional tools to help you simplify the problem.

Your First Structure

Structures allow you to encapsulate related properties and behaviors. You can declare a new type, give it a name and then use it in your code.

In the pizza business example, you've used x/y coordinate tuples to represent locations.

As a first example of structures, promote locations from tuples to a structure type:

```
struct Location {
   let x: Int
   let y: Int
}
```

This block of code demonstrates the basic syntax for defining a structure. In this case, the code declares a type named Location that combines x and y coordinates.

The basic syntax begins with the struct keyword followed by the name of the type and a pair of curly braces. Everything between the curly braces is a *member* of the struct.

In Location, both members, x and y, are **properties**. Properties are constants or variables that are declared as part of a type. Every instance of this type will have these properties. In our example, every Location will have both an x and a y property.

You can instantiate a structure and store it in a constant or variable just like any other type you've worked with:

```
let storeLocation = Location(x: 3, y: 3)
```

To create the Location value, you use the name of the type along with a parameter list in parentheses. This parameter list provides a way to specify the values for the properties x and y. This is an example of an **initializer**.

Initializers enforce that all properties are set before you start using them. This guarantee is one of the key safety features of Swift. Accidentally using uninitialized variables is a significant source of bugs in other languages. Another handy Swift feature is that you don't need to declare this initializer in the Location type. Swift automatically provides initializers for structures with all the properties in the parameter list. You'll learn much more about initializers in Chapter 13, "Methods."

You may remember that there's also a range involved, and now that the pizza business is expanding, there may be different ranges associated with different restaurants. You can create another struct to represent the delivery area of a restaurant, like so:

```
struct DeliveryArea {
  let center: Location
  var radius: Double
}

var storeArea = DeliveryArea(center: storeLocation, radius: 2.5)
```

Now there's a new structure named `DeliveryArea` that contains a constant `center` property along with a variable `radius` property. As you can see, you can have a structure value inside a structure value; here, you use the `Location` type as the type of the `center` property of the `DeliveryArea` struct.

Mini-Exercise

Write a structure that represents a pizza order. Include toppings, size and any other option you'd want for a pizza.

Accessing Members

With your `DeliveryArea` defined and an instantiated value in hand, you may be wondering how you can *use* these values. Just as you have been doing with `Strings`, `Arrays`, and `Dictionaries`, you use **dot syntax** to access members:

```
storeArea.radius // 2.5
```

You can even access *members of members* using dot syntax:

```
storeArea.center.x // 3
```

Similar to how you can read values with dot syntax, you can also *assign* them. If the delivery radius of one pizza location becomes larger, you could assign the new value to the existing property:

```
storeArea.radius = 3.5
```

Defining a property as a constant or variable determines if you can change it. In this case, you can modify `radius` because you declared it with `var`.

On the other hand, you declared `center` with `let`, so you can't modify it. Your `DeliveryArea` struct allows a pizza restaurant's delivery range to be changed, but not its location!

In addition to choosing whether your properties should be variable or constants, you must also declare the structure itself as a variable if you want to be able to modify it after it is initialized:

```
let fixedArea = DeliveryArea(center: storeLocation, radius: 4)

// Error: Cannot assign to property
fixedArea.radius = 3.5
```

Even though `radius` was declared with `var`, the enclosing type `fixedArea` is constant, so you can't change it. The compiler correctly emits an error. Change `fixedArea` from a `let` constant to a `var` variable to make it mutable, so it compiles.

Now you've learned how to control the mutability of the properties in your structure.

Mini-Exercise

Rewrite `isInDeliveryRange` to use `Location` and `DeliveryArea`.

Introducing Methods

Using some of the capabilities of structures, you could now make a pizza delivery range calculator that looks something like this:

```
let areas = [
  DeliveryArea(center: Location(x: 3, y: 3), radius: 2.5),
  DeliveryArea(center: Location(x: 8, y: 8), radius: 2.5)
]

func isInDeliveryRange(_ location: Location) -> Bool {
  for area in areas {
    let distanceToStore =
      distance(from: (area.center.x, area.center.y),
               to: (location.x, location.y))

    if distanceToStore < area.radius {
      return true
    }
  }
  return false
}
```

```
let customerLocation1 = Location(x: 5, y: 5)
let customerLocation2 = Location(x: 7, y: 7)

isInDeliveryRange(customerLocation1) // false
isInDeliveryRange(customerLocation2) // true
```

In this example, the function `isInDeliveryRange()` uses the `areas` array to determine if a customer's location is within any of the delivery areas.

Being in range is something you want to know about for a particular restaurant. It'd be great if `DeliveryArea` could tell you if the restaurant could deliver to a location.

Much like a structure can have constants and variables, it can also define its own functions. In your playground, locate the implementation of `DeliveryArea`. Just before the closing curly brace and add the following code:

```
func contains(_ location: Location) -> Bool {
    let distanceFromCenter =
      distance(from: (center.x, center.y),
               to: (location.x, location.y))

    return distanceFromCenter < radius
}
```

This code defines a function `contains` as a member of `DeliveryArea`. Functions that are members of types are called **methods**. Notice how `contains` uses the `center` and `radius` properties of the current location. This implicit access to properties and other members inside the structure makes methods different from regular functions. You'll learn more about methods in Chapter 13, "Methods".

Just like other members of structures, you can use dot syntax to access a method:

```
let area = DeliveryArea(center: Location(x: 8, y: 8), radius:
2.5)
let customerLocation = Location(x: 7, y: 7)
area.contains(customerLocation) // true
```

Mini-Exercises

1. Change `distance(from:to:)` to use `Location` as your parameters instead of x-y tuples.

2. Change `contains(_:)` to call the new `distance(from:to:)` with `Location`.

3. Add a method `overlaps(with:)` on `DeliveryArea` that can tell you if the area overlaps with another area.

Structures as Values

The term **value** has an important meaning for structures in Swift, and that's because structures create what are known as **value types**.

A value type is a type whose instances are *copied* on assignment.

```
var a = 5
var b = a

a // 5
b // 5

a = 10

a // 10
b // 5
```

This **copy-on-assignment** behavior means that when a is assigned to b, the value of a is copied into b. But later, when you change the value of a, the value of b stays the same. That's why it's important to read = as "assign", not "is equal to". Read the statement b = a as "Assign the value of a to b".

> **Note**: You use == to calculate equality: 2 + 2 == 4. Read this expression as a question: "Is 2 + 2 equal to 4?".

How about the same principle, except with the `DeliveryArea` struct:

```
var area1 = DeliveryArea(center: Location(x: 3, y: 3), radius:
2.5)
var area2 = area1

area1.radius // 2.5
area2.radius // 2.5

area1.radius = 4

area1.radius // 4.0
area2.radius // 2.5
```

As with the previous example, `area2.radius` didn't pick up the new value set in `area1.radius`. The disconnection demonstrates the **value semantics** of working with structures. When you assign `area2` the value of `area1`, it gets an exact copy of this value. `area1` and `area2` are still completely independent!

Thanks to value semantics and copying, structures are *safe*, so you'll never need to worry about values being shared and possibly being changed behind your back by another piece of code.

Structures Everywhere

You saw how the `Location` struct and a simple `Int` share the same copy-on-assignment behavior. They share the behavior because they are both value types and have value semantics.

You know structures represent values, so what exactly is an `Int` then? If you were to look at the definition of `Int` in the Swift library, you might be a bit surprised:

```
struct Int : FixedWidthInteger, SignedInteger {
  // …
}
```

The `Int` type is *also* a structure. Many standard Swift types are structures, such as: `Double`, `String`, `Bool`, `Array` and `Dictionary`. As you'll learn in future chapters, the value semantics of structures provide many other advantages over their reference type counterparts that make them ideal for representing core Swift types.

Conforming to a Protocol

You may have noticed some unfamiliar parts to the `Int` definition from the Swift standard library above. The types `FixedWidthInteger` and `SignedInteger` appear right after the declaration of `Int`:

```
struct Int : FixedWidthInteger, SignedInteger {
  // …
}
```

These types are known as *protocols*. By putting them after a colon when `Int` is declared, you signal that `Int` *conforms* to these protocols.

Protocols contain a set of requirements that conforming types **must** satisfy. A simple example from the standard library is `CustomStringConvertible`:

```
public protocol CustomStringConvertible {
  /// A textual representation of this instance.
  var description: String { get }
}
```

This protocol contains one property requirement: `description`. The documentation refers to `description` as "A textual representation of this instance."

If you were to modify `DeliveryArea` to conform to `CustomStringConvertible`, you would be required to add a `description` property with a "textual representation" of the instance. Try this now. Change `DeliveryArea` to:

```swift
struct DeliveryArea: CustomStringConvertible {
  let center: Location
  var radius: Double
  var description: String {
    """
    Area with center: (x: \(center.x), y: \(center.y)),
    radius: \(radius)
    """
  }

  func contains(_ location: Location) -> Bool {
    distance(from: center, to: location) < radius
  }

  func overlaps(with area: DeliveryArea) -> Bool {
    distance(from: center, to: area.center) <=
    (radius + area.radius)
  }
}
```

The value of the `description` property contains the center and current radius. A value that updates in response to changes elsewhere is called a *computed* property.

You'll learn all about computed properties — and more — in Chapter 12, "Properties"!

So what exactly does conforming to a protocol do? Because any type conforming to `CustomStringConvertible` must define `description`, so you can call `description` on any instance of any type that conforms to `CustomStringConvertible`. The Swift standard library takes advantage of this with the `print()` function. That function will use `description` in the console instead of a rather noisy default description:

```swift
print(area1) // Area with center: (x: 3, y: 3), radius: 4.0
print(area2) // Area with center: (x: 3, y: 3), radius: 2.5
```

Any named type can use protocols to extend its behavior. In this case, you conformed your structure to a protocol defined in the Swift standard library. In Chapter 17, "Protocols", you'll learn more about defining, using and conforming to protocols.

Challenges

Before moving on, here are some challenges to test your knowledge of structures. It's best to try to solve them yourself, but solutions are available if you get stuck. These came with the download or are available at the printed book's source code link listed in the introduction.

Challenge 1: Fruit Tree Farm

Imagine you're at a fruit tree farm and you grow different kinds of fruits: pears, apples and oranges. After the fruits are picked, a truck brings them in to be processed at the central facility. Since the fruits are all mixed together on the truck, the workers in the central facility have to sort them into the correct inventory container one by one.

Implement an algorithm that receives a truck full of different kinds of fruits and places each fruit into the correct inventory container.

Keep track of the total weight of fruit processed by the facility and print out how many of each fruit are in the inventory.

Challenge 2: A T-shirt Model

Create a T-shirt structure that has size, color and material options. Provide a method to calculate the cost of a shirt based on its attributes.

Challenge 3: Battleship

Write the engine for a Battleship-like game. If you aren't familiar with Battleship, you can brush up on the details at this webpage: http://bit.ly/2nT3JBU

- Use an (x, y) coordinate system for your locations modeled using a structure.

- Ships should also be modeled with structures. Record an origin, direction and length.

- Each ship should be able to report if a "shot" has resulted in a "hit".

Key Points

- Structures are named types you can define and use in your code.

- Structures are **value types**, which means their values are copied on assignment.

- You use dot syntax to access the members of named types, such as structures.

- Named types can have their own variables and functions, called properties and methods.

- Conforming to a protocol requires implementing the properties and methods required by that protocol.

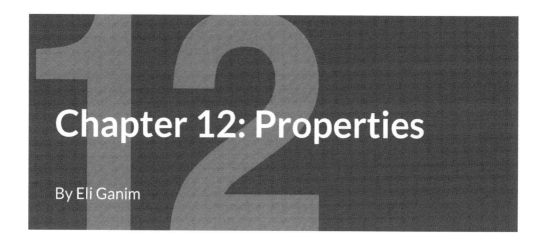

Chapter 12: Properties

By Eli Ganim

Chapter 11, "Structures", showed that you can use structures to group related properties and behaviors into a custom type.

In the example below, the Car structure has two properties; both are constants that store String values:

```
struct Car {
    let make: String
    let color: String
}
```

The values inside a structure are called **properties**. The two properties of Car are **stored properties**, which means they store actual string values for each instance of Car.

Some properties calculate values rather than store them. In other words, there's no actual memory allocated for them; instead, they get calculated on-the-fly each time you access them. Naturally, these are called **computed properties**.

In this chapter, you'll learn about both kinds of properties. You'll also learn some other neat tricks for working with properties, such as how to monitor changes in a property's value and delay the initialization of a stored property.

Stored Properties

As you may have guessed from the example in the introduction, you're already familiar with the features of stored properties.

To review, imagine you're building an address book. You'll need a Contact type:

```
struct Contact {
  var fullName: String
  var emailAddress: String
}
```

You can use this structure repeatedly, letting you build an array of contacts, each with a different value. The properties you want to store are an individual's full name and email address.

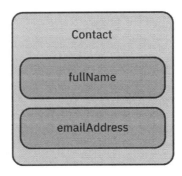

These are the properties of the Contact structure. You provide a data type for each but opt not to assign a default value because you plan to assign the value upon initialization. After all, the values will differ for each instance of Contact.

Remember that Swift automatically creates an initializer for you based on the properties you defined in your structure:

```
var person = Contact(fullName: "Grace Murray",
             emailAddress: "grace@navy.mil")
```

You can access the individual properties using dot notation:

```
person.fullName // Grace Murray
person.emailAddress // grace@navy.mil
```

You can assign values to properties as long as they're defined as variables and the parent instance is stored in a variable. That means both the property and the structure containing the property must be declared with var instead of let.

When Grace married, she changed her last name:

```
person.fullName = "Grace Hopper"
person.fullName // Grace Hopper
```

Since the property is a variable, she could update her name.

If you'd like to prevent a value from changing, you can define a property as a constant using let, like so:

```
struct Contact {
    var fullName: String
    let emailAddress: String
}

// Error: cannot assign to a constant
person.emailAddress = "grace@gmail.com"
```

Once you've initialized an instance of this structure, you can't change emailAddress.

Default Values

If you can make a reasonable assumption about the value of a property when the type is initialized, you can give that property a default value.

It doesn't make sense to create a default name or email address for a contact, but imagine you add a new property relationship to indicate what kind of contact it is:

```
struct Contact {
    var fullName: String
    let emailAddress: String
    var relationship = "Friend"
}
```

By assigning a value in the definition of relationship, you give this property a default value. Any contact created will automatically be a friend unless you change the value of relationship to something like "Work" or "Family".

Swift will notice which properties you have defaulted and create the member-wise initializer with parameters also defaulted, so you don't need to specify them unless you want to.

```
var person = Contact(fullName: "Grace Murray",
                     emailAddress: "grace@navy.mil")
person.relationship // Friend

var boss = Contact(fullName: "Ray Wenderlich",
                   emailAddress: "ray@raywenderlich.com",
                   relationship: "Boss")
```

You can choose to specify the `relationship` if you want to; otherwise, it takes on the value `"Friend"`.

Computed Properties

Most of the time, properties are stored data, but some can just be computed, which means they perform a calculation before returning a value.

While a stored property can be a constant or a variable, a computed property must be defined as a variable.

Computed properties must also include a type because the compiler needs to know what to expect as a return value.

The measurement for a TV is the perfect use case for a computed property:

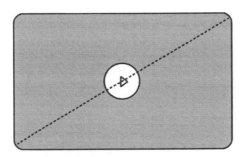

The industry definition of the screen size of a TV isn't the screen's height or width but its diagonal measurement:

```
struct TV {
  var height: Double
  var width: Double
```

```
// 1
var diagonal: Int {
  // 2
  let result = (height * height +
    width * width).squareRoot().rounded()
  // 3
  return Int(result)
}
}
```

Let's go through this code one step at a time:

1. You use an `Int` type for your `diagonal` property. Although `height` and `width` are `Double` types, TV sizes are usually advertised as nice, round numbers such as 50" rather than 49.52". Instead of the usual assignment operator = to assign a value as you would for a stored property, you use curly braces to enclose your computed property's calculation.

2. As you've seen in this book, geometry can be handy; once you have the width and height, you can use the Pythagorean theorem to calculate the diagonal length. You use the `rounded` method to round the value with the standard rule: If the decimal is 0.5 or above, it rounds up; otherwise, it rounds down.

3. Now that you've got a properly-rounded number, you return it as an `Int`. Had you converted `result` directly to `Int` without rounding first, the result would have been truncated, so 109.99 would have become 109.

Computed properties don't store any values; they return values based on calculations. From outside of the structure, a computed property can be accessed just like a stored property.

Test this with the TV size calculation:

```
var tv = TV(height: 53.93, width: 95.87)
tv.diagonal // 110
```

You have a 110-inch TV. Let's say you decide you don't like the standard movie aspect ratio and would instead prefer a square screen. You cut off some of the screen's width to make it equivalent to the height:

```
tv.width = tv.height
tv.diagonal // 76
```

Now you *only* have a 76-inch square screen. The computed property automatically provides the new value based on the new width.

Mini-Exercise

Do you have a television or a computer monitor? Measure the height and width, plug it into a TV struct, and see if the diagonal measurement matches what you think it is.

Getter and Setter

The computed property you wrote in the previous section is called a **read-only computed property**. It has a block of code to compute the property's value, called the **getter**.

It's also possible to create a **read-write computed property** with two code blocks: a **getter** and a **setter**.

This **setter** works differently than you might expect.

As the computed property has no place to store a value, the setter usually sets one or more related *stored* properties indirectly:

```swift
var diagonal: Int {
  // 1
  get {
    // 2
    let result = (height * height +
      width * width).squareRoot().rounded()
    return Int(result)
  }
  set {
    // 3
    let ratioWidth = 16.0
    let ratioHeight = 9.0
    // 4
    let ratioDiagonal = (ratioWidth * ratioWidth +
      ratioHeight * ratioHeight).squareRoot()
    height = Double(newValue) * ratioHeight / ratioDiagonal
    width = height * ratioWidth / ratioHeight
  }
}
```

Here's what's happening in this code:

1. Because you want to include a setter, you now have to be explicit about which calculations comprise the getter and which the setter, so you surround each code block with curly braces and precede it with either get or set. This specificity isn't required for read-only computed properties, as their single code block is implicitly a getter.

2. You use the same code as before to get the computed value.

3. For a setter, you usually have to make some kind of assumption. In this case, you provide a reasonable default value for the screen ratio.

4. The formulas to calculate height and width, given a diagonal and a ratio, are a bit deep. You could work them out with a bit of time, but I've done the dirty work for you and provided them here. The important parts to focus on are:

- The `newValue` constant lets you use whatever value was passed in during the assignment.

- Remember, the `newValue` is an `Int`, so to use it in a calculation with a `Double`, you must first convert it to a `Double`.

- Once you've done the calculations, you assign the height and width properties of the `TV` structure.

In addition to setting the height and width directly, you can set them *indirectly* by setting the `diagonal` computed property. When you set this value, your setter will calculate and store the height and width.

Notice there's no `return` statement in a setter — it only modifies the other stored properties. With the setter in place, you have a nice little screen size calculator:

```
tv.diagonal = 70
tv.height // 34.32...
tv.width // 61.01...
```

Now you can finally figure out the biggest TV you can cram into your cabinet — you're so welcome. :]

Type Properties

In the previous section, you learned how to declare stored and computed properties for instances of a particular type. The properties on your instance of TV are separate from the properties on my instance of TV.

However, the type *itself* may also need properties that are common across all instances. These properties are called **type properties**.

Imagine you're building a game with many levels. Each level has a few attributes or stored properties:

```
struct Level {
  let id: Int
  var boss: String
  var unlocked: Bool
}

let level1 = Level(id: 1, boss: "Chameleon", unlocked: true)
let level2 = Level(id: 2, boss: "Squid", unlocked: false)
let level3 = Level(id: 3, boss: "Chupacabra", unlocked: false)
let level4 = Level(id: 4, boss: "Yeti", unlocked: false)
```

You can use a type property to store the game's progress as the player unlocks each level. A type property is declared with the modifier `static`:

```
struct Level {
  static var highestLevel = 1
  let id: Int
  var boss: String
  var unlocked: Bool
}
```

Here, `highestLevel` is a property on `Level` itself rather than on the instances. That means you don't access this property on an instance:

```
// Error: you can't access a type property on an instance
let highestLevel = level3.highestLevel
```

Instead, you access it on the type itself:

```
Level.highestLevel // 1
```

Using a type property means you can retrieve the same stored property value from anywhere in the code for your app or algorithm. The game's progress is accessible from any level or any other place in the game, like the main menu.

Property Observers

For your `Level` implementation, it would be useful to automatically set the `highestLevel` when the player unlocks a new one. For that, you'll need a way to listen to property changes. Thankfully, there are a couple of **property observers** that get called before and after property changes.

The `willSet` observer is called when a property is about to be changed. The `didSet` observer is called after a property has been changed. Their syntax is similar to getters and setters:

```
struct Level {
    static var highestLevel = 1
    let id: Int
    var boss: String
    var unlocked: Bool {
        didSet {
            if unlocked && id > Self.highestLevel {
                Self.highestLevel = id
            }
        }
    }
}
```

When the player unlocks a new level, it will update the `highestLevel` type property if the level is a new high. There are a couple of things to note here:

- You *can* access the value of `unlocked` from inside the `didSet` observer. Remember that `didSet` gets called *after* the value has been set.

- Even though you're inside an instance of the type, you still have to access type properties with the type name prefix. You must use the full name `Level.highestLevel` rather than just `highestLevel` to indicate you're accessing a type property. You can also refer to the static property from within the type as `Self.highestLevel`. Using `Self` here is preferred because even if you change the name of the type to something else — say, `GameLevel` — the code would still work. The uppercase `Self` indicates you're accessing a property on the type itself, not an instance property.

`willSet` and `didSet` observers are only available for stored properties. If you want to listen for changes to a computed property, add the relevant code to the property's setter.

Also, remember that the `willSet` and `didSet` observers are *not* called when a property is set during initialization; they only get called when you assign a new value to a fully initialized instance. That means property observers are only useful for variable properties since constant properties are only set during initialization.

Limiting a Variable

You can also use property observers to limit the value of a variable. Say you had a light bulb that could only support a maximum current flowing through its filament.

```
struct LightBulb {
  static let maxCurrent = 40
  var current = 0 {
    didSet {
      if current > LightBulb.maxCurrent {
        print("""
              Current is too high,
              falling back to previous setting.
              """)
        current = oldValue
      }
    }
  }
}
```

In this example, if the current flowing into the bulb exceeds the maximum value, it will revert to its last successful value. Notice there's a helpful oldValue constant available in didSet to access the previous value.

Give it a try:

```
var light = LightBulb()
light.current = 50
light.current // 0
light.current = 40
light.current // 40
```

When you try to set the light bulb to 50 amps, the bulb rejects that input. Pretty cool!

Note: Do not confuse property observers with getters and setters. A stored property can have a didSet and a willSet observer. A computed property has a getter and, optionally, a setter. These, even though the syntax is similar, are entirely different concepts!

Mini-Exercise

In the light bulb example, the bulb goes back to a successful setting if the current gets too high. In real life, that wouldn't work, and the bulb would burn out! Your task is to rewrite the structure so the bulb turns off before the current burns it out.

Hint: You'll need to use the `willSet` observer that gets called before the value is changed. The value about to be set is available in the constant `newValue`. The trick is that you can't change this `newValue`, and it will still be set, so you'll have to go beyond adding a `willSet` observer. :]

Lazy Properties

If you have a property that might take some time to calculate, you don't want to slow things down until you need the property. Say hello to the **lazy stored property**. It is useful for such things as downloading a user's profile picture or making a serious calculation.

Look at this example of a `Circle` structure that uses pi in its circumference calculation:

```
struct Circle {
  lazy var pi = {
    ((4.0 * atan(1.0 / 5.0)) - atan(1.0 / 239.0)) * 4.0
  }()
  var radius = 0.0
  var circumference: Double {
    mutating get {
      pi * radius * 2
    }
  }
  init(radius: Double) {
    self.radius = radius
  }
}
```

For the sake of this example, you're not using the value of pi available from the standard library; you calculate it explicitly.

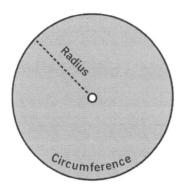

You can create a new `Circle` with its initializer, and the pi calculation won't run yet:

```
var circle = Circle(radius: 5) // got a circle, pi has not been
run
```

The calculation of `pi` defers until you need it. Only when you ask for the circumference property is `pi` calculated and assigned a value.

```
circle.circumference // 31.42
// also, pi now has a value
```

Since you've got eagle eyes, you've noticed that `pi` uses a `{ }()` self-executing closure pattern to calculate its value, even though it's a stored property. The trailing parentheses execute the code inside the closure curly braces immediately. But since `pi` is marked as `lazy`, this calculation is postponed until the first time you access the property.

For comparison, `circumference` is a computed property calculated every time it's accessed. You expect the circumference's value to change if the radius changes. `pi`, as a lazy stored property, is only calculated the first time. That's great because who wants to calculate the same thing repeatedly?

The lazy property must be a variable, defined with `var`, instead of a constant defined with `let`. When you first initialize the structure, the property effectively has no value. Then when some part of your code requests the property, its value will be calculated. So even though the value only changes once, you still use `var`.

Here are two more advanced features of the code:

- Since the value of `pi` changes, the `circumference` getter must be marked as `mutating`. Accessing the value of `pi` changes the value of the structure.

- Since `pi` is a stored property of the structure, you need a custom initializer to use only the `radius`. Remember, a structure's automatic memberwise initializer includes all the stored properties.

In the next chapter, "Methods", you'll learn about the `mutating` keyword and custom initializers. The important concept to understand here is how the `lazy` stored property works. The rest of the details are window dressing that you'll get more comfortable with in time.

> **Note**: `lazy` is a kind of *property wrapper*. By historical accident, `lazy` omits the @ symbol and capitalization that usually prefix property wrappers. When you build apps with SwiftUI, you will see many other property wrappers, like `@State`, `@Binding`, and `@EnvironmentObject`. When you apply a property wrapper to a property, it gives that property some additional behavior. In *Swift Apprentice: Beyond the Basics*, you will learn how to make your own custom property wrappers.

Mini-Exercises

Of course, you should trust the value of pi from the standard library. It's a type property, and you can access it as `Double.pi`. Given the `Circle` example above:

1. Remove the lazy stored property `pi`. Use the value of pi from the Swift standard library instead.

2. Remove the initializer. Since `radius` is the only stored property now, you can rely on the automatically included memberwise initializer.

Challenges

Before moving on, here are some challenges to test your knowledge of properties. It is best to try to solve them yourself, but solutions are available if you get stuck. These came with the download or are available at the printed book's source code link listed in the introduction.

Challenge 1: Ice Cream

Rewrite the `IceCream` structure below to use default values and lazy initialization:

```
struct IceCream {
  let name: String
  let ingredients: [String]
}
```

1. Use default values for the properties.

2. Lazily initialize the `ingredients` array.

Challenge 2: Car and Fuel Tank

At the beginning of the chapter, you saw a `Car` structure. Dive into the inner workings of the car and rewrite the `FuelTank` structure below with property observer functionality:

```
struct FuelTank {
  var level: Double // decimal percentage between 0 and 1
}
```

1. Add a `lowFuel` Boolean stored property to the structure.

2. Flip the `lowFuel` Boolean when the `level` drops below 10%.

3. Ensure that when the tank fills back up, the `lowFuel` warning will turn off.

4. Set the `level` to a minimum of 0 or a maximum of 1 if it gets set above or below the expected values.

5. Add a `FuelTank` property to `Car`.

Key Points

- **Properties** are variables and constants that are part of a named type.

- **Stored properties** allocate memory to store a value.

- **Computed properties** are calculated each time your code requests them and aren't stored as a value in memory.

- The **static** modifier marks a **type property** that's universal to all instances of a particular type.

- The **lazy** modifier prevents a value of a stored property from being calculated until your code uses it for the first time. You'll want to use **lazy initialization** when a property's initial value is computationally intensive or when you won't know the initial value of a property until after you've initialized the object.

Chapter 13: Methods

By Eli Ganim

In Chapter 12, "Properties", you learned about properties, constants and variables that are part of structures. **Methods**, as you've already seen, are functions that reside inside a structure.

In this chapter, you'll take a closer look at methods and initializers. As with properties, you'll begin to design more complex structures. The things you learn in this chapter will apply to methods across all named types, including classes and enumerations, which you'll see in later chapters.

Method Refresher

Remember `Array.removeLast()`? It pops the last item off an instance of an array:

```
var numbers = [1, 2, 3]
numbers.removeLast()
numbers // [1, 2]
```

Methods like `removeLast()` help you control the data in the structure.

Comparing Methods to Computed Properties

With computed properties, you saw in Chapter 12, "Properties", that you could run code from inside a structure. That sounds a lot like a method. What's the difference? It comes down to style, but there are a few helpful thoughts to help you decide. Properties hold values that you can get and set while methods perform work. Sometimes this distinction gets fuzzy when a method's sole purpose is to return a single value.

Should I implement this value getter as a method or as a computed property?

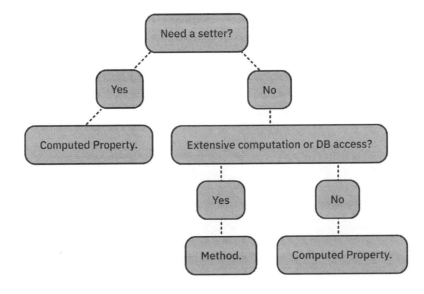

Ask yourself whether you want to be able to set a value as well as get the value. A computed property can have a setter component inside to write values. Another question to consider is whether the calculation requires extensive computation or reads from a database. Even for a simple value, a method helps you indicate to future developers that the call is expensive in time and computational resources. If the call is cheap (as in constant time O(1)), stick with a computed property.

Turning a Function Into a Method

To explore methods and initializers, you will create a simple model for dates called `SimpleDate`. Be aware that Apple's `Foundation` framework contains a robust, production-ready `Date` class that correctly handles all of the subtle intricacies of dealing with dates and times. For learning purposes, though, we'll explore how you might construct `SimpleDate` to be useful in many contexts.

In the code below, how could you convert `monthsUntilWinterBreak(date:)` into a method?

```
let months = ["January", "February", "March",
              "April", "May", "June",
              "July", "August", "September",
              "October", "November", "December"]

struct SimpleDate {
   var month: String
}

func monthsUntilWinterBreak(from date: SimpleDate) -> Int {
   months.firstIndex(of: "December")! -
   months.firstIndex(of: date.month)!
}
```

Note: This example is fragile because it force unwraps an index that might not be valid. You would not want to do this in production code. Also, if you live in the southern hemisphere, you might be disappointed with the result since the winter season starts in June. Dealing with time is hard. :]

Making a method is as easy as moving the function inside the structure definition:

```
struct SimpleDate {
   var month: String

   func monthsUntilWinterBreak(from date: SimpleDate) -> Int {
```

```
    months.firstIndex(of: "December")! -
    months.firstIndex(of: date.month)!
  }
}
```

There's no identifying keyword for a method; it is just a function inside a named type. You call methods on an instance using dot syntax just as you do for properties:

```
let date = SimpleDate(month: "October")
date.monthsUntilWinterBreak(from: date) // 2
```

And just like properties, as soon as you start typing a method name, Xcode will provide suggestions. You can select one with the Up and Down arrow keys on your keyboard, and you can autocomplete the call by pressing Tab:

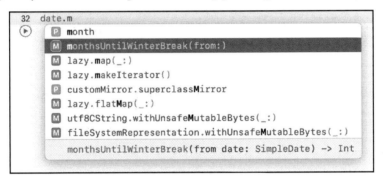

If you think about this code for a minute, you'll realize that the method's definition is awkward. There must be an alternative for accessing content stored by the instance instead of passing the instance itself as a parameter to the method. It would be so much nicer to call this:

```
date.monthsUntilWinterBreak() // Error!
```

Introducing self

You already saw Self (spelled with an uppercase S) in Chapter 12, "Properties", as a way to access static properties from inside a struct. Now we look at lowercase self. A structure definition (uppercase first letter) is like a blueprint, whereas an instance (lowercase first letter) is a real object. To access the value of an *instance*, you use the keyword **self** inside the structure. The Swift compiler passes it into your method as a secret parameter.

The method definition transforms into this:

```
// 1
func monthsUntilWinterBreak() -> Int {
  // 2
  months.firstIndex(of: "December")! -
    months.firstIndex(of: self.month)!
}
```

Here's what changed:

1. Now, there's no parameter in the method definition.

2. In the implementation, self replaces the old parameter name.

You can now call the method without passing a parameter:

```
date.monthsUntilWinterBreak() // 2
```

That's looking a lot cleaner! One more thing you can do to simplify the code is to remove self.....and you're saying to yourself, "But you just told me to add it!"

While you can always use self to access the properties and methods of the current instance, most of the time, you don't need to. In monthsUntilWinterBreak(), you can say month instead of self.month:

```
months.firstIndex(of: "December")! -
  months.firstIndex(of: month)!
```

Most programmers use self only when required, such as disambiguating between an input parameter and a property with the same name. You'll get more practice using self a little later.

Mini-Exercise

Since monthsUntilWinterBreak() returns a single value and there's not much calculation involved, transform the method into a computed property with a getter component.

Introducing Initializers

You learned about initializers in Chapter 11, "Structures", and Chapter 12, "Properties", but let's look at them again with your newfound knowledge of methods.

Initializers are special methods you call to create a new instance. They omit the `func` keyword and even a name; instead, they use `init`. An initializer can have parameters, but it doesn't have to.

Right now, when you create a new instance of the `SimpleDate` structure, you have to specify a value for the `month` property:

```
let date = SimpleDate(month: "October")
```

It is often convenient to have a no-parameter initializer. An empty initializer would create a new `SimpleDate` instance with a reasonable default value:

```
let date = SimpleDate() // Error!
```

While the compiler gives you an error now, you can fix it by making a no-parameter initializer like this:

```
struct SimpleDate {
  var month: String

  init() {
    month = "January"
  }

  func monthsUntilWinterBreak() -> Int {
    months.firstIndex(of: "December")! -
      months.firstIndex(of: month)!
  }
}
```

Here's what's happening in that code:

1. The `init()` definition requires neither the `func` keyword nor a name. You use the name of the type to call an initializer.

2. Like a function, an initializer must have a parameter list, even if it is empty.

3. In the initializer, you assign values for all the stored properties of a structure.

4. An initializer never returns a value. Its task is solely to initialize a new instance.

When you write your own custom initializer, the automatic **memberwise initializer** is no longer generated. So this code doesn't work right now:

```
let date = SimpleDate(month: "October") // Error!
```

For now, comment out that code. Click somewhere in that line and press **Command**-/ to comment it out. You'll add the memberwise initializer back in soon.

For now, use your new simple, empty initializer to create an instance:

```
let date = SimpleDate()
date.month // January
date.monthsUntilWinterBreak() // 11
```

You can test a change to the value in the initializer:

```
init() {
   month = "March"
}
```

The value of monthsUntilWinterBreak() will change accordingly:

```
let date = SimpleDate()
date.month // March
date.monthsUntilWinterBreak() // 9
```

As you think about the implementation, a good user experience optimization would have the initializer use a default value based on today's date.

In the future, you'll be capable of retrieving the current date. Eventually, you'll use the Date class from the Foundation framework to work with dates.

Before you get carried away with all the power that these frameworks provide, let's continue implementing your own SimpleDate type from the ground up.

Initializers in Structures

Add a day property to SimpleDate:

```
struct SimpleDate {
   var month: String
   var day: Int

   init() {
     month = "January"
     day = 1
   }
}
```

```
    func monthsUntilWinterBreak() -> Int {
      months.firstIndex(of: "December")! -
      months.firstIndex(of: month)!
    }
  }
```

Since initializers ensure all properties are set before the instance is ready to use, you must set day inside init(). The compiler would complain if you tried to create an initializer without setting the day property.

Again, recall that the auto-generated memberwise initializer takes all stored properties as parameters. For the SimpleDate structure, that is init(month: String, day: Int). However, when you add a custom initializer, the compiler scraps it.

So this code won't work right now:

```
let valentinesDay = SimpleDate(month: "February",
                               day: 14) // Error!
```

To make it work again, you'll have to define your own like so:

```
init(month: String, day: Int) {
  self.month = month
  self.day = day
}
```

In this code, you assign the incoming parameters to the properties of the structure. Notice how self tells the compiler that you're referring to the property rather than the local parameter.

self wasn't necessary in the simple initializer:

```
init() {
  month = "January"
  day = 1
}
```

There aren't any parameters with the same name as the properties in this code. Therefore, self isn't necessary for the compiler to understand you're referring to properties.

You can now use the initializer the same way you used to use the automatically generated one:

```
let valentinesDay = SimpleDate(month: "February", day: 14)
```

```
valentinesDay.month // February
valentinesDay.day // 14
```

Default Values and Initializers

There is a more straightforward way to make a no-argument initializer.

When you set default values for parameters, the automatic memberwise initializer will use them.

In your structure, remove both initializers and then add default values for month and day:

```
struct SimpleDate {
  // 1
  var month = "January"
  var day = 1

  //2

  func monthsUntilWinterBreak() -> Int {
    months.firstIndex(of: "December")! -
    months.firstIndex(of: month)!
  }
}
```

Here's what's happening in this code:

1. You assign a reasonable default to each declared property: January 1st.

2. Both initializers, init() and init(month:day:) have been removed. ...Look ma', no initializers!

Even though both custom initializers are gone, you can still use both initializer styles:

```
let newYearsDay = SimpleDate()
newYearsDay.month // January
newYearsDay.day // 1

let valentinesDay = SimpleDate(month: "February", day: 14)
valentinesDay.month // February
valentinesDay.day // 14
```

Once again, the automatic memberwise initializer is available since you didn't declare any custom ones. The compiler provides init(month:day:) for you since those parameters are the properties.

However, it is also smart enough to realize that the properties have default values when declared and therefore do not need to be passed into the initializer. So that is how you get init() as well. What's cool is that you can also mix and match, passing only the properties that you care to set:

```
let octoberFirst = SimpleDate(month: "October")
octoberFirst.month // October
octoberFirst.day // 1

let januaryTwentySecond = SimpleDate(day: 22)
januaryTwentySecond.month // January
januaryTwentySecond.day // 22
```

In that code, you only passed the month into the first instance and only the day into the second instance. Pretty slick, eh!

Introducing Mutating Methods

Methods in structures cannot change the values of the instance without being marked as mutating. You can imagine a method in the SimpleDate structure that advances to the next day:

```
mutating func advance() {
    day += 1
}
```

> **Note**: The implementation above is a naive way of writing advance() because it doesn't account for what happens at the end of a month. In a challenge at the end of this chapter, you'll create a more robust version.

The mutating keyword marks any method that may change one or more of the structure's values. By marking a method as mutating, you're telling the Swift compiler this method must not be called on constant instances declared with let. If you call a mutating method on a constant instance of a structure, the compiler will flag it as an error.

Swift secretly passes in self to mutating methods, just like non-mutating methods. But for mutating methods, the secret self gets marked as an inout parameter. Whatever happens inside the mutating method will impact everything that relies on the type externally.

Type Methods

Like type properties, you can use **type methods** to access data across all instances. You call type methods on the type itself instead of on an instance. To define a type method, you prefix it with the `static` modifier.

Type methods are useful for things that are *about* a type in general rather than something about specific instances.

For example, you could use type methods to group similar methods into a structure:

```
struct Math {
  // 1
  static func factorial(of number: Int) -> Int {
    // 2
    (1...number).reduce(1, *)
  }
}
// 3
Math.factorial(of: 6) // 720
```

You might have custom calculations for things such as factorial. Instead of having many free-standing functions, you can group related functions as type methods in a structure. The structure is said to act as a **namespace**.

Here's what's happening:

1. You use `static` to declare the type method, which accepts an integer and returns an integer.

2. The implementation uses a higher-order function called `reduce(_:_:)`. It effectively follows the formula for calculating a factorial: "The product of all the whole numbers from 1 to n". You could write this using a `for` loop, but the higher-order function expresses your intent in a cleaner way.

3. You call the type method on `Math` rather than on an instance of the type.

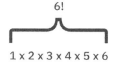

Type methods gathered into a structure will code complete in Xcode. In this example, you can see all the math utility methods available by typing `Math.`.

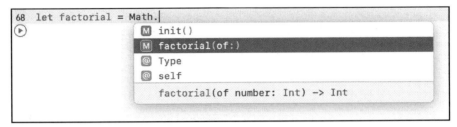

Mini-Exercise

Add a type method to the `Math` structure that calculates the *n*-th triangle number. It will be very similar to the factorial formula, except instead of multiplying the numbers, you add them.

Adding to an Existing Structure With Extensions

Sometimes you want to add functionality to a structure but don't want to muddy up the original definition. And sometimes, you can't add the functionality because you don't have access to the source code.

It is possible to *open* an existing structure (even one you do not have the source code for) and add methods, initializers and computed properties to it. This feature is useful for code organization. Doing so is as easy as typing the keyword `extension`.

At the bottom of your playground, outside the definition of `Math`, add this type method named `primeFactors(of:)` using an extension:

```
extension Math {
  static func primeFactors(of value: Int) -> [Int] {
    // 1
    var remainingValue = value
    // 2
    var testFactor = 2
    var primes: [Int] = []
    // 3
    while testFactor * testFactor <= remainingValue {
      if remainingValue % testFactor == 0 {
        primes.append(testFactor)
        remainingValue /= testFactor
```

```
      }
      else {
        testFactor += 1
      }
    }
    if remainingValue > 1 {
      primes.append(remainingValue)
    }
    return primes
  }
}
```

This method finds the prime factors for a given number. For example, 81 returns `[3, 3, 3, 3]`. Here's what's happening in the code:

1. The `value` passed in as a parameter is assigned to the mutable variable, `remainingValue`, so that it can be changed as the calculation runs.

2. The `testFactor` starts as two and will be divided into `remainingValue`.

3. The logic runs a loop until the `remainingValue` is exhausted. If it evenly divides, meaning there's no remainder, that value of the `testFactor` is set aside as a prime factor. If it doesn't evenly divide, `testFactor` is incremented for the next loop.

This algorithm is a brute force one but does contain one optimization: the square of the `testFactor` should never be larger than the `remainingValue`. If it is, the `remainingValue` itself must be prime and added to the `primes` list.

You've now added a method to `Math` without changing its original definition. Verify that the extension works with this code:

```
Math.primeFactors(of: 81) // [3, 3, 3, 3]
```

Pretty slick! You're about to see how that can be powerful in practice.

> **Note**: In an extension, you cannot add stored properties to an existing structure because that would change the size and memory layout of the structure and break existing code.

Keeping the Compiler-generated Initializer Using Extensions

With the `SimpleDate` structure, you saw that once you added your own `init()`, the compiler-generated one disappeared. You can keep both if you add your `init()` to an extension to `SimpleDate`. The code looks like this:

```
struct SimpleDate {
  var month = "January"
  var day = 1

  func monthsUntilWinterBreak() -> Int {
    months.firstIndex(of: "December")! -
    months.firstIndex(of: month)!
  }

  mutating func advance() {
    day += 1
  }
}

extension SimpleDate {
  init(month: Int, day: Int) {
    self.month = months[month-1]
    self.day = day
  }
}
```

`init(month:day:)` gets added to `SimpleDate` without sacrificing the automatically generated memberwise initializer. You can create an instance using the month index `Int` instead of the month name `String`:

```
let halloween = SimpleDate(month: 10, day: 31)
halloween.month // October
halloween.day // 31
```

Hooray!

Challenges

Before moving on, here are some challenges to test your knowledge of methods. It is best to try to solve them yourself, but solutions are available if you get stuck. These came with the download or are available at the printed book's source code link listed in the introduction.

Challenge 1: Grow a Circle

Given the `Circle` structure below:

```
struct Circle {

   var radius = 0.0

   var area: Double {
      .pi * radius * radius
   }

}
```

Write a method that can change an instance's area by a growth factor. For example, if you call `circle.grow(byFactor: 3)`, the area of the instance will triple.

Hint: Add a setter to `area`.

Challenge 2: A More Advanced advance()

Here is a naïve way of writing `advance()` for the `SimpleDate` structure you saw earlier in the chapter:

```
let months = ["January", "February", "March",
              "April", "May", "June",
              "July", "August", "September",
              "October", "November", "December"]

struct SimpleDate {
  var month: String
  var day: Int

  mutating func advance() {
     day += 1
  }
}

var date = SimpleDate(month: "December", day: 31)
date.advance()
date.month // December; should be January!
date.day // 32; should be 1!
```

What happens when the function should go from the end of one month to the start of the next? Rewrite `advance()` to account for advancing from December 31st to January 1st.

Challenge 3: Odd and Even Math

Add type methods named `isEven` and `isOdd` to your `Math` namespace that return `true` if a number is even or odd, respectively.

Challenge 4: Odd and Even Int

It turns out that `Int` is simply a struct. Add the computed properties `isEven` and `isOdd` to `Int` using an extension.

> **Note**: Generally, you want to be careful about what functionality you add to standard library types as it can confuse readers.

Challenge 5: Prime Factors

Add the method `primeFactors()` to `Int`. Since this is an expensive operation, this is best left as an actual method and not a computed property.

Key Points

- **Methods** are functions associated with a type.
- Methods are the behaviors that define the functionality of a type.
- A method can access the data of an instance by using the keyword `self`.
- **Initializers** create new instances of a type. They look like functions called `init` without the `func` keyword and no return value.
- A **type method** adds behavior to a type instead of the instances of that type. To define a type method, you prefix it with the `static` modifier.
- You can open an existing structure and add methods, initializers and computed properties to it by using an `extension`.
- Adding custom initializers as extensions allows you to keep the compiler-generated memberwise initializer.
- Methods can exist in all the named types — structures, classes and enumerations.

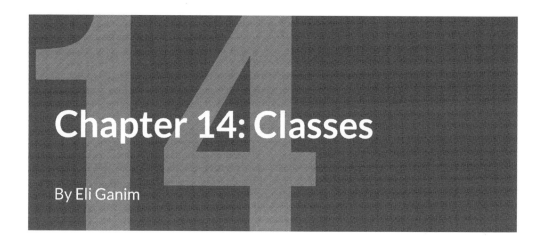

Chapter 14: Classes

By Eli Ganim

Structures introduced you to named types. In this chapter, you'll get acquainted with **classes**, which are much like structures — they are named types with properties and methods.

You'll learn classes are *reference* types, as opposed to *value* types, and have substantially different capabilities and benefits than their structure counterparts. While you'll often use structures in your apps to represent values, you'll generally use classes to represent *objects*.

What does *values* vs. *objects* mean, though?

Creating Classes

Consider the following class definition in Swift:

```swift
class Person {
  var firstName: String
  var lastName: String

  init(firstName: String, lastName: String) {
    self.firstName = firstName
    self.lastName = lastName
  }

  var fullName: String {
    "\(firstName) \(lastName)"
  }
}

let john = Person(firstName: "Johnny", lastName: "Appleseed")
```

That's simple enough! It may surprise you that the definition is almost identical to its struct counterpart. The keyword `class` is followed by the name of the class, and everything in the curly braces is a member of that class.

But you can also see some differences between a class and a struct: The class above defines an initializer that sets both `firstName` and `lastName` to initial values. Unlike a struct, a class doesn't provide a memberwise initializer automatically — which means you must provide it yourself if you need it. If you forget to provide an initializer, the Swift compiler will flag that as an error:

```swift
class Person {                    ⊙ Class 'Person' has no initializers
  var firstName: String
  var lastName: String

  var fullName: String {
    "\(firstName) \(lastName)"
  }
}
```

Default initialization aside, the initialization rules for classes and structs are very similar. Class initializers are functions marked `init`, and all stored properties must be assigned initial values before the end of `init`.

There is *much* more to class initialization, but you'll have to wait until Chapter 15, "Advanced Classes", which will introduce the concept of **inheritance** and its effect on initialization rules. This chapter will stick with basic class initializers so that you can get comfortable with classes in Swift.

Reference Types

In Swift, an instance of a structure is an immutable value, whereas an instance of a class is a mutable object. Classes are reference types, so a variable of a class type doesn't store an actual instance — it stores a **reference** to a location in memory that stores the instance.

If you created a SimplePerson class instance with only a name like this:

```swift
class SimplePerson {
    let name: String
    init(name: String) {
        self.name = name
    }
}

var var1 = SimplePerson(name: "John")
```

It would look something like this in memory:

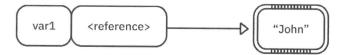

If you were to create a new variable var2 and assign to it the value of var1:

```swift
var var2 = var1
```

Then the references inside both var1 and var2 would reference the same place in memory:

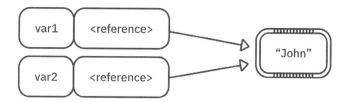

Conversely, a structure as a value type stores the actual value, providing direct access to it. Replace the SimplePerson class implementation with a struct like this:

```swift
struct SimplePerson {
    let name: String
}
```

The variable would not reference an external, shared place in memory but instead belong to var1 exclusively:

The assignment var var2 = var1 would **copy** the *value* of var1 in this case:

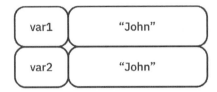

Value types and reference types each have their own distinct advantages — and disadvantages. Later in the chapter, you'll consider which type to use in a given situation. You'll now examine how classes and structs work under the hood.

The Heap vs. the Stack

When you create a reference type using a class, the system often stores the actual instance in a region of memory known as the **heap** that has a dynamic lifetime. Instances of value types typically reside in a region of memory called the **stack** that lives only as long as the current scope.

Both the heap and the stack have essential roles in the execution of any program. A general understanding of what they are and how they work will help you visualize the functional differences between a class and a structure:

- The system uses the **stack** to store anything on the immediate thread of execution; it's tightly managed and optimized by the CPU. A function allocates stack variables on entry and deallocates them on exit. Since the stack is so strictly organized, it's very efficient.

- The system uses the **heap** to store instances of reference types. The heap is generally a large pool of memory from which the system can request and dynamically allocate memory blocks. Heap variables' lifetimes are flexible and dynamic.

The heap doesn't automatically deallocate as the stack does; additional work is required. This extra work makes creating and removing data on the heap more involved.

You may have already figured out how this relates to structs and classes. Take a look at the diagram below:

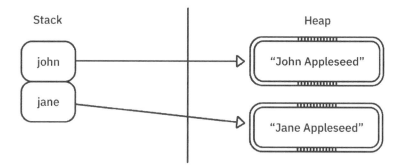

- When you create an instance of a class, your code requests a block of memory on the heap to store the instance itself; that's the first name and last name inside the instance on the right side of the diagram. It stores the *address* of that memory in your named variable on the stack; that's the *reference* stored on the left side of the diagram.

- When you create an instance of a struct (that is not part of an instance of a class), the instance itself is stored on the stack, and the heap is never involved.

This essential mental model of heaps and stacks is enough to understand the reference semantics of classes. You'll now get some additional experience working with them.

Working with References

In Chapter 11, "Structures", you saw the copy semantics involved when working with structures and other value types. Here's a little reminder, using the Location and DeliveryArea structures from that chapter:

```
struct Location {
    let x: Int
    let y: Int
}

struct DeliveryArea {
    var range: Double
    let center: Location
}

var area1 = DeliveryArea(range: 2.5,
                         center: Location(x: 2, y: 4))
```

```
var area2 = area1
print(area1.range) // 2.5
print(area2.range) // 2.5

area1.range = 4
print(area1.range) // 4.0
print(area2.range) // 2.5
```

When you assign the value of area1 into area2, area2 receives a *copy* of the area1 value. That way, when area1.range receives a new value of 4, the number is only reflected in area1 while area2 still has the original value of 2.5.

Since a class is a reference type, when you assign a class type variable, the system does *not* copy the instance; it only copies a reference.

Compare the previous code with the following code:

```
var homeOwner = john     // "Johnny Appleseed"
john.firstName = "John"  // John wants to use his short name!
john.firstName           // "John"
homeOwner.firstName      // "John"
```

As you can see, john and homeOwner truly have the same value!

This implied sharing among class instances results in a new way of thinking when passing things around. For instance, anything that references john will automatically see the update if the john object changes. If you were using a structure, you would have to update each copy individually, or it would still have the old value of "Johnny".

Mini-Exercise

Change the value of lastName on homeOwner, then try reading fullName on both john and homeOwner. What do you observe?

Object Identity

In the previous code sample, it's easy to see that john and homeOwner are pointing to the same object. The code is short, and both references are named variables. What if you want to see if the value behind a variable *is* John?

You might think to check the value of `firstName`, but how would you know it's the John you're looking for and not an imposter? Or worse, what if John changed his name again?

In Swift, the === operator lets you check if the *identity* of one object is equal to the identity of another:

```
john === homeOwner // true
```

Just as the == operator checks if two *values* are equal, the === identity operator compares the memory address of two *references*. It tells you whether the references are the same; that is, they point to the same block of data on the heap.

That means this === operator can tell the difference between the John you're looking for and an imposter-John:

```
let imposterJohn = Person(firstName: "Johnny",
                          lastName: "Appleseed")

john === homeOwner         // true
john === imposterJohn      // false
imposterJohn === homeOwner // false

// Assignment of existing variables changes the instances the
variables reference.
homeOwner = imposterJohn
john === homeOwner // false

homeOwner = john
john === homeOwner // true
```

This form of reference equality can be handy when you cannot rely on regular equality (==) to compare and identify objects you care about:

```
// Create fake, imposter Johns. Use === to see if any of these
imposters are our real John.
var imposters = (0...100).map { _ in
  Person(firstName: "John", lastName: "Appleseed")
}

// Equality (==) is not effective when John cannot be identified
by his name alone
imposters.contains {
  $0.firstName == john.firstName && $0.lastName == john.lastName
} // true
```

By using the identity operator, you can verify that the *references* themselves are equal and separate our real John from the crowd:

```
// Check to ensure the real John is not found among the
imposters.
imposters.contains {
  $0 === john
} // false

// Now hide the "real" John somewhere among the imposters.
imposters.insert(john, at: Int.random(in: 0..<100))

// John can now be found among the imposters.
imposters.contains {
  $0 === john
} // true

// Since `Person` is a reference type, you can use === to grab
the real John out of the list of imposters and modify the value.
// The original `john` variable will print the new last name!
if let indexOfJohn = imposters.firstIndex(where:
                                       { $0 === john }) {
  imposters[indexOfJohn].lastName = "Bananapeel"
}

john.fullName // John Bananapeel
```

Because Swift emphasizes value types, you'll find the reference identity operator === isn't used that often. What's important is to understand what it does and what it demonstrates about the properties of reference types.

Mini-Exercise

Write a function memberOf(person: Person, group: [Person]) -> Bool that will return true if person can be found inside group and false if it can not.

Test it by creating two arrays of five Person objects for group and using john as the person. Put john in one of the arrays but not in the other.

Methods and Mutability

As you've read before, instances of classes are mutable objects, whereas instances of structures are immutable values. The following example illustrates this difference:

```
struct Grade {
  let letter: String
  let points: Double
  let credits: Double
}

class Student {
  var firstName: String
  var lastName: String
  var grades: [Grade] = []

  init(firstName: String, lastName: String) {
    self.firstName = firstName
    self.lastName = lastName
  }

  func recordGrade(_ grade: Grade) {
    grades.append(grade)
  }
}

let jane = Student(firstName: "Jane", lastName: "Appleseed")
var history = Grade(letter: "B", points: 9.0, credits: 3.0)
var math = Grade(letter: "A", points: 16.0, credits: 4.0)

jane.recordGrade(history)
jane.recordGrade(math)
```

Note that recordGrade(_:) can mutate the array grades by adding more values to the end. The keyword mutating is not required because it mutates the underlying object, not the reference itself.

If you had tried this with a struct, you'd get a compiler error because structure methods are, by default, immutable and can't change any of their properties. The keyword mutating marks structure methods that can change stored properties. This keyword is not used with classes because a class is just a reference to some storage that another client could share and mutate. It would give you a false sense of security about a guarantee that doesn't exist for methods not marked mutating.

Mutability and Constants

The previous example may have had you wondering how you could modify jane even though it was a constant. After all, when you define a constant, it doesn't change. If you recall the discussion of value types vs. reference types, it's important to remember that, with reference types, the value is a *reference*.

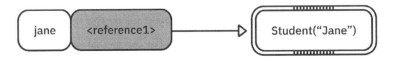

The value of "reference1" in red is the value stored in jane. This value is a reference, and because jane is declared a constant, this reference is constant. If you were to attempt to assign another student to jane, you would get a compiler error.

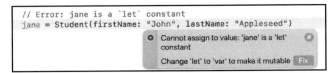

If you declared jane as a variable instead, you would be able to assign to it another instance of Student on the heap:

```
var jane = Student(firstName: "Jane", lastName: "Appleseed")
jane = Student(firstName: "John", lastName: "Appleseed")
```

After assigning another Student to jane, the reference value behind jane would be updated to point to the new Student object.

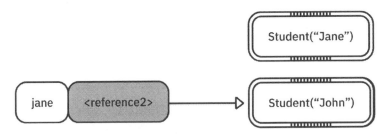

Since nothing would be referencing the original "Jane" object, its memory would be freed to use elsewhere.

Any individual member of a class can be protected from modification through the use of constants. Still, because reference types are not treated as values, they are not protected as a whole from mutation.

Mini-Exercise

Add a computed property to `Student` that returns the student's Grade Point Average or GPA. A GPA is defined as the number of points earned divided by the number of credits taken. For the example above, Jane earned (9 + 16 = **25**) points while taking (3 + 4 = **7**) credits, making her GPA (25 / 7 = **3.57**).

> **Note**: Points in most American universities range from 4 per credit for an A, down to 1 point for a D (with an F being 0 points). For this exercise, you may, of course, use any scale that you want!

Understanding State and Side Effects

Since the very nature of classes is that they are both referenced and mutable, programmers have many possibilities and many concerns. Remember: If you update a class instance with a new value, every reference to that instance will also see the new value.

You can use this to your advantage. Perhaps you pass a `Student` instance to a sports team, a report card and a class roster. Imagine all of these entities need to know the student's grades, and because they all point to the same instance, they'll all see new grades as the instance records them.

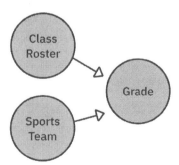

The result of this sharing is that class instances have **state**. State changes can sometimes be obvious, but often they're not.

To illustrate this, add a `credits` property to the `Student` class.

```
var credits = 0.0
```

and update `recordGrade(_:)` to use this new property:

```
func recordGrade(_ grade: Grade) {
  grades.append(grade)
  credits += grade.credits
}
```

In this slightly modified example of `Student`, `recordGrade(_:)` now adds the number of credits to the `credits` property. Calling `recordGrade(_:)` has the side effect of updating `credits`.

Now, observe how side effects can result in non-obvious behavior:

```
jane.credits // 7

// The teacher made a mistake; math has 5 credits
math = Grade(letter: "A", points: 20.0, credits: 5.0)
jane.recordGrade(math)

jane.credits // 12, not 8!
```

Whoever wrote the modified `Student` class did so somewhat naïvely by assuming that the same grade won't get recorded twice!

Because class instances are mutable, you need to be careful about unexpected behavior around shared references.

While confusing in a small example, mutability and state could be highly jarring as classes grow in size and complexity.

Situations like this would be much more common as the `Student` class grows to include additional properties and methods.

Extending a Class Using an Extension

As you saw with structs, classes can be *re-opened* using the `extension` keyword to add methods and computed properties. Add a `fullName` computed property to `Student`:

```
extension Student {
  var fullName: String {
```

```
        "\(firstName) \(lastName)"
    }
}
```

Functionality can also be added to classes using *inheritance*. You can even add new stored properties to inheriting classes. In Chapter 15, "Advanced Classes", you'll explore this technique in detail.

When to Use a Class Versus a Struct

You may wonder when to use a class vs. a struct. Here are some general guidelines.

Values vs. Objects

While there are no hard-and-fast rules, you should consider value versus reference semantics and use structures as *values* and classes as *objects with identity*.

An **object** is an instance of a reference type, and such instances have **identity**, meaning that every object is unique. Two objects may not be equal simply because they hold the same state. Hence, you use === to see if objects refer to the same place in memory. In contrast, instances of value types, which *are* values, are considered equal if they are the same value.

For example: A delivery range is a value, so you implement it as a struct. A student is an object, so you implement it as a class. In non-technical terms, no two students are equal, even if they have the same name!

Speed

Speed considerations are a thing, as structs rely on the faster stack while classes rely on the slower heap. If you'll have many more instances (hundreds and greater), or if these instances will only exist in memory for a short time — lean towards using a struct. If your instance will have a longer lifecycle in memory, or if you'll create relatively few instances, then class instances on the heap shouldn't create too much overhead.

For example, you'd use a struct to calculate the total distance of a running route using many GPS-based waypoints, such as the Location struct you used in Chapter 11, "Structures". You'll create many waypoints, but they'll be quickly created and destroyed as you modify the route.

You could also use a class for an object to store route history, as there would be only one object for each user, and you'd likely use the same history object for the user's lifetime.

Minimalist Approach

Another approach is to use only what you need. Use structures if your data will never change or you need a simple data store. If you need to update your data and it contains logic to update its state, then use a class. Often, it's best to begin with a struct. If you need the behavior of a class sometime later, you can convert the struct to a class.

Structures vs. Classes Recap

Structures

- Useful for representing values.

- Implicit copying of values.

- Becomes completely immutable when declared with `let`.

- Fast memory allocation (stack).

Classes

- Useful for representing objects with an identity.

- Implicit sharing of objects.

- Internals can remain mutable even when declared with `let`.

- Slower memory allocation (heap).

Challenges

Before moving on, here are some challenges to test your knowledge of classes. It's best to try and solve them yourself, but solutions are available if you get stuck. These came with the download or are available at the printed book's source code link listed in the introduction.

Challenge 1: Movie Lists

Imagine you're writing a movie-viewing app in Swift. Users can create lists of movies and share those lists with other users. Create a User and a List class that uses reference semantics to help maintain lists between users.

- User: Has a method addList(_:) that adds the given list to a dictionary of List objects (using the name as a key), and list(forName:) -> List? that returns the List for the provided name.

- List: Contains a name and an array of movie titles. A report method will print all the movies in the list.

- Create jane and john users and create a list that they share. Have both jane and john modify the list and call report from both users. Are all the changes reflected?

- What happens when you implement the same with structs? What problems do you run into?

Challenge 2: T-shirt Store

Your challenge here is to build a set of entities to support a T-shirt store. Decide if each entity should be a class or a struct and why.

- TShirt: Represents a shirt style you can buy. Each TShirt has a size, color, price, and an optional image on the front.

- User: A registered user of the t-shirt store app. A user has a name, email, and a ShoppingCart (see below).

- Address: This represents a shipping address and contains the name, street, city, and zip code.

- ShoppingCart: Holds a current order, composed of an array of TShirt that the User wants to buy, as well as a method to calculate the total cost. Additionally, an Address represents where the order will be shipped.

> **Bonus:** After you've decided on whether to use a class or struct for each entity, go ahead and implement them all!

Key Points

- Like structures, **classes** are a named type that can have properties and methods.

- Classes use **references** that are shared on assignment.

- Class instances are called **objects**.

- Objects are **mutable**.

- Mutability introduces **state**, which adds complexity when managing your objects.

- Use classes when you want **reference semantics**; structures for **value semantics**.

Chapter 15: Advanced Classes

By Eli Ganim

Chapter 14, "Classes", introduced you to the basics of defining and using classes in Swift. Classes are reference types and can be used to support traditional object-oriented programming.

Classes introduce inheritance, overriding, and polymorphism, making them suited for this purpose. These extra features require special consideration for initialization, class hierarchies, and understanding the class lifecycle in memory.

This chapter will introduce you to the finer points of classes in Swift and help you understand how you can create full-featured classes and class hierarchies.

Introducing Inheritance

In Chapter 14, "Classes", you saw a `Grade` struct and a pair of class examples: `Person` and `Student`.

```swift
struct Grade {
  var letter: Character
  var points: Double
  var credits: Double
}

class Person {
  var firstName: String
  var lastName: String

  init(firstName: String, lastName: String) {
    self.firstName = firstName
    self.lastName = lastName
  }
}

class Student {
  var firstName: String
  var lastName: String
  var grades: [Grade] = []

  init(firstName: String, lastName: String) {
    self.firstName = firstName
    self.lastName = lastName
  }

  func recordGrade(_ grade: Grade) {
    grades.append(grade)
  }
}
```

It's not difficult to see redundancy between `Person` and `Student`. Maybe you've also noticed that a `Student` *is* a `Person`! This simple case demonstrates the idea behind class inheritance. Much like in the real world, where you can think of a student as a person, you can represent the same relationship in code by replacing the original `Student` class implementation with the following:

```swift
class Student: Person {
  var grades: [Grade] = []

  func recordGrade(_ grade: Grade) {
    grades.append(grade)
  }
}
```

In this modified example, the Student class now **inherits** from Person, indicated by a colon after the declaration of Student, followed by the class from which Student inherits, which in this case is Person. Through inheritance, Student automatically gets the properties and methods declared in the Person class. In code, it would be accurate to say that a Student *is-a* Person.

With much less duplication of code, you can now create Student objects that have all the properties and methods of a Person:

```
let john = Person(firstName: "Johnny", lastName: "Appleseed")
let jane = Student(firstName: "Jane", lastName: "Appleseed")

john.firstName // "John"
jane.firstName // "Jane"
```

Additionally, only the Student object will have all of the properties and methods defined in Student:

```
let history = Grade(letter: "B", points: 9.0, credits: 3.0)
jane.recordGrade(history)
john.recordGrade(history)   ⊗ Value of type 'Person' has no member 'r...
                             ⊗ Value of type 'Person' has no member  ⊗
                               'recordGrade'
```

A class inheriting from another class is known as a **subclass** or a **derived class**. The class it inherits is known as a **superclass** or a **base class**.

The rules for subclassing are relatively simple:

- A Swift class can inherit from only one class, a concept known as **single inheritance**.

- There's no limit to the depth of subclassing, meaning you can subclass from a class that is *also* a subclass, like below:

```
class BandMember: Student {
  var minimumPracticeTime = 2
}

class OboePlayer: BandMember {
  // This is an example of an override, which we'll cover soon.
  override var minimumPracticeTime: Int {
    get {
      super.minimumPracticeTime * 2
    }
    set {
      super.minimumPracticeTime = newValue / 2
    }
  }
}
```

A chain of subclasses is called a **class hierarchy**. In this example, the hierarchy would be OboePlayer -> BandMember -> Student -> Person. A class hierarchy is analogous to a family tree. Because of this analogy, a superclass is also called the **parent class** of its **child class**.

Polymorphism

The Student/Person relationship demonstrates a computer science concept known as **polymorphism**. In brief, polymorphism is a programming language's ability to treat an object differently based on context.

An OboePlayer is also a Person. Because it derives from Person, you could use an OboePlayer object anywhere you'd use a Person object.

This example demonstrates how you can treat an OboePlayer as a Person:

```swift
func phonebookName(_ person: Person) -> String {
  "\(person.lastName), \(person.firstName)"
}

let person = Person(firstName: "Johnny", lastName: "Appleseed")
let oboePlayer = OboePlayer(firstName: "Jane",
                           lastName: "Appleseed")

phonebookName(person)     // Appleseed, Johnny
phonebookName(oboePlayer) // Appleseed, Jane
```

Because OboePlayer derives from Person, it's a valid input into the function phonebookName(_:). More importantly, the function has no idea that the object passed in is anything *other* than a regular Person. It can only observe the elements of OboePlayer that are defined in the Person base class.

With the polymorphism characteristics provided by class inheritance, Swift treats the object referred to by oboePlayer differently based on the context. This distilled behavior can be advantageous when you have many specialized derived types but want to code that operates on a common base class.

Runtime Hierarchy Checks

Now that you are coding with polymorphism, you'll likely find situations where the specific type backing a variable can differ. For instance, you could define a variable hallMonitor as a Student:

```swift
var hallMonitor = Student(firstName: "Jill",
                         lastName: "Bananapeel")
```

But what if `hallMonitor` were a more derived type, such as an `OboePlayer`?

```
hallMonitor = oboePlayer
```

This assignment works because `hallMonitor` is a `Student`. However, the compiler won't allow you to use properties or methods for the more derived type `OboePlayer` with the `hallMonitor` instance.

Fortunately, Swift provides the as casting-operator to treat a property or a variable as another type:

- `as`: Cast to a type known at compile-time to succeed, such as casting to a supertype. It is guaranteed to succeed.

- `as?`: An optional downcast (to a subtype). If the downcast fails, the result of the expression will be `nil`.

- `as!`: A forced downcast. If the downcast fails, the program will halt execution. Use this rarely and only when you are sure the cast will always succeed.

Casts can be used in various contexts to treat the `hallMonitor` as a `BandMember` or the `oboePlayer` as a less-derived `Student`.

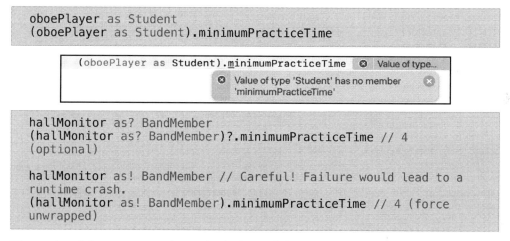

```
oboePlayer as Student
(oboePlayer as Student).minimumPracticeTime
```

```
(oboePlayer as Student).minimumPracticeTime   ⊗  Value of type...
                                        ⊗  Value of type 'Student' has no member    ⊗
                                           'minimumPracticeTime'
```

```
hallMonitor as? BandMember
(hallMonitor as? BandMember)?.minimumPracticeTime // 4
(optional)

hallMonitor as! BandMember // Careful! Failure would lead to a
runtime crash.
(hallMonitor as! BandMember).minimumPracticeTime // 4 (force
unwrapped)
```

The optional downcast as? is particularly useful in `if let` or `guard` statements:

```
if let hallMonitor = hallMonitor as? BandMember {
  print("This hall monitor is a band member and practices
        at least \(hallMonitor.minimumPracticeTime)
        hours per week.")
}
```

You may wonder under what contexts you would use the as operator by itself. Any object contains all the properties and methods of its parent class, so what use is casting it to something it already is?

Swift has a strong type system, and the interpretation of a specific type can affect **static dispatch**, aka the process of deciding which operation to use at compile-time.

Sound confusing? Let's see an example.

Assume you have two functions with identical names and parameter names for two different parameter types:

```
func afterClassActivity(for student: Student) -> String {
  "Goes home!"
}

func afterClassActivity(for student: BandMember) -> String {
  "Goes to practice!"
}
```

If you were to pass oboePlayer into afterClassActivity(for:), which one of these implementations would get called? The answer lies in Swift's dispatch rules, which will select the more specific version that takes in an OboePlayer.

If, instead, you were to cast oboePlayer to a Student, the Student version would be called:

```
afterClassActivity(for: oboePlayer)              // Goes to
practice!
afterClassActivity(for: oboePlayer as Student) // Goes home!
```

Inheritance, Methods and Overrides

Subclasses receive all properties and methods defined in their superclass, plus any additional properties and methods the subclass defines for itself. In that sense, subclasses are additive.

For example, you saw that the Student class can add additional properties and methods to handle a student's grades. These properties and methods are available to any Person class instances but fully available to Student subclasses.

Besides creating their own methods, subclasses can *override* methods defined in their superclass. For another example, assume that student-athletes become ineligible for the athletics program if they fail three or more classes. That means you need to keep track of failing grades somehow, like so:

```
class StudentAthlete: Student {
  var failedClasses: [Grade] = []

  override func recordGrade(_ grade: Grade) {
    super.recordGrade(grade)

    if grade.letter == "F" {
      failedClasses.append(grade)
    }
  }

  var isEligible: Bool {
    failedClasses.count < 3
  }
}
```

In this example, the StudentAthlete class overrides recordGrade(_:) to keep track of any courses the student has failed. StudentAthlete has isEligible, its own computed property that uses this information to determine the athlete's eligibility.

When overriding a method, use the override keyword before the method declaration.

If your subclass were to have an identical method declaration as its superclass, but you omitted the override keyword, Swift would emit a compiler error:

```
class StudentAthlete: Student {
  var failedClasses: [Grade] = []

  func recordGrade(_ grade: Grade) {    ⊙ Overriding declaration requires an 'override' keyword
    super.recordGrade(grade)

    if grade.letter == "F" {
      failedClasses.append(grade)
    }
  }

  var isEligible: Bool {
    failedClasses.count < 3
  }
}
```

This requirement makes it very clear whether a method is an override of an existing one or not.

Introducing Super

You may have also noticed the line `super.recordGrade(grade)` in the overridden method. The `super` keyword is similar to `self`, except it will invoke the method in the nearest implementing superclass. In the example of `recordGrade(_:)` in `StudentAthlete`, calling `super.recordGrade(grade)` will execute the method defined in the `Student` class.

Remember how inheritance lets you define `Person` with first name and last name properties and avoid repeating those properties in subclasses? Similarly, calling the superclass methods means you can write the code to record the grade once in `Student` and then call "up" to it as needed in subclasses.

Although it isn't always required, it's often important to call `super` when overriding a method in Swift. The `super` call will record the grade in the `grades` array because that behavior isn't duplicated in `StudentAthlete`. Calling `super` is also a way of avoiding the need for duplicate code in `StudentAthlete` and `Student`.

When to Call Super

As you may notice, exactly *when* you call super can significantly affect your overridden method.

Suppose you replace the overridden `recordGrade(_:)` method in the `StudentAthlete` class with the following version that recalculates the `failedClasses` each time a grade is recorded:

```
override func recordGrade(_ grade: Grade) {
  var newFailedClasses: [Grade] = []
  for grade in grades {
    if grade.letter == "F" {
      newFailedClasses.append(grade)
    }
  }
  failedClasses = newFailedClasses

  super.recordGrade(grade)
}
```

This version of recordGrade(_:) uses the grades array to find the current list of failed classes. If you've spotted a bug in the code above, good job! Since you call super last, if the new grade.letter is an F, the code won't update failedClasses properly.

It's best practice to call the super version of a method first when overriding. That way, the superclass won't experience any side effects introduced by its subclass, and the subclass won't need to know the superclass's implementation details.

Preventing Inheritance

Sometimes you'll want to disallow subclasses of a particular class. Swift provides the final keyword for you to guarantee a class will never get a subclass:

```
final class FinalStudent: Person {}
class FinalStudentAthlete: FinalStudent {}
            ⊗  Inheritance from a final class 'FinalStudent'    ⊗
```

By marking the FinalStudent class final, you tell the compiler to prevent any classes from inheriting from FinalStudent. This requirement can remind you — or others on your team! — that a class wasn't designed to have subclasses.

Additionally, you can mark individual *methods* as final if you want to allow a class to have subclasses but protect individual methods from being overridden:

```
class AnotherStudent: Person {
    final func recordGrade(_ grade: Grade) {}
}
```

```
class AnotherStudentAthlete: AnotherStudent {
    override func recordGrade(_ grade: Grade) {}  ⊗  Instance...
}
            ⊗  Instance method overrides a 'final' instance
               method
```

There are benefits to initially marking any new class you write as final. This keyword tells the compiler it doesn't need to look for any more subclasses, which can shorten compile time, and it also requires you to be very explicit when deciding to subclass a class previously marked final.

Inheritance and Class Initialization

Chapter 14, "Classes", briefly introduced you to class initializers, which are similar to their struct counterparts. With subclasses, there are a few more considerations about setting up instances.

> **Note**: In the chapter's playground, I have renamed `Student` and `StudentAthlete` to `NewStudent` and `NewStudentAthlete` to keep both versions working side-by-side.

Modify the `StudentAthlete` class to add a list of sports an athlete plays:

```
class StudentAthlete: Student {
  var sports: [String]
  // original code
}
```

Because `sports` doesn't have an initial value, `StudentAthlete` must provide one in its initializer:

```
class StudentAthlete: Student {
  var sports: [String]

  init(sports: [String]) {
    self.sports = sports
    // Build error - super.init isn't called before
    // returning from initializer
  }
  // original code
}
```

Uh-oh! The compiler complains that you didn't call `super.init` by the end of the initializer:

```
27
28 class StudentAthlete: Student {
29     var sports: [String]
30
31     init(sports: [String]) {
32         self.sports = sports
33         // Build error - super.init isn't called before
34         // returning from initializer
35     }                                    🛑 Super.init isn't called before returning from initializer
36 }
```

Initializers in subclasses are *required* to call `super.init` because, without it, the superclass won't be able to provide initial states for all its stored properties — in this case, `firstName` and `lastName`.

Let's make the compiler happy:

```
class StudentAthlete: Student {
  var sports: [String]

  init(firstName: String, lastName: String, sports: [String]) {
    self.sports = sports
    super.init(firstName: firstName, lastName: lastName)
  }
  // original code
}
```

The initializer now calls the initializer of its superclass, and the build error is gone.

Notice that the initializer now takes in a `firstName` and a `lastName` to call the `Person` initializer.

You also call `super.init` *after* you initialize the `sports` property, an enforced rule.

Two-Phase Initialization

Because Swift requires that all stored properties have initial values, initializers in subclasses must adhere to Swift's convention of **two-phase initialization**.

• **Phase one:** Initialize all of the stored properties in the class instance, from the bottom to the top of the class hierarchy. You can't use properties and methods until phase one is complete.

• **Phase two:** You can now use properties, methods and initializations that require the use of `self`.

Without two-phase initialization, methods and operations on the class might interact with properties before they've been initialized.

The transition from phase one to phase two happens after you've initialized all stored properties in the base class of a class hierarchy.

In the scope of a subclass initializer, you can think of this as coming after the call to `super.init`.

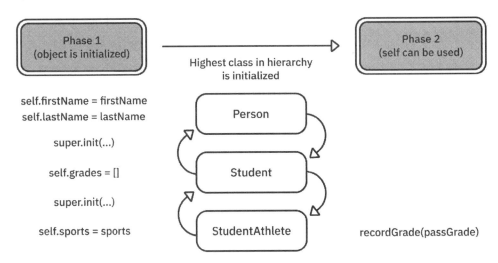

Here's the `StudentAthlete` class again, with athletes automatically getting a starter grade:

```swift
class StudentAthlete: Student {
  var sports: [String]

  init(firstName: String, lastName: String, sports: [String]) {
    // 1
    self.sports = sports
    // 2
    let passGrade = Grade(letter: "P", points: 0.0,
                          credits: 0.0)
    // 3
    super.init(firstName: firstName, lastName: lastName)
    // 4
    recordGrade(passGrade)
  }
  // original code
}
```

The above initializer shows two-phase initialization in action.

1. First, you initialize the `sports` property of `StudentAthlete`. This is part of the first initialization phase and must be done before you call the superclass initializer.

2. Although you can create local variables for things like grades, you can't call `recordGrade(_:)` yet because the object is still in the first phase.

3. Call `super.init`. When this returns, you know that you've also initialized every class in the hierarchy because the same rules apply at every level.

4. After `super.init` returns, the initializer is in phase 2, so you call `recordGrade(_:)`.

Mini-Exercise

What's different in the two-phase initialization in the base class `Person` compared to the others?

Required and Convenience Initializers

You already know it's possible to have multiple initializers in a class, which means you could potentially call *any* of those initializers from a subclass.

Often, you'll find that your classes have various initializers that simply provide a "convenient" way to initialize an object:

```
class Student {
  let firstName: String
  let lastName: String
  var grades: [Grade] = []

  init(firstName: String, lastName: String) {
    self.firstName = firstName
    self.lastName = lastName
  }

  init(transfer: Student) {
    self.firstName = transfer.firstName
    self.lastName = transfer.lastName
  }

  func recordGrade(_ grade: Grade) {
    grades.append(grade)
  }
}
```

In this example, the `Student` class can be built with another `Student` object. The student may come from another school. Both initializers fully set the first and last names.

Subclasses of `Student` could potentially rely on the `Student`-based initializer when they call `super.init`. Subclasses might not even provide a method to initialize with first and last names.

You might decide the first and last name-based initializer is important enough that you want it to be available to *all* subclasses.

Swift supports this through the language feature known as **required initializers**.

```
class Student {
  let firstName: String
  let lastName: String
  var grades: [Grade] = []

  required init(firstName: String, lastName: String) {
    self.firstName = firstName
    self.lastName = lastName
  }
  // original code
}
```

In the modified version of Student above, the first and last name-based initializer has been marked with the keyword `required`. This keyword will force all subclasses of Student to implement this initializer.

Now that there's a required initializer on Student, StudentAthlete *must* override and implement it.

```
class StudentAthlete: Student {
  // Now required by the compiler!
  required init(firstName: String, lastName: String) {
    self.sports = []
    super.init(firstName: firstName, lastName: lastName)
  }
  // original code
}
```

Notice how the `override` keyword isn't needed with required initializers. In its place, the `required` keyword must be used to ensure that any subclass of StudentAthlete implements this required initializer.

You can also mark an initializer as a **convenience** initializer:

```
class Student {
  convenience init(transfer: Student) {
    self.init(firstName: transfer.firstName,
              lastName: transfer.lastName)
  }
  // original code
}
```

The compiler forces a convenience initializer to call a non-convenience initializer (directly or indirectly) instead of handling the initialization of stored properties itself. A non-convenience initializer is called a **designated** initializer and is subject to the rules of two-phase initialization. All initializers you've written in previous examples were, in fact, designated initializers.

You might want to mark an initializer as convenience if you only use it as an easy way to initialize an object. However, you still want it to leverage one of your designated initializers.

Here's a summary of the compiler rules for using designated and convenience initializers:

1. A designated initializer must call a designated initializer from its immediate superclass.

2. A convenience initializer must call another initializer from the same class.

3. A convenience initializer must ultimately call a designated initializer.

Mini-Exercise

Create two more convenience initializers on Student. Which other initializers are you able to call?

When and Why to Subclass

This chapter has introduced you to class inheritance and the numerous programming techniques that subclassing enables.

But you might be asking, "When should I subclass?"

Rarely is there a right or wrong answer, so you need an understanding of the trade-offs to make an informed decision for a particular case.

Using the Student and StudentAthlete classes as an example, you might decide you can simply put all of the characteristics of StudentAthlete into Student:

```
class Student: Person {
  var grades: [Grade]
  var sports: [Sport]
  // original code
}
```

In reality, this *could* solve all of the use cases for your needs. A Student that doesn't play sports would simply have an empty sports array, and you would avoid some of the added complexities of subclassing.

Adhering to the Single Responsibility Principle

The guideline known as the **single responsibility principle** in software development states that any entity should have a single concern. Having more components with a single responsibility makes mixing and matching (composing) your components easier to build up functionality. When it comes time to change and add features, it is easier to augment your system when everything has a single, well-understood job.

This principle is true for object-oriented design. For example, in Student/ StudentAthlete, you might argue that it shouldn't be the Student class's job to encapsulate responsibilities that only make sense to student-athletes. That way, if you later need to support students in student government, you can do so without worrying about their athletic standing.

Leveraging Strong Types

Subclassing creates an additional type. With Swift's type system, you can declare properties or behavior based on objects that are student-athletes, not regular students:

```
class Team {
  var players: [StudentAthlete] = []

  var isEligible: Bool {
    for player in players {
      if !player.isEligible {
        return false
      }
    }
    return true
  }
}
```

A team has players who are student-athletes. If you tried to add a regular Student object to the array of players, the type system wouldn't allow it. This new type is helpful as the compiler can help you enforce the logic and requirement of your system.

Note: This is also where single-inheritance classes in Swift fall a bit short. This design might not work if you later added a `StudentPresident` type, but the student president was on the track team for one year. To overcome this limitation, Swift also comes with protocol inheritance which effectively allows multiple inheritances. You will learn about this in Chapter 17 - "Protocols".

Shared Base Classes

You can subclass a shared base class multiple times by classes that have mutually exclusive behavior:

```
// A button that can be pressed.
class Button {
  func press() {}
}

// An image that can be rendered on a button
class Image {}

// A button that is composed entirely of an image.
class ImageButton: Button {
  var image: Image

  init(image: Image) {
    self.image = image
  }
}

// A button that renders as text.
class TextButton: Button {
  var text: String

  init(text: String) {
    self.text = text
  }
}
```

In this example, you can imagine numerous `Button` subclasses sharing only that they can be pressed. The `ImageButton` and `TextButton` classes likely use different mechanisms to render a given button, so they might have to implement their own behavior to handle presses. You can see here how storing `image` and `text` in the `Button` class — not to mention any other kind of button there might be — would quickly become impractical. It makes sense for `Button` to be concerned with the press behavior and the subclasses to handle the actual look and feel of the button.

Extensibility

Sometimes you need to extend the behavior of code you don't own. In the example above, it's possible `Button` is part of an external framework you're using, so there's no way you can modify the source code to fit your specific case.

But you can subclass `Button` and add your custom subclass to use with code that's expecting an object of type `Button`.

Identity

Finally, it's important to understand that classes and class hierarchies model what objects *are*. If your goal is to share behavior (what objects *can do*) between types, more often than not, you should prefer protocols over subclassing. Again, you'll learn about protocols in Chapter 17, "Protocols".

Understanding the Class Lifecycle

In Chapter 14, "Classes", you learned that objects are created in memory and stored on the heap. Objects on the heap are *not* automatically destroyed because the heap is simply a giant pool of memory. Without the utility of the call stack, there's no automatic way for a process to know that a piece of memory will no longer be in use.

In Swift, the mechanism for deciding when to clean up unused objects on the heap is known as **reference counting**. Each object has a reference count incremented for each constant or variable with a reference to that object and decremented each time a reference is removed.

> **Note**: You might see the reference count called a "retain count" in other books and online resources. They refer to the same thing!

The object is abandoned when a reference count reaches zero since nothing in the system holds a reference to it. When that happens, Swift will clean up the object.

Here's a demonstration of how the reference count changes for an object. Note that only one actual object is created in this example; the one object has many references to it.

```
var someone = Person(firstName: "Johnny", lastName: "Appleseed")
// Person object has a reference count of 1 (someone variable)

var anotherSomeone: Person? = someone
// Reference count 2 (someone, anotherSomeone)

var lotsOfPeople = [someone, someone, anotherSomeone, someone]
// Reference count 6 (someone, anotherSomeone, 4 references in
lotsOfPeople)

anotherSomeone = nil
// Reference count 5 (someone, 4 references in lotsOfPeople)

lotsOfPeople = []
// Reference count 1 (someone)
```

Now we create another object and replace someone with that reference.

```
someone = Person(firstName: "Johnny", lastName: "Appleseed")
// Reference count 0 for the original Person object!
// Variable someone now references a new object
```

In this example, you don't have to do any work yourself to increase or decrease the object's reference count. That's because Swift has a feature known as **automatic reference counting** or **ARC**. While some older languages require you to increment and decrement reference counts in *your* code, the Swift compiler adds these calls automatically at compile-time.

> **Note**: If you use a low-level language like C, you're required to manually free memory you're no longer using yourself. Higher-level languages like Java and C# use something called **garbage collection**. In that case, the language's runtime will search your process for references to objects before cleaning up those no longer in use. While more automatic and behind the scenes than ARC, Garbage collection comes with a memory utilization and performance cost that Apple decided wasn't acceptable for mobile devices or a general systems language.

Deinitialization

Swift removes the object from memory and marks that memory as free when an object's reference count reaches zero.

A **deinitializer** is a special method on classes that runs when an object's reference count reaches zero but before Swift removes the object from memory.

Modify Person as follows:

```
class Person {
  // original code
  deinit {
    print("\(firstName) \(lastName) is being removed
          from memory!")
  }
}
```

Much like init is a special method in class initialization, deinit is a special method that handles deinitialization. Unlike init, deinit isn't required and is automatically invoked by Swift. You also aren't required to override it or call super within it. Swift will make sure to call each class deinitializer.

If you add this deinitializer, you'll see the message Johnny Appleseed is being removed from memory! in the debug area after running the previous example.

What you do in a deinitializer is up to you. Often you'll use it to clean up other resources, save state to a disk or execute any other logic you might want when an object goes out of scope.

Mini-Exercises

Modify the Student class to have the ability to record the student's name to a list of graduates. Add the student's name to the list when the object is deallocated.

Retain Cycles and Weak References

Because classes in Swift rely on reference counting to remove them from memory, it's essential to understand the concept of a **retain cycle**.

Add a field representing a classmate — for example, a lab partner — and a deinitializer to class `Student` like this:

```
class Student: Person {
  var partner: Student?
  // original code
  deinit {
    print("\(firstName) is being deallocated!")
  }
}

var alice: Student? = Student(firstName: "Alice",
                              lastName: "Appleseed")
var bob: Student? = Student(firstName: "Bob",
                            lastName: "Appleseed")

alice?.partner = bob
bob?.partner = alice
```

Now suppose both `alice` and `bob` drop out of school:

```
alice = nil
bob = nil
```

If you run this in your playground, you'll notice that you don't see the message `Alice/Bob is being deallocated!`, and Swift doesn't call `deinit`. Why is that?

Alice and Bob each have a reference to *each other*, so the reference count never reaches zero! To make things worse, by assigning `nil` to `alice` and `bob`, there are no more references to the initial objects. This situation is a classic case of a retain cycle, which leads to a software bug known as a **memory leak**.

With a memory leak, memory isn't freed up even though its practical lifecycle has ended. Retain cycles are the most common cause of memory leaks. Fortunately, there's a way that the `Student` object can reference another `Student` without being prone to retain cycles, and that's by making the reference **weak**:

```
class Student: Person {
  weak var partner: Student?
  // original code
}
```

This simple modification marks the `partner` variable as weak, which means the reference in this variable will not take part in reference counting. When a reference isn't weak, it's called a **strong reference**, which is the default in Swift. Weak references must be declared as optional types so that when the object they are referencing is released, it automatically becomes `nil`.

Challenges

Before moving on, here are some challenges to test your advanced class knowledge. It's best to try and solve them yourself, but solutions are available if you get stuck. These came with the download or are available at the printed book's source code link listed in the introduction.

Challenge 1: Initialization Order

Create three simple classes called A, B, and C where C inherits from B and B inherits from A. In each class initializer, call print("I'm <X>!") both before and after super.init(). Create an instance of C called c. What order do you see each print() called in?

Challenge 2: Deinitialization Order

Implement deinit for each class. Create your instance c inside a do { } scope, causing the reference count to go to zero when it exits the scope. Which order do the classes deinitialize?

Challenge 3: Type Casting

Cast the instance of type C to an instance of type A. Which casting operation do you use and why?

Challenge 4: To Subclass or Not

Create a subclass of StudentAthlete called StudentBaseballPlayer and include properties for position, number, and battingAverage. What are the benefits and drawbacks of subclassing StudentAthlete in this scenario?

Key Points

- **Class inheritance** is a feature of classes that enables **polymorphism**.

- **Subclassing** is a powerful tool, but it's good to know when to subclass. Subclass when you want to extend an object and could benefit from an "is-a" relationship between subclass and superclass, but be mindful of the inherited state and deep class hierarchies.

- The keyword `override` makes it clear when you are overriding a method in a subclass.

- The keyword `final` prevents a class from being subclassed.

- Swift classes use **two-phase initialization** as a safety measure to ensure all stored properties are initialized before they are used.

- Class instances have lifecycles which their **reference counts** control.

- **Automatic reference counting**, or **ARC**, handles reference counting for you automatically, but it's essential to watch out for **retain cycles**.

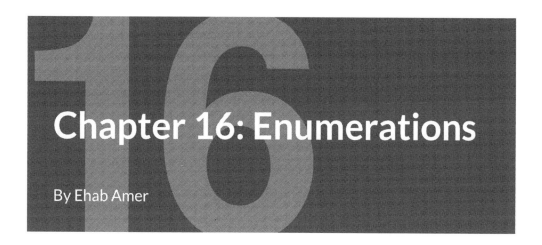

Chapter 16: Enumerations

By Ehab Amer

One day in your life as a developer, you realize you're being held captive by your laptop. Determined to break from convention, you set off on a long trek on foot. Of course, you need a map of the terrain you'll encounter. Since it's the 21st century and you're fluent in Swift, you decide to create a custom map app.

As you code away, you think it would be swell to represent the cardinal directions as variables: north, south, east and west. But what's the best way to do this in code?

You could represent each value as an integer, like so:

- North: 1

- South: 2

- East: 3

- West: 4

This encoding could quickly get confusing if you or your users happen to think of the directions in a different order. "What does 3 mean again?" To alleviate that, you might represent the values as strings, like so:

- North: "north"

- South: "south"

- East: "east"

- West: "west"

The trouble with strings, though, is that the value can be any string. What would your app do if it received "up" instead of "north"? Furthermore, it's all too easy to make a typo like "nrth".

Wouldn't it be great if there were a way to create a group of related, compiler-checked values? If you find yourself headed in this... *direction*, you'll want to use an **enumeration**.

An enumeration is a list of related values that define a common type and let you work with values in a type-safe way. The compiler will catch your mistake if your code expects a Direction and you try to pass in a float like 10.7 or a misspelled direction like "Souuth".

Besides cardinal directions, other good examples of related values are colors (black, red, blue), card suits (hearts, spades, clubs, diamonds) and roles (administrator, editor, reader).

Enumerations in Swift are more powerful than they are in other languages, such as C or Objective-C. They share features with the structure and class types you learned about in Chapter 11, "Structures", and Chapter 14, "Classes". An enumeration can have methods and computed properties while holding a particular state.

In this chapter, you'll learn how enumerations work and when they're useful. As a bonus, you'll finally discover what an optional is under the hood. Hint: They are implemented with enumerations!

Your First Enumeration

Your challenge: Construct a function to determine the school semester based on the month. One way to solve this would be to use an array of strings and match the semesters with a switch statement:

```
let months = ["January", "February", "March", "April", "May",
              "June", "July", "August", "September", "October",
              "November", "December"]

func semester(for month: String) -> String {
  switch month {
  case "August", "September", "October", "November", "December":
    return "Autumn"
  case "January", "February", "March", "April", "May":
```

```
      return "Spring"
  default:
    return "Not in the school year"
    }
  }

semester(for: "April") // Spring
```

Running this code in a playground, you can see that the function correctly returns "Spring". But as you saw in the introduction, it's easy to mistype a string. A better way to tackle this would be with an enumeration.

Declaring an Enumeration

To declare an enumeration, you list out all the possible member values as case clauses:

```
enum Month {
    case january
    case february
    case march
    case april
    case may
    case june
    case july
    case august
    case september
    case october
    case november
    case december
}
```

This code creates a new enumeration called Month with 12 possible member values. The commonly accepted best practice is to start each member value with a lowercase first letter, just like a property.

You can simplify the code a bit by collapsing the case clauses down to one line, with each value separated by a comma:

```
enum Month {
    case january, february, march, april, may, june, july, august,
    september, october, november, december
}
```

That looks snazzy and simple. So far, so good.

Deciphering an Enumeration in a Function

You can rewrite the function that determines the semester to use enumeration values instead of string matching.

```
func semester(for month: Month) -> String {
  switch month {
  case Month.august, Month.september, Month.october,
      Month.november, Month.december:
    return "Autumn"
  case Month.january, Month.february, Month.march,
      Month.april, Month.may:
    return "Spring"
  default:
    return "Not in the school year"
  }
}
```

Since Swift is strongly typed and uses type inference, you can simplify `semester(for:)` by removing the enumeration name in places where the compiler already knows the type. Keep the dot prefix, but lose the enumeration name, as shown below for the cases inside the `switch` statement:

```
func semester(for month: Month) -> String {
  switch month {
  case .august, .september, .october, .november, .december:
    return "Autumn"
  case .january, .february, .march, .april, .may:
    return "Spring"
  default:
    return "Not in the school year"
  }
}
```

Also, recall that `switch` statements must be exhaustive with their cases. The compiler will warn you if they aren't. When case patterns are `String` elements, you need a `default` case because it's impossible to create cases to match every possible `String` value.

However, enumerations have a limited set of values you can match against. So if you have cases for each member value of the enumeration, you can safely remove the `default` case of the `switch` statement:

```
func semester(for month: Month) -> String {
  switch month {
  case .august, .september, .october, .november, .december:
    return "Autumn"
  case .january, .february, .march, .april, .may:
    return "Spring"
  case .june, .july:
    return "Not in the school year"
  }
}
```

That's much more readable. There is another huge benefit to getting rid of the `default`. If in a future update, someone added `.undecember` or `.duodecember` to the Month enumeration, the compiler would automatically flag this and any other `switch` statement as being non-exhaustive, allowing you to handle this specific case.

You can test this function in a playground like so:

```
var month = Month.april
semester(for: month) // "Spring"

month = .september
semester(for: month) // "Autumn"
```

The variable declaration for `month` uses the full enumeration type and value. You can use the shorthand `.september` in the second assignment since the compiler already knows the type. Alternatively, you could have strongly typed the variable using `var month: Month = .april` if you find that easier to read. Finally, you pass both months to `semester(for:)`, where a `switch` statement returns the strings `"Spring"` and `"Autumn"` respectively.

Mini-Exercise

Wouldn't it be nice to request the semester from an instance like `month.semester` instead of using the function? Add a `semester` computed property to the `month` enumeration so that you can run this code:

```
let semester = month.semester // "Autumn"
```

Using Code Completion to Prevent Typos

Another advantage of using enumerations instead of strings is that you'll never have a typo in your member values. Xcode provides code completion:

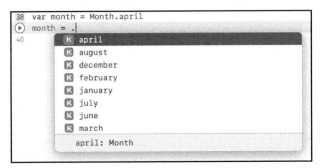

And if you do misspell an enumeration value, the compiler will complain with an error, so you won't get too far down the line without recognizing your mistake:

Raw Values

Unlike enumeration values in C, Swift enum values are *not* backed by integers as a default. That means january is *itself* the value.

You can specify that an integer backs the enumeration by declaring it with `:  Int` like this:

```
enum Month: Int {
```

Swift enumerations are flexible: you can specify other raw value types like String, Float or Character. As in C, if you use integers and don't specify values as you've done here, Swift will automatically assign the values 0, 1, 2 and up.

In this case, it would be better if January had the raw value of 1 rather than 0. To specify your own raw values, use the = assignment operator:

```
enum Month: Int {
  case january = 1, february = 2, march = 3, april = 4, may = 5,
  june = 6, july = 7, august = 8, september = 9,
  october = 10, november = 11, december = 12
}
```

This code assigns an integer value to each enumeration case.

There's another handy shortcut here. The compiler will automatically increment the values if you provide the first one and leave out the rest:

```
enum Month: Int {
  case january = 1, february, march, april, may, june, july,
    august, september, october, november, december
}
```

You can use the enumeration values alone and never refer to the raw values if you don't want to. But the raw values will be there behind the scenes if you ever need them!

Accessing the Raw Value

Enumeration instances with raw values have a handy `rawValue` property. With the raw values in place, your enumeration has a sense of order, and you can calculate the number of months left until winter break:

```
func monthsUntilWinterBreak(from month: Month) -> Int {
  Month.december.rawValue - month.rawValue
}
monthsUntilWinterBreak(from: .april) // 8
```

Initializing With the Raw Value

You can use the raw value to instantiate an enumeration value with an initializer. You can use `init(rawValue:)` to do this, but if you try to use the value afterward, you'll get an error:

```
let fifthMonth = Month(rawValue: 5)
monthsUntilWinterBreak(from: fifthMonth) // Error: not unwrapped
```

There's no guarantee that the raw value you pass in exists in the enumeration, so the initializer can fail. An optional value expresses this possibility for failure. For example, you could have used 13 as the input for a month that does not exist. Enumeration initializers with the `rawValue:` parameter are **failable initializers**, meaning if things go wrong, the initializer will return `nil`.

If you're using these raw value initializers in your own projects, remember that they return optionals. If you're unsure if the raw value is correct, you'll need to either check for nil or use optional binding. In this case, the value 5 must be correct, so it's appropriate to force unwrap the optional:

```
let fifthMonth = Month(rawValue: 5)! // may
monthsUntilWinterBreak(from: fifthMonth) // 7
```

That's better! You used the exclamation mark, !, to force unwrap the optional. Now there's no error, and monthsUntilWinterBreak(from:) returns 7 as expected.

Mini-Exercise

Make monthsUntilWinterBreak a computed property of the Month enumeration so that you can execute the following code:

```
let monthsLeft = fifthMonth.monthsUntilWinterBreak // 7
```

String Raw Values

Similar to the handy trick of incrementing an Int raw value, if you specify a raw value type of String, you'll get another automatic conversion. Pretend you're building a news app that has tabs for each section. Each section has an icon. Icons are a good opportunity to deploy enumerations because, by their nature, they are a limited set:

```
// 1
enum Icon: String {
  case music
  case sports
  case weather

  var filename: String {
    // 2
    "\(rawValue).png"
  }
}
let icon = Icon.weather
icon.filename // weather.png
```

Here's what's happening in this code:

1. The enumeration declares Icon with a String raw value type.

2. Calling rawValue inside the enumeration definition is equivalent to calling self.rawValue. Since the raw value is a string, you can use it to build a file name.

Note you didn't have to specify a String for each member value. If you set the raw value type of the enumeration to String and don't specify any raw values yourself, the compiler will use the enumeration case names as the raw values. The filename computed property will generate an image asset name for you. You can now fetch and display images for the tab icons in your app.

Next, let's jump back to working with raw numerical values and learn how to use enumerations for banking.

Unordered Raw Values

Integer raw values don't have to be in an incremental order. Coins are a good use case:

```
enum Coin: Int {
  case penny = 1
  case nickel = 5
  case dime = 10
  case quarter = 25
}
```

You can instantiate values of this type and access their raw values as usual:

```
let coin = Coin.quarter
coin.rawValue // 25

let aSmallCoin = Coin.dime
coin.rawValue > aSmallCoin.rawValue    //true

aSmallCoin.rawValue + coin.rawValue    //35
```

It's important to understand that the `Coin` enum is not an `Int`; it just has `Int` raw values. You will get a compiler error if you try to add two `Coin` variables, but you can add their raw values:

```
let thirtyFiveCents = coin + aSmallCoin
    ⊗ Binary operator '+' cannot be applied to two
      'Coin' operands
```

Mini-Exercise

Create an array called `coinPurse` that contains coins. Add an assortment of pennies, nickels, dimes and quarters to it.

Associated Values

Associated values take Swift enumerations to the next level in expressive power. They let you associate a custom value (or values) with each enumeration case.

Here are some unique qualities of associated values:

1. Each enumeration case has zero or more associated values.

2. The associated values for each enumeration case have their own data type.

3. You can define associated values with label names as you would for named function parameters.

An enumeration can have raw values or associated values, but not both.

In the last mini-exercise, you defined a coin purse. Let's say you took your money to the bank and deposited it. You could then go to an ATM and withdraw your money:

```
var balance = 100

func withdraw(amount: Int) {
  balance -= amount
}
```

The ATM will only let you withdraw what you put in, so it needs a way to let you know whether the transaction was successful. You can implement this as an enumeration with associated values:

```
enum WithdrawalResult {
  case success(newBalance: Int)
```

```
    case error(message: String)
}
```

Each case has a required value to go along with it. For the success case, the associated Int will hold the new balance; for the error case, the associated String will have some kind of error message.

Then you can rewrite the withdraw function to use the enumeration cases:

```
func withdraw(amount: Int) -> WithdrawalResult {
  if amount <= balance {
    balance -= amount
    return .success(newBalance: balance)
  } else {
    return .error(message: "Not enough money!")
  }
}
```

Now you can perform a withdrawal and handle the result:

```
let result = withdraw(amount: 99)

switch result {
case .success(let newBalance):
  print("Your new balance is: \(newBalance)")
case .error(let message):
  print(message)
}
```

Notice how you used let bindings to read the associated values. Associated values aren't properties you can access freely, so you'll need bindings like these to read them.

Remember that the newly bound constants newBalance and message are local to the switch cases. They aren't required to have the same name as the associated values, although it's common to do so.

This prints out the following in the debug console:

```
Your new balance is: 1
```

Many real-world contexts function by accessing associated values in an enumeration. For example, internet servers often use enumerations to differentiate between types of requests:

```
enum HTTPMethod {
  case get
  case post(body: String)
}
```

In the bank account example, you had multiple values you wanted to check for in the enumeration. In places where you only have one, you could instead use pattern matching in an `if case` or `guard case` statement. Here's how that works:

```
let request = HTTPMethod.post(body: "Hi there")
guard case .post(let body) = request else {
  fatalError("No message was posted")
}
print(body)
```

In this code, `guard case` checks to see if `request` contains the `post` enumeration case and, if so, reads and binds the associated value.

You'll also see enumerations used in error handling. The bank account example had multiple cases but one generic error case with an associated string.

Enumeration as a State Machine

An enumeration is an example of a state machine, meaning it can only ever be a single case at a time, never more. The friendly traffic light illustrates this concept well:

```
enum TrafficLight {
  case red, yellow, green
}
let trafficLight = TrafficLight.red
```

A working traffic light will never be red and green simultaneously. You can observe this state machine behavior in other modern devices that follow a predetermined sequence of actions in response to events.

Examples of state machines include:

- Vending machines that dispense soda when the customer deposits the proper amount of money.

- Elevators that drop riders off at upper floors before going down.

- Combination locks that require combination numbers in the proper order.

To operate as expected, these devices depend on an enumeration's guarantee that they will only ever be in one state at a time.

Mini-Exercise

A household light switch is another example of a state machine. Create an enumeration for a light that can switch .on and .off.

Iterating Through All Cases

Sometimes you want to loop through all of the cases in an enumeration. This is easy to do:

```
enum Pet: CaseIterable {
  case cat, dog, bird, turtle, fish, hamster
}

for pet in Pet.allCases {
  print(pet)
}
```

When you conform to the CaseIterable protocol, your enumeration gains a class method called allCases that lets you loop through each case in the order it was declared. This prints:

```
cat
dog
bird
turtle
fish
hamster
```

Enumerations Without Any Cases

In Chapter 13, "Methods," you learned how to create a namespace for a group of related type methods. The example in that chapter looked like this:

```
struct Math {
  static func factorial(of number: Int) -> Int {
    (1...number).reduce(1, *)
  }
}
let factorial = Math.factorial(of: 6) // 720
```

One thing you may not have realized at the time is that you could create an instance of Math, like so:

```
let math = Math()
```

The math instance doesn't serve any purpose since it is empty; it has no stored properties. In situations like this, the better design is actually to transform Math from a structure to an enumeration:

```
enum Math {
  static func factorial(of number: Int) -> Int {
    (1...number).reduce(1, *)
  }
}
let factorial = Math.factorial(of: 6) // 720
```

Now, if you try to make an instance, the compiler will give you an error:

```
let math = Math()
```

⊗ 'Math' cannot be constructed because it has no accessible initializers   ⊗

Enumerations with no cases are sometimes referred to as **uninhabited types** or **bottom types**.

As you learned at the beginning of this chapter, enumerations are powerful. They can do almost everything a structure can, including having custom initializers, computed properties and methods. To create an enumeration instance, though, you have to assign a member value as the state. If there are no member values, you won't be able to create an instance.

That works perfectly for you in this case (pun intended). There's no reason to have an instance of `Math`. You should make the design decision that there will *never* be an instance of the type.

That will prevent future developers from accidentally creating an instance and help enforce its use as you intended. So, choose a case-less enumeration if it would be confusing if a valueless instance existed.

Mini-Exercise

Euler's number is useful in calculating statistical bell curves and compound growth rates. Add the constant *e*, 2.7183, to your `Math` namespace. Then you can figure out how much money you'll have if you invest $25,000 at 7% continuous interest for 20 years:

```
let nestEgg = 25000 * pow(Math.e, 0.07 * 20) // $101,380.95
```

> **Note:** In everyday life, you should use `M_E` from the Foundation library for the value of *e*. The `Math` namespace here is just for practice.

Optionals

Since you've made it this far, the time has come to let you in on a little secret. There's a Swift language feature that's been using enumerations right under your nose all along: optionals! In this section, you'll explore their underlying mechanism.

Optionals act like containers that have either something or nothing inside:

```
var age: Int?
age = 17
age = nil
```

Optionals are enumerations with two cases:

1. `.none` means there's no value.

2. `.some` means a value attached to the enumeration case as an associated value.

You can extract the associated value from an optional with a `switch` statement, as you've already seen:

```
switch age {
case .none:
  print("No value")
case .some(let value):
  print("Got a value: \(value)")
}
```

You'll see this printed to the debug console:

```
No value
```

Although optionals are enumerations under the hood, Swift hides the implementation details by using optional binding, the ? and ! operators, and keywords such as `nil`.

```
let optionalNil: Int? = .none
optionalNil == nil     // true
optionalNil == .none   // true
```

If you try this in a playground, you'll see that `nil` and `.none` are equivalent.

In Chapter 18, "Generics," you'll learn a bit more about the underlying mechanism for optionals, including how to write your code to function in the same manner as optionals.

Now that you know how optionals work, you'll have the right tool for the job the next time you need a value container.

Challenges

Before moving on, here are some challenges to test your knowledge of enumerations. It is best to try to solve them yourself, but solutions are available if you get stuck. These came with the download or are available at the printed book's source code link listed in the introduction.

Challenge 1: Adding Raw Values

Take the coin example from earlier in the chapter and begin with the following array of coins:

```
enum Coin: Int {
    case penny = 1
    case nickel = 5
    case dime = 10
    case quarter = 25
}

let coinPurse: [Coin] =
[.penny, .quarter, .nickel, .dime, .penny, .dime, .quarter]
```

Write a function where you can pass in the array of coins, add up the value and then return the number of cents.

Challenge 2: Computing With Raw Values

Take the example from earlier in the chapter and begin with the Month enumeration:

```
enum Month: Int {
    case january = 1, february, march, april, may, june, july,
        august, september, october, november, december
}
```

Write a computed property to calculate the number of months until summer.

Hint: You'll need to account for a negative value if summer has already passed in the current year. To do that, imagine looping back around for the next full year.

Challenge 3: Pattern Matching Enumeration Values

Take the map example from earlier in the chapter and begin with the `Direction` enumeration:

```
enum Direction {
  case north
  case south
  case east
  case west
}
```

Imagine starting a new level in a video game. The character makes a series of movements in the game. Calculate the position of the character on a top-down level map after making a set of movements:

```
let movements: [Direction] = [.north, .north, .west, .south,
   .west, .south, .south, .east, .east, .south, .east]
```

Hint: Use a tuple for the location:

```
var location = (x: 0, y: 0)
```

Key Points

- An **enumeration** is a list of mutually exclusive cases that define a common type.

- Enumerations provide a type-safe alternative to old-fashioned integer values or strings.

- You can use enumerations to handle responses, store state and encapsulate values.

- `CaseIterable` lets you loop through an enumeration with `allCases`.

- **Uninhabited enumerations** can be used as namespaces and prevent the creation of instances.

- The Swift `Optional` type is a generic enumeration with cases `.none` and `.some`.

Chapter 17: Protocols

By Ehab Amer

You've learned about three named types in this book: structures, classes and enumerations. There is another very special one: the **protocol**.

Unlike the other named types, protocols don't define anything you instantiate directly. Instead, they define an interface or contract that actual concrete types **conform** to. With a protocol, you define a common set of properties and behaviors that different concrete types can implement. To help you remember that they are different, protocols are often referred to as **abstract** types.

You've been using protocols behind the scenes since the beginning of this book. In this chapter, you'll learn the details about protocols and see why they're central to Swift.

Introducing Protocols

You define a protocol much as you do any other named type. Start with this definition for a Vehicle:

```
protocol Vehicle {
    /// Return a description of the state of the vehicle.
    func describe() -> String

    // more to come...
}
```

Following the keyword, protocol is its name, followed by curly braces with the requirements inside. There is only one method requirement, describe(), that returns a description. The big difference you'll notice is that the protocol *doesn't contain any implementation.*

That means you can't instantiate a Vehicle directly:

```
7
8  let vehicle = Vehicle()   ⓘ 'Vehicle' cannot be constructed because it has no accessible initializers
⊙
```

Delete that line and continue building the Vehicle abstraction. Add the following to the protocol body:

```
/// Increases speed until it reaches its maximum speed.
mutating func accelerate()

/// Stop moving. Reducing the speed to zero miles per hour.
mutating func stop()
```

You mark these methods mutating because when they are implemented, they need to change the instance's state. You can also add a couple of property requirements:

```
/// The speed of the vehicle in miles per hour.
var speed: Double { get set }

/// The maximum speed attainable by this Vehicle type.
static var maxSpeed: Double { get }
```

When defining properties in a protocol, you must explicitly mark them as get or get set, similar to how you declare computed properties. However, much like methods, you don't include any implementation for properties.

The fact that you must mark `get` and `set` on properties shows that a protocol doesn't know about a property's implementation, which makes no assumption about the property's *storage*. You can implement these property requirements as computed properties *or* as regular variables. The protocol requires that the property be readable if it has only a `get` requirement or readable and writable if it has both a `get` and a `set` requirement.

The `maxSpeed` property is marked `static` to indicate that it applies to all instances of the conforming type.

In short, you use protocols to describe the requirements of a type. What you've defined here is the abstract *idea* of a vehicle.

Protocol Adoption

A protocol can be **adopted** by a class, struct or enum — and when another type adopts a protocol, it's required to implement the methods and properties defined in the protocol. Once a type implements all members of a protocol, the type is said to **conform** to the protocol.

Here's how you declare protocol conformance for your type. In the playground, define a new class that will conform to `Vehicle`:

```
class Unicycle: Vehicle {
}
```

You follow the name of the named type with a colon and the name of the protocol you want to adopt. This syntax might look familiar since it's the same syntax you use to make a class inherit from another class. In this example, `Unicycle` conforms to the `Vehicle` protocol.

Since you haven't fulfilled the requirements of the protocol, you get an error:

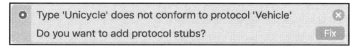

The fix-it button provided by Xcode is a quick way to add all the properties and methods you need to conform to the protocol. Fill in an implementation for `Unicycle`:

```
class Unicycle: Vehicle {
    func describe() -> String {
      "Unicycle @ \(speed) mph"
    }
```

```
    func accelerate() {
      speed = min(speed + 2, Self.maxSpeed)
    }
    func stop() {
      speed = 0
    }
    var speed: Double = 0
    static var maxSpeed: Double { 15 }
  }
```

With this implementation, Unicycle now conforms to Vehicle. For this type (a class), accelerate() and stop() don't need to be marked mutating even though they modify the state of the instance.

Use a struct to define a Car:

```
  struct Car {
    func describe() -> String {
      "Car @ \(speed) mph"
    }
    mutating func accelerate() {
      speed = min(speed + 20, Self.maxSpeed)
    }
    mutating func stop() {
      speed = 0
    }
    var speed: Double = 0
    static var maxSpeed: Double { 150 }
  }
```

This Car type implements all of the methods required by Vehicle but does not conform to Vehicle. You must explicitly write that it conforms to the type to get conformance. You can do that by either adding it to the declaration as you did in with Unicycleor add conformance using an extension like this:

```
  extension Car: Vehicle {}
```

With this code, Car now conforms to Vehicle. Since the definition of Car already contains everything it needs to be a Vehicle, the extension body is empty.

If you needed to, you could add code here to make it conform properly. This technique of re-opening the type helps adapt code you might not have the source code for. The fancy term for it is **retroactive modeling**.

> **Note:** You can't declare *stored* properties in extensions. You can only declare stored properties in the original type declaration or derived classes in the case of a class type. This limitation can present a challenge to implementing arbitrary protocol conformance for some types.

Defining Implementations

Protocol extensions allow you to define default implementation for protocol definitions. You might notice duplicated code in the example above. You can write a general purpose `stop()` method like so:

```
extension Vehicle {
    mutating func stop() {
        speed = 0
    }
}
```

Now when you conform to `Vehicle`, you don't have to write an implementation for `stop()` if you are okay with this default one. However, if you need to do additional work, such as managing a fuel or peddling status, you can define your own `stop()` method in your conforming type.

You can also create extensions on protocols that aren't part of the formal protocol definition, like this:

```
extension Vehicle {
    /// Return the speed as a value between 0-1.
    var normalizedSpeed: Double {
        speed / Self.maxSpeed
    }
}
```

Unlike an extension that implements a method or property part of the formal protocol, this implementation cannot be overridden by a conforming type. Every conforming type (`Unicycle`, `Car`, etc.) must accept this definition of `normalizedSpeed`.

Default Parameters

Protocols do not let you define default parameters like you can with functions or methods. But you can work around this limitation. To see how, create the following abstraction for `Turnable` types:

```
/// Different pressure options.
enum BrakePressure {
  case light
  case normal
  case hard
}

protocol Braking {
  /// Apply the brakes.
  mutating func brake(_ pressure: BrakePressure = .normal) //
ERROR
}
```

You can simulate having a default argument like this:

```
protocol Braking {
  /// Apply the brakes.
  mutating func brake(_ pressure: BrakePressure)
}

extension Braking {
  /// Apply normal brakes.
  mutating func brake() {
    brake(.normal)
  }
}
```

The adopting type still needs to implement `brake(_:)` for all brake pressures, but gets access to a normal pressure `brake()` automatically.

Initializers in Protocols

While protocols themselves can't be initialized, they can declare initializers that conforming types must implement:

```
protocol Account {
  var value: Double { get set }
  init(initialAmount: Double)
  init?(transferAccount: Account)
}
```

In the `Account` protocol above, you define two initializers as part of the protocol. Any type that conforms to `Account` is required to have these initializers. If you conform to a protocol with initializers using a `class` type, those initializers must use the `required` keyword:

```
class BitcoinAccount: Account {
    var value: Double
    required init(initialAmount: Double) {
        value = initialAmount
    }
    required init?(transferAccount: Account) {
        guard transferAccount.value > 0.0 else {
            return nil
        }
        value = transferAccount.value
    }
}
```

Using the `required` keyword will help you ensure that subclasses of your class also conform to the protocol. Swift is smart enough to realize that class marked `final` does not need to mark the initializers with `required` since there aren't any subclasses.

To instantiate a `BitcoinAccount`, you can use `BitcoinAccount(initialAmount: 30)` like normal. However, to prove that you can create one *strictly* through the `Account` protocol, you can use a **meta type** of `Account` like so:

```
let accountType: Account.Type = BitcoinAccount.self
let account = accountType.init(initialAmount: 30)
let transferAccount = accountType.init(transferAccount:
account)!
```

All types, including `BitcoinAccount`, have a property `self` that returns a descriptor to the type itself. The descriptor type is a so-called **meta type** and expressed as `BitcoinAccount.Type`. Since you know `BitcoinAccount` conforms to `Account`, you can assign it `Account`'s meta type, `Account.Type`. With this protocol meta type instance, you can use the `init()` methods directly to create new `BitcoinAccount` instances.

Protocol Inheritance

The `Vehicle` protocol contains a set of methods that could apply to any vehicle, such as a bike, car, snowmobile, or airplane!

You may wish to define a protocol that contains all the qualities of a `Vehicle` but is also specific to vehicles with wheels. For this, you can have protocols that inherit from other protocols, much like you can have classes that inherit from other classes:

```
protocol WheeledVehicle: Vehicle {
  var numberOfWheels: Int { get }
  var wheelSize: Double { get }
}
```

Any type you mark as conforming to the `WheeledVehicle` protocol will have all the members defined within the braces and the members of `Vehicle`. As with subclassing, any type you mark as a `WheeledVehicle` will have an "is-a" relationship with the protocol `Vehicle`.

You could extend `Unicycle` to be a `WheeledVehicle` like this:

```
extension Unicycle: WheeledVehicle {
  var numberOfWheels: Int { 1 }
  var wheelSize: Double { 20.0 }
}
```

`Unicycle` now conforms to to `WheeledVehicle`.

Using Protocols

Because each conforming type can supply its own implementation, protocols can be used with any type (structures, enumeration, classes) to achieve polymorphism like traditional base classes. Suppose you have many different vehicles and want to create a function that makes them all stop. You might try to implement it like this:

```
func stop(vehicles: [Vehicle]) {
  vehicles.forEach { vehicle in
    vehicle.stop() // ERROR: Cannot call a mutating method on a
constant array!
  }
}
```

Because you marked stop() as mutating the compiler knows that this implementation will be problematic for non-reference conforming types like structs. To fix this, you can clarify what is being mutated:

```
func stop(vehicles: inout [Vehicle]) {
  vehicles.indices.forEach {
    vehicles[$0].stop()
  }
}
```

Notice that you're not looping on the elements in the vehicles array directly. You're looping on the indices then using that index to reach the vehicle in the array then call stop(). The inout keyword on vehicles makes the array modifiable so that calling a mutating method succeeds. You can get more information on inout in Chapter 5: "Functions".

There is one more stylistic improvement you can make. In this code and the previous code, vehicles is an array of different types that all conform to the Vehicle protocol. In newer versions of Swift, you can distinguish between the protocol Vehicle and a box type that contains any kind of Vehicle. This is done by writing any Vehicle instead of just Vehicle. You can update the above function with this better style:

```
func stop(vehicles: inout [any Vehicle]) {
  vehicles.indices.forEach {
    vehicles[$0].stop()
  }
}
```

This use of any Vehicle makes it clear that vehicles is an array of **existential box** (any Vehicle) types. There is a small runtime cost to being able to work with all kinds of Vehicle types, and any Vehicle (while not required) highlights this cost. A future version of Swift may require you to use any here. Not doing so will likely become a warning or error.

Mini-Exercises

1. Create an Area protocol that defines a read-only property area of type Double.

2. Implement Area with structs representing Square, Triangle and Circle.

3. Add a circle, a square and a triangle to an array. Compute the total area of shapes in the array.

Associated Types in Protocols

Some types are naturally associated together with others. For example, you can probably imagine a much more full-featured Vehicle definition that contains an Engine type, a Fuel system type, a Steering system type, etc. Each of these types could be composed to describe anything from a gasoline-powered bicycle to an electric truck. Swift gives you the power to do this.

You can add an **associated type** as a protocol member. When using associatedtype in a protocol, you're simply stating there *is* a type used in this protocol without specifying what type this should be. It's up to the protocol adopter to decide the exact type.

Rather than sticking with the Vehicle example, you can make a simple protocol to explore this feature.

```swift
protocol WeightCalculatable {
  associatedtype WeightType
  var weight: WeightType { get }
}
```

By defining the stand-in WeightType associated type, you delegate the decision of the type of weight to whatever adopts the protocol.

You can see how this works in the two examples below:

```swift
struct HeavyThing: WeightCalculatable {
  // This heavy thing only needs integer accuracy
  typealias WeightType = Int

  var weight: Int { 100 }
}

struct LightThing: WeightCalculatable {
  // This light thing needs decimal places
  typealias WeightType = Double

  var weight: Double { 0.0025 }
}
```

You use typealias in these examples to be explicit about the associated type. This explicitness usually isn't required, as the compiler can often infer the type. In the previous examples, the type of weight clarifies what the associated type should be so that you can remove typealias.

You may have noticed that the contract of WeightCalculatable now changes depending on the choice of associated type in the adopting type.

Note that this prevents you from using the protocol as a simple variable type because the compiler doesn't know what WeightType will be ahead of time. But it'll recommend a solution for you:

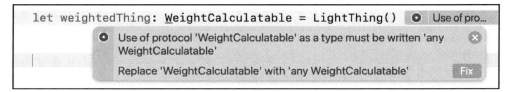

If you press the fix button, Xcode will change the type from WeightCalculatable to any WeightCalculatable. For protocols that do not contain associated types, Swift doesn't strictly require you to use the any keyword as you saw before. It is, however, required in protocols with associated types. This ensures you understand that the compiler is doing a lot for you to hide the size and implementation details of the underlying type with an existential type.

Implementing Multiple Protocols

A class can only inherit from a single class — this is the property of "single inheritance". By contrast, a class, structure or enumeration can conform to as many protocols as you'd like! Suppose you made Wheeled a protocol instead of the WheeledVehicle protocol earlier. It might look like this:

```
protocol Wheeled {
  var numberOfWheels: Int { get }
  var wheelSize: Double { get }
}
```

You could conform Car to it like this with an extension:

```
extension Car: Wheeled {
  var numberOfWheels: Int { 4 }
  var wheelSize: Double { 17 }
}
```

Now Car conforms to both Vehicle and Wheeled. Protocols support multiple conformances. You can add any number of protocol conformances to classes, structures and enumerations. In the example above, the Car has to implement all members defined in all of the protocols it adopts.

> **Note**: With a class that inherits from a base class *and* adopts many protocols, you must write the base class first in the list and then all the protocols it adopts.

Protocol Composition and some

In the previous section, you learned how to implement multiple protocols. Sometimes you need a function to take a data type that must conform to multiple protocols. That is where **protocol composition** comes in. Imagine you need a function that needs access to the Vehicle protocol's mutable stop() function and the Wheeled protocol's numberOfWheels property. You can do this using the & composition operator.

```swift
func freeze(transportation: inout any Vehicle & Wheeled) {
    transportation.stop()
    print("Stopping the rotation of \
(transportation.numberOfWheels) wheel(s).")
}
```

You can call it like this:

```swift
var car: any Wheeled & Vehicle = Car()
freeze(transportation: &car)
// Stopping the rotation of 4 wheel(s).
```

You might be wondering why car needs to be any Wheeled & Vehicle. In order mutate a existential type, you must pass exactly that type. It wouldn't be useful to pass a Car because the compiler would box it into a temporary any Wheeled & Vehicle mutate that box and then return leaving the original car value mysteriously untouched. Fortunately, trying to pass a Car type will result in a compiler error.

To fix this, instead of any Wheeled & Vehicle you can use some Wheeled & Vehicle. Unlike any which creates a existential box, the some keyword creates a **generic function** for every concrete type that is Wheeled & Vehicle.

```swift
func freeze(transportation: inout some Vehicle & Wheeled) {
    transportation.stop()
    print("Stopping the rotation of \
(transportation.numberOfWheels) wheel(s).")
}
```

Now you can write it like this:

```
var car = Car()
freeze(transportation: &car)
// Stopping the rotation of 4 wheel(s).
```

`freeze(transportation:)` is a fully generic function! It turns out that protocols and generics are language features completely intertwined with one another. This relationship is why protocols are the basis for generic code. You will learn more about generics in the next chapter.

Requiring Reference Semantics

Protocols can be adopted by both value types (structs and enums) and reference types (such as classes), so you might wonder if protocols have reference or value semantics.

The truth is that it depends! If you have an instance of a class or struct assigned to a variable of a protocol type, it will express value or reference semantics that match the conforming type.

To illustrate, take the simple example of a Named protocol below, implemented as a struct and a class:

```
protocol Named {
  var name: String { get set }
}

class ClassyName: Named {
  var name: String
  init(name: String) {
    self.name = name
  }
}

struct StructyName: Named {
  var name: String
}
```

If you were to assign a `Named` variable an instance of a reference type, you would see the behavior of reference semantics:

```
var named: Named = ClassyName(name: "Classy")
var copy = named

named.name = "Still Classy"
named.name // Still Classy
copy.name  // Still Classy
```

Likewise, if you assign an instance of a value type, you will see the behavior of value semantics:

```
named = StructyName(name: "Structy")
copy = named

named.name = "Still Structy?"
named.name // Still Structy?
copy.name  // Structy
```

The situation isn't always this clear. You'll notice that most of the time, Swift will favor value semantics over reference semantics. If you're designing a protocol adopted exclusively by classes, it's best to request that Swift uses reference semantics when using this protocol as a type.

```
protocol Named: AnyObject {
    var name: String { get set }
}
```

Using the `AnyObject` protocol constraint above indicates that only classes may adopt this protocol. This declaration makes it clear that Swift should use reference semantics.

The `class` keyword provides the same constraint. However, it is preferable to use the protocol `AnyObject` instead.

> **Note**: You can learn more about the difference between value type and reference type semantics in the "Value Types & Reference Types" chapter of *Swift Apprentice: Beyond the Basics*.

Protocols: More Than Bags of Syntax

As you have seen, protocols let you specify many syntax requirements for conforming types. However, they can't (and never will) let you specify every conceivable requirement for the compiler to check. For example, a protocol may need to specify complexity requirements (O(1) vs. O(n)) for an operation, and it can do this only by stating it in comments. You need to understand all of these requirements that a protocol makes to conform correctly. This reality has led to the refrain that protocols are "more than bags of syntax" that the compiler can check. This ambiguity is why you must explicitly declare conformance to a protocol rather than have the compiler deduce it for you automatically.

Protocols in the Standard Library

The Swift standard library uses protocols extensively in ways that may surprise you. Understanding the roles protocols play in Swift can help you write clean, decoupled "Swifty" code.

Equatable

Some of the simplest code compares two integers with the == operator:

```
let a = 5
let b = 5

a == b // true
```

You can do the same thing with strings:

```
let swiftA = "Swift"
let swiftB = "Swift"

swiftA == swiftB // true
```

But you can't use == on *any* type. Suppose you wrote a class to represent a team's record and wanted to determine if two records were equal:

```
class Record {

  var wins: Int
  var losses: Int

  init(wins: Int, losses: Int) {
```

```
        self.wins = wins
        self.losses = losses
    }
}

let recordA = Record(wins: 10, losses: 5)
let recordB = Record(wins: 10, losses: 5)

recordA == recordB // Build error!
```

You can't apply the == operator to the class you just defined. But the use of the equality operator isn't simply "magic" reserved for standard Swift types like Int and String; they're structs, just like Record. You can extend the use of this operator to your own types!

Both Int and String conform to the Equatable protocol from the standard library that defines a single static method:

```
protocol Equatable {
    static func ==(lhs: Self, rhs: Self) -> Bool
}
```

You can apply this protocol to Record like so:

```
extension Record: Equatable {
    static func ==(lhs: Record, rhs: Record) -> Bool {
        lhs.wins == rhs.wins &&
        lhs.losses == rhs.losses
    }
}
```

Here, you're defining (or *overloading*) the == operator for comparing two Record instances. In this case, two records are equal if they have the same number of wins and losses.

Now, you're able to use the == operator to compare two Record types, just like you can with String or Int:

```
recordA == recordB // true
```

Note: The compiler will often automatically write (or **codegen**) the function== for you. This automatic code generation happens for structures and enumerations that conform to Equatable. All stored properties and associated values must also be Equatable.

Comparable

A subprotocol of `Equatable` is `Comparable`:

```
protocol Comparable: Equatable {
  static func <(lhs: Self, rhs: Self) -> Bool
  static func <=(lhs: Self, rhs: Self) -> Bool
  static func >=(lhs: Self, rhs: Self) -> Bool
  static func >(lhs: Self, rhs: Self) -> Bool
}
```

In addition to the equality operator ==, `Comparable` requires you to overload the comparison operators <, <=, > and >= for your type. In practice, you'll usually only provide <, as the standard library can implement <=, > and >= for you, using your implementations of == and <.

Now you can make `Record` adopt `Comparable` as shown below:

```
extension Record: Comparable {
  static func <(lhs: Record, rhs: Record) -> Bool {
    if lhs.wins == rhs.wins {
      return lhs.losses > rhs.losses
    }
    return lhs.wins < rhs.wins
  }
}
```

This implementation of < considers one record lesser than another record if the first record either has fewer wins than the second record or an equal number of wins but a greater number of losses.

"Free" Functions

While == and < are useful in their own right, the Swift library provides you with many "free" functions and methods for types that conform to `Equatable` and `Comparable`.

For any collection you define that contains a `Comparable` type, such as an `Array`, you have access to methods such as `sort()` that are part of the standard library:

```
let teamA = Record(wins: 14, losses: 11)
let teamB = Record(wins: 23, losses: 8)
let teamC = Record(wins: 23, losses: 9)
var leagueRecords = [teamA, teamB, teamC]

leagueRecords.sort()
// {wins 14, losses 11}
// {wins 23, losses 9}
```

```
// {wins 23, losses 8}
```

Since you've given `Record` the ability to compare two values, the standard library has all the information it needs to sort an array of `Record`s! As you can see, implementing `Comparable` and `Equatable` gives you quite an arsenal of tools:

```
leagueRecords.max() // {wins 23, losses 8}
leagueRecords.min() // {wins 14, losses 11}
leagueRecords.starts(with: [teamA, teamC]) // true
leagueRecords.contains(teamA) // true
```

Other Useful Protocols

You'll find a few essential protocols in the Swift standard library that are helpful in almost any project.

Hashable

The `Hashable` protocol, a subprotocol of `Equatable`, is required for any type you want to use as a key to a `Dictionary`. As with `Equatable`, the compiler will automatically code generate `Hashable` conformance for you, but you must do it yourself for reference types such as classes.

Hash values help you quickly find elements in a collection. For this to work, values considered equal by == must also have the same hash value. Because the number of hash values is limited, there's a finite probability that non-equal values can have the same hash. The mathematics behind hash values is quite complex, but you can let Swift handle the details. Make sure that everything you include in the == comparison is combined using the `hasher`.

For example:

```
class Student {
  let email: String
  let firstName: String
  let lastName: String

  init(email: String, firstName: String, lastName: String) {
    self.email = email
    self.firstName = firstName
    self.lastName = lastName
  }
}

extension Student: Hashable {
  static func ==(lhs: Student, rhs: Student) -> Bool {
```

```
      lhs.email == rhs.email &&
      lhs.firstName == rhs.firstName &&
      lhs.lastName == rhs.lastName
  }

  func hash(into hasher: inout Hasher) {
    hasher.combine(email)
    hasher.combine(firstName)
    hasher.combine(lastName)
  }
}
```

You use `email`, `firstName` and `lastName` as the basis for equality. An exemplary implementation of `hash` would be to use all of these properties by combining them using the `Hasher` type passed in. The `hasher` does the heavy lifting of properly composing the values.

You can now use the `Student` type as the key in a `Dictionary`:

```
let john = Student(email: "johnny.appleseed@apple.com",
                   firstName: "Johnny",
                   lastName: "Appleseed")
let lockerMap = [john: "14B"]
```

Identifiable

The `Identifiable` protocol vends a unique `id` property. Specifically, `Identifiable` requires only a `get` property named `id` whose type must be `Hashable`.

For example, you could make `Student` identifiable like this:

```
extension Student: Identifiable {
  var id: String {
    email
  }
}
```

This implementation works because `email` is unique for each student. (If two students shared the same email address, it would not work.) Also, the `id` is of type `String` which is `Hashable`.

You would not want to use `firstName` to fulfill the `id` requirement because two or more students might have the same first name.

CustomStringConvertible

The convenient `CustomStringConvertible` protocol helps you log and debug instances.

When you call `print()` on an instance such as a `Student`, Swift prints a vague description:

```
print(john)
// Student
```

As if you didn't already know that! The `CustomStringConvertible` protocol has only a `description` property requirement. This property customizes how the instance appears in `print()` statements and in the debugger:

```
protocol CustomStringConvertible {
  var description: String { get }
}
```

You can provide a more readable representation by adopting `CustomStringConvertible` on the `Student` type.

```
extension Student: CustomStringConvertible {
  var description: String {
    "\(firstName) \(lastName)"
  }
}
print(john)
// Johnny Appleseed
```

`CustomDebugStringConvertible` is similar to `CustomStringConvertible`: It behaves exactly like `CustomStringConvertible` except it also defines a `debugDescription`. Use `CustomDebugStringConvertible` and `debugPrint()` to print to the output only in debug configurations.

Challenge

Before moving on, here is a challenge to test your knowledge of protocols. It is best to try to solve it yourself, but, as always, a solution is available if you get stuck.

Challenge 1: Pet Shop Tasks

Create a collection of protocols for tasks at a pet shop with dogs, cats, fish and birds.

The pet shop duties include these tasks:

- All pets need to be fed.

- Pets that can fly need to be caged.

- Pets that can swim need to be put in a tank.

- Pets that walk need exercise.

- Tanks and cages need to be cleaned occasionally.

1. Create classes or structs for each animal and adopt the appropriate protocols. Feel free to simply use a `print()` statement for the method implementations.

2. Create homogeneous arrays for animals that need to be fed, caged, cleaned, walked, and tanked. Add the appropriate animals to these arrays. The arrays should be declared using the protocol as the element type, for example, `var caged: [Cageable]`

3. Write a loop that will perform the proper tasks (such as feed, cage and walk) on each array element.

Key Points

- Protocols define a contract that classes, structs and enums can **adopt**.

- Adopting a protocol requires a type to **conform** to the protocol by implementing all methods and properties of the protocol.

- You must declare protocol conformance explicitly; it is not enough to implement all protocol requirements.

- You can use extensions for protocol adoption and conformance.

- If you create an extension on a protocol that isn't declared in the protocol, conforming types *cannot* override the extension.

- If you create an implementation in an extension declared in the protocol, conforming types *can* override the extension.

- A type can adopt any number of protocols, which allows for a quasi-multiple inheritance not permitted through subclassing.

- `any Protocol` creates an existential box type to access the underlying type similar to a class base class.

- `some Protocol` creates generic access to a concrete type.

- Protocols are the basis for creating generic code.

- The Swift standard library uses protocols extensively. You can use many of them, such as `Equatable` and `Hashable`, with your own types.

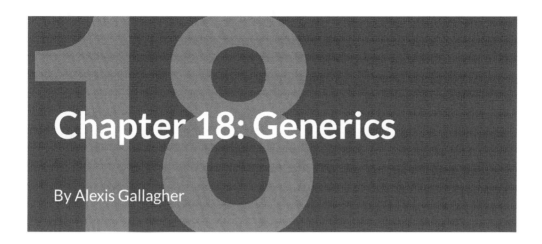

Chapter 18: Generics

By Alexis Gallagher

The truth is, you already know about generics. Every time you use a Swift array, you're using generics. This observation might give the impression that generics are *about* collections, but that impression is incorrect. In this chapter, you'll learn the fundamentals of generics, giving you a solid foundation for understanding how to write generic code. Finally, you'll loop back to look at generic types in the Swift standard library — arrays, dictionaries and optionals — using this new perspective.

Introducing Generics

To get started, consider how you might model pets and their keepers. You could do this using different values for each or by using different types for each. You'll see that by using types, instead of values, the Swift **type checker** can reason about your code at compile time. Not only do you need to do less at runtime, but you can catch problems that would have gone under the radar had you just used values. Your code also runs faster.

Values Defined by Other Values

Suppose you're running a pet shop that sells only dogs and cats and want to use Swift to model that business. To start, you define a type, PetKind, that can hold two possible values corresponding to the two kinds of pets that you sell:

```
enum PetKind {
  case cat
  case dog
}
```

So far, so good. Now you want to model the animals and the employees, the pet keepers who look after them. Your employees are highly specialized. Some keepers only look after cats, and others only dogs.

So you define a KeeperKind type as follows:

```
struct KeeperKind {
  var keeperOf: PetKind
}
```

Then you can initialize a catKeeper and dogKeeper in the following way:

```
let catKeeper = KeeperKind(keeperOf: .cat)
let dogKeeper = KeeperKind(keeperOf: .dog)
```

There are two points to note about how you're modeling your shop.

First, you're representing the different kinds of pets and keepers by *varying the values of types*. There's only one type for pet kinds — PetKind — and one type for keeper kinds — KeeperKind. Different kinds of pets are represented only by distinct values of the PetKind type, just as different kinds of keepers are represented by distinct values of the KeeperKind type.

Second, *one range of possible values determines another range of possible values.* Specifically, the range of possible KeeperKind values mirrors the range of possible PetKind values.

If your store started selling birds, you'd simply add a .bird member to the PetKind enumeration, and you'd immediately be able to initialize a value describing a bird keeper, KeeperKind(keeperOf: .bird). And if you started selling a hundred different kinds of pets, you'd immediately be able to represent a hundred different kinds of keepers.

In contrast, you could have defined a second unrelated enumeration instead of KeeperKind:

```
enum EnumKeeperKind {
    case catKeeper
    case dogKeeper
}
```

In this case, only your diligence in always updating one type to mirror the other would enforce this relationship. If you added PetKind.snake but forgot to add EnumKeeperKind.snakeKeeper, things would get out of whack.

But with KeeperKind, you explicitly established the relationship via a property of type PetKind. Every possible PetKind value implies a corresponding KeeperKind value. Or you could say the set of potential PetKind values defines the set of possible KeeperKind values.

To summarize, you can depict the relationship like so:

PetKind values	KeeperKind values
.cat	KeeperKind(keeperOf:.cat)
.dog	KeeperKind(keeperOf:.dog)
.etc	etc.

Types Defined by Other Types

The model above fundamentally works by varying the *values of types*. Now consider another way to model the pet-to-keeper system — by varying *the types themselves*.

Suppose that instead of defining a single type, `PetKind`, representing all kinds of pets, you chose to define a distinct type for every kind of pet you sell.

Distinct types are a plausible choice if you're working in an object-oriented style, where you model the pets' behaviors with different methods for each pet. Then you'd have the following:

```
class Cat {}
class Dog {}
```

Now how do you represent the corresponding kinds of keepers? You could simply write the following:

```
class KeeperOfCats {}
class KeeperOfDogs {}
```

But that's no good. This approach has *exactly* the same problem as manually defining a parallel enum of `KeeperKind` values — it relies on you to enforce the required domain relationship of one kind of keeper for every kind of pet.

What you'd like is a way to *declare* a relationship just like the one you established for values.

You'd like to declare that every possible pet type implies the existence of a corresponding keeper type, a correspondence that you'd depict like so:

Pet types	Keeper types
Cat	Keeper (of Cat...)
Dog	Keeper (of Dog...)
etc.	etc.

You'd like to establish that, for every possible pet type, there's a corresponding Keeper type. But you don't want to do this manually. You want a way to *automatically* define a set of new types for all the keepers.

Automatic type generation, it turns out, is the problem generics solve!

Anatomy of Generic Types

Generics provide a mechanism for using one set of types to define a new set of types.

In your example, you can define a **generic type** for keepers, like so:

```
class Keeper<Animal> {}
```

This definition immediately defines all the corresponding keeper types, as desired:

Pet types	Keeper types
Cat	Keeper<Cat>
Dog	Keeper<Dog>

You can verify these types are real by creating values of them, specifying the entire type in the initializer:

```
var aCatKeeper = Keeper<Cat>()
```

What's going on here? First, Keeper is the name of a generic type.

But you might say that a generic type isn't a type at all. It's more like a recipe for making real types or **concrete types**. One sign of this is the error you get if you try to instantiate it in isolation:

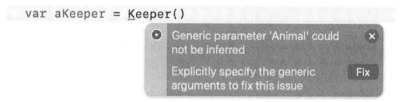

The compiler complains here that "generic parameter 'Animal' could not be inferred" because it doesn't know what kind of keeper you want. That Animal in angle brackets is the **type parameter** that specifies the type for the kind of animal you're keeping.

Once you provide the required type parameter, as in Keeper<Cat>, the generic Keeper becomes a new concrete type. Keeper<Cat> is different from Keeper<Dog>, even though they started from the same generic type. These resulting concrete types are called **specializations** of the generic type.

To summarize the mechanics, to define a generic type like Keeper<Animal>, you only need to choose the name of the generic type and the type parameter. The name of the type parameter, also called a **placeholder**, should clarify the relationship between the type parameter and the generic type. You'll encounter names like T (short for Type) from time to time but avoid these names when the placeholder has a well-defined role, such as Animal.

In one stroke, the generic type Keeper<Animal> defines a *family* of new types. Those are all the specializations of Keeper<Animal> implied by all possible concrete types that could substitute for the type parameter Animal.

Notice that the type Keeper doesn't currently store anything or even use the type parameter Animal in any way. Essentially, generics are a way to systematically define sets of types.

Using Type Parameters

Usually, though, you'll want to *do* something with type parameters.

Suppose you want to keep better track of individuals. First, you enrich your type definitions to include identifiers, such as names. Adding it lets every value represent the identity of an individual animal or keeper:

```swift
class Cat {
  var name: String

  init(name: String) {
    self.name = name
  }
}

class Dog {
  var name: String

  init(name: String) {
    self.name = name
  }
}

class Keeper<Animal> {
  var name: String

  init(name: String) {
    self.name = name
  }
}
```

You also want to track which keeper looks after which animals. Suppose every keeper is responsible for one animal in the morning and another in the afternoon. You can express this by adding properties for the morning and afternoon animals. But what type should those properties have?

If a particular keeper only manages dogs, then the properties must only hold dogs. And if cats, then cats. In general, if it's a keeper of Animal, then the morning and afternoon animal properties should be of type Animal.

To express this, you merely need to *use* the type parameter that previously only distinguished the nature of your keeper types:

```
class Keeper<Animal> {
  var name: String
  var morningCare: Animal
  var afternoonCare: Animal

  init(name: String, morningCare: Animal, afternoonCare: Animal)
{
    self.name = name
    self.morningCare = morningCare
    self.afternoonCare = afternoonCare
  }
}
```

Using Animal in the body of the generic type definition above, you can express that the morning and afternoon animals must be the kind of animal the keeper knows best. Just as function parameters become constants to use within the body of your function definition, you can use type parameters such as Animal throughout your type definitions. You can use the type parameter anywhere in the definition of Keeper<Animal> for stored properties, computed properties, method signatures and nested types.

Now when you instantiate a Keeper, Swift will make sure, at compile-time, that the morning and afternoon types are the same:

```
let jason = Keeper(name: "Jason",
                   morningCare: Cat(name: "Whiskers"),
                   afternoonCare: Cat(name: "Sleepy"))
```

Here, the keeper, Jason, manages the cat Whiskers in the morning and the cat Sleepy in the afternoon. The type of jason is Keeper<Cat>. Note that you did not have to specify a value for the type parameter.

Because you used instances of Cat as the values for morningCare and afternoonCare, Swift knows the type of jason should be Keeper<Cat>.

Generic Function Parameters

Functions can be generic as well. A function's **type parameter list** comes after the function name. You can then use the generic parameters in the rest of the definition.

This function takes two arguments and swaps their order:

```
func swapped<T, U>(_ x: T, _ y: U) -> (U, T) {
  (y, x)
}

swapped(33, "Jay")  // returns ("Jay", 33)
```

A generic function definition demonstrates a confusing aspect of the syntax: having both type parameters and function parameters. You have both the generic parameter list of type parameters `<T, U>` and the list of function parameters `(_ x: T, _ y: U)`.

Think of the type parameters as arguments *for the compiler*, which it uses to define one possible function. Just as your generic Keeper type meant the compiler could make dog keepers, cat keepers and any other kind of keeper, the compiler can now make a non-generic specialized swapped function for any two types for you to use.

Mini-Exercises

- Try instantiating another Keeper, but this time for dogs.

- What would happen if you tried to instantiate a Keeper with a dog in the morning and a cat in the afternoon?

- What happens if you try instantiating a Keeper but for strings?

Type Constrained Generics

In your definition of Keeper, the identifier Animal serves as a type parameter, a named placeholder for some concrete type you supply later.

This is much like the parameter name cat in an ordinary function like `func feed(cat: Cat) { /* open can, etc... */ }`. But when calling this function, you can't simply pass any argument. You can only pass values of type Cat.

However, at present, you could offer any type for Animal, even something nonsensically unlike an animal, like a String or Int.

Being able to use anything is no good. You'd like a mechanism more closely analogous to a function parameter. You want a feature that lets you restrict the types allowed in the type parameter. In Swift, you do this with various kinds of **type constraints**.

A simple kind of type constraint applies directly to a type parameter, and it looks like this:

```
class Keeper<Animal: Pet> {
    /* definition body as before */
}
```

Here, the constraint : Pet requires that the type assigned to Animal must be a subclass of Pet if Pet is a class or must implement the Pet protocol if Pet is a protocol.

For instance, to comply with the constraint established by the revised Keeper definition, you could redefine Cat and other animals to implement Pet, or you could **retro-actively model** conformance to the protocol by using an extension as you did in the previous Chapter:

```
protocol Pet {
    var name: String { get }  // all pets respond to a name
}
extension Cat: Pet {}
extension Dog: Pet {}
```

This code works because Cat and Dog already implement a name stored property. Now you can use this new protocol.

Suppose you want to implement a generic function that works with any type. You can start by writing this:

```
func callForDinner<Animal>(_ pet: Animal) {
    // What can you write here?
}
```

Here you have a generic type of Animal that could literally be anything. Because it can be anything, the compiler can't make assumptions about what it is. That makes it very challenging to write the implementation. That's where a protocol comes in. Add a Pet protocol constraint like so:

```
func callForDinner<Animal: Pet>(_ pet: Animal) {
    print("Here \(pet.name)-\(pet.name)! Dinner time!")
}
```

The generic type `Animal` conforms to `Pet` and can use the `name` property in the body to properly call the pet in for dinner. You can write the same function in a better way using the `some` keyword. It looks like this:

```
func callForDinner(_ pet: some Pet) {
  print("Here \(pet.name)-\(pet.name)! Dinner time!")
}
```

This generic function expresses the same thing as the previous version. This style is preferable because it's more readable without angle brackets, and it more directly states the constraints.

There is a more full-featured way of expressing constraints that you'll learn about next.

Conditional Conformance

In addition to simple type constraints, you can define more complex type constraints using a *generic where clause*. You can use a `where` clause in defining functions, types, member functions, protocols, and extensions. It can constrain type parameters and associated types, letting you define rich relationships on top of generic types.

To begin with, this is how you could use a where clause to implement the `callForDinner()` function. It looks like this:

```
func callForDinner<Animal>(_ pet: Animal) where Animal: Pet {
  print("Here \(pet.name)-\(pet.name)! Dinner time!")
}
```

Even though `callForDinner(_ pet: some Pet)` is the preferred style for this case, this shows how you can use the `where` clause to accomplish the same thing. The real power happens with more complex relationships.

Type constraints on extensions are instrumental. For example, suppose you want all `Cat` arrays to support the method `meow()`. You can use an extension to specify that when the array's `Element` is a `Cat`, then the array provides `meow()`:

```
extension Array where Element: Cat {
  func meow() {
    forEach { print("\($0.name) says meow!") }
  }
}
```

You can even specify that a type should conform to some protocol only if it meets certain constraints. Suppose that anything that can meow is a Meowable. You could write that every Array is Meowable if its elements are Meowable, as follows:

```
protocol Meowable {
  func meow()
}

extension Cat: Meowable {
  func meow() {
    print("\(self.name) says meow!")
  }
}

extension Array: Meowable where Element: Meowable {
  func meow() {
    forEach { $0.meow() }
  }
}
```

This code demonstrates **conditional conformance**, a subtle but powerful mechanism of composition.

Advanced Generic Parameters

Suppose you wish to write a function to find a lost animal. You start with an array of lost animals:

```
let lost: [any Pet] = [Cat(name: "Whiskers"), Dog(name:
"Hachiko")]
```

Since all types of pets can become lost, you use the existential box type any Pet. Strictly speaking, since protocol Pet doesn't contain associated types, you can drop the any keyword, and it will still compile, but it is better style to include it.

You can implement a non-generic find function like this:

```
/// Return a lost Cat.
func findLostCat(name: String) -> Cat? {
  lost.lazy.compactMap {
    $0 as? Cat
  }.first {
    $0.name == name
  }
}
```

This method lazily iterates over the `lost` list looking for `Cat`s and returning the first with a matching name. Now define one for dogs:

```
/// Return a lost Dog.
func findLostDog(name: String) -> Dog? {
  lost.lazy.compactMap {
    $0 as? Dog
  }.first {
    $0.name == name
  }
}
```

You probably notice a lot of repetition in that code except for the type `Cat` and `Dog`. Every time there is a new `Pet` type such as a `Goldfish`, `Chinchilla` or `Iguana`, you need to write a new function. That could be better.

You could write something more "generic":

```
func findLostPet(name: String) -> (any Pet)? {
  lost.first { $0.name == name}
}
```

This code will find all kinds of pets, in fact, any `Pet` by returning an existential boxed type that can contain any concrete type conforming to the `Pet` protocol. However, it tosses away valuable type information. What if someone was looking for a `Cat` and it returned a `Goldfish` named "Whiskers"?

You can use a generic to get back that lost type information:

```
func findLost<Animal: Pet>(_ petType: Animal.Type, name: String)
  -> (some Pet)? {
  lost.lazy.compactMap {
    $0 as? Animal
  }.first {
    $0.name == name
  }
}
```

You can call it this way:

```
findLost(Cat.self, name: "Whiskers")
findLost(Dog.self, name: "Hachiko")
```

The first parameter lets the compiler infer the generic type. It has the requirement that it must conform to the `Pet` protocol. `findLost(_:name:)` works for any `Pet` conforming Animal type you can dream up. The function body can use the inferred type to filter down to the correct type.

The return type is a concrete type, some Pet, that conceals the details of the specific type. This some Protocol return type is called an **opaque return type** and is used to hide complexity.

In this case, such hiding doesn't provide any advantage, and you are better off returning the concrete type, which was constrained to the input type.

```
func findLost<Animal: Pet>(_ petType: Animal.Type, name: String)
-> Animal? {
  lost.lazy.compactMap {
    $0 as? Animal
  }.first {
    $0.name == name
  }
}
```

Now you have *complete* type information so can call any method that the concrete type implements.

```
findLost(Cat.self, name: "Whiskers")?.meow()
// Whiskers says meow!
```

Because findLost(_:name:) returns a Cat type, you can call meow(). The same code used with Dog.self would not compile since Dog has no meow() method.

Arrays

While the original Keeper type illustrates that a generic type doesn't need to store anything or use its type parameter, Array, one of the most common generic types, does both.

The need for generic arrays was part of the original motivation to invent generic types. Since many programs need homogeneous arrays, generic arrays make all that code safer. Once the compiler infers (or is told) the type of an array's elements at one point in the code, it can spot any deviations at other points before the program runs.

You've been using Array all along, but only with **syntactic sugar**: [Element] instead of Array<Element>. Consider an array declared like so:

```
let animalAges: [Int] = [2,5,7,9]
```

This code is equivalent to the following:

```
let animalAges: Array<Int> = [2,5,7,9]
```

Array<Element> and [Element] are completely interchangeable. So you could even call an array's default initializer by writing [Int]() instead of Array<Int>().

Since Swift arrays allow indexed access to a sequence of elements, they impose no requirements on their Element type. But this isn't always the case.

Dictionaries

Swift generics allow multiple type parameters, each with unique constraints. A Dictionary is a straightforward example of this.

Dictionary has two type parameters in the comma-separated generic parameter list that falls between the angle brackets, as you can see in its declaration:

```
struct Dictionary<Key: Hashable, Value> // etc..
```

Key and Value represent the types of the dictionary's keys and values. The type constraint Key: Hashable requires that any type serving as the dictionary's key be hashable because the dictionary is a hash map and must hash its keys to enable fast lookup.

To instantiate types such as Dictionary with multiple type parameters, simply provide a comma-separated type argument list:

```
let intNames: Dictionary<Int, String> = [42: "forty-two"]
```

As with arrays, dictionaries get special treatment in Swift since they're built-in and rather common. You've already seen the shorthand notation [Key: Value], and you can also use type inference:

```
let intNames2: [Int: String] = [42: "forty-two", 7: "seven"]
let intNames3 = [42: "forty-two", 7: "seven"]
```

Optionals

Finally, no discussion of generics would be complete without mentioning optionals. Optionals are enumerations, but they're just another generic type, which you could have defined yourself.

Suppose you were writing an app that lets a user enter her birthdate in a form but doesn't require it. You might find it handy to define an enum type as follows:

```
enum OptionalDate {
   case none
   case some(Date)
}
```

Similarly, if another form allowed but didn't require the user to enter her last name, you might define the following type:

```
enum OptionalString {
   case none
   case some(String)
}
```

Then you could capture all the information a user did or did not enter into a struct with properties of those types:

```
struct FormResults {
   // other properties here
   var birthday: OptionalDate
   var lastName: OptionalString
}
```

And if you found yourself doing this repeatedly for new types, at some point, you'd want to generalize this into a generic type that could support any type in the future. Therefore, you'd write the following:

```
enum Optional<Wrapped> {
   case none
   case some(Wrapped)
}
```

At this point, you would have reproduced Swift's own Optional<Wrapped> type since this is quite close to the definition in the Swift standard library! It turns out Optional<Wrapped> is close to being a plain old generic type, like one you could write yourself.

Why "close"? It would *only* be a plain old generic type if you interacted with optionals only by writing out their full types, like so:

```
var birthdate: Optional<Date> = .none
if birthdate == .none {
  // no birthdate
}
```

But, of course, it's more common and conventional to write something like this:

```
var birthdate: Date? = nil
if birthdate == nil {
  // no birthdate
}
```

Those two code blocks say the same thing. The second relies on special language support for optionals: the `Wrapped?` shorthand syntax for specifying the optional type `Optional<Wrapped>` and `nil`, which can stand for the `.none` value of an `Optional<Wrapped>` specialized on any type.

As with arrays and dictionaries, optionals get a privileged place in the language with this syntax to be more concise. But all of these features provide more convenient ways to access the underlying type, which is simply a generic enumeration type.

Challenge

Before moving on, here is a challenge to test your knowledge of generics. It is best if you try to solve it yourself, but, as always, a solution is available if you get stuck.

Challenge 1: Build a Collection

Consider the pet and keeper examples from earlier in the chapter:

```
class Cat {
  var name: String

  init(name: String) {
    self.name = name
  }
}

class Dog {
  var name: String

  init(name: String) {
    self.name = name
  }
}

class Keeper<Animal> {
  var name: String
  var morningCare: Animal
  var afternoonCare: Animal

  init(name: String, morningCare: Animal, afternoonCare: Animal)
  {
    self.name = name
    self.morningCare = morningCare
    self.afternoonCare = afternoonCare
  }
}
```

Imagine that instead of looking after only two animals, every keeper looks after a changing number of animals throughout the day. It could be one, two, or ten animals per keeper instead of just morning and afternoon ones. You'd have to do things like the following:

```
let christine = Keeper<Cat>(name: "Christine")

christine.lookAfter(someCat)
christine.lookAfter(anotherCat)
```

You'd want access to the count of animals for a keeper like `christine.countAnimals` and to access the 51st animal via a zero-based index like `christine.animalAtIndex(50)`.

Of course, you're describing your old friend, the array type, `Array<Element>`!

Your challenge is updating the `Keeper` type to have this interface. You'll probably want to include a private array inside `Keeper` and then provide methods and properties on `Keeper` to allow outside access to the array.

Key Points

- Generics are everywhere in Swift: optionals, arrays, dictionaries, other collection structures, and most basic operators like + and ==.

- Generics express systematic variation at the level of types via **type parameters** that range over possible concrete types.

- Generics are like functions *for the compiler*. They are evaluated at compile-time and result in new types – specializations of the generic type.

- A generic type is not a concrete type but more like a recipe, program, or template for defining new types.

- Swift provides a rich system of **type constraints**, which lets you specify what types are allowed for various type parameters.

- `some Protocol` refers to a concrete, generic type, while `any Protocol` refers to a concrete type in an existential box.

- There are many ways to write generics with constraints, the most general being the generic `where` clause.

Conclusion

We hope you learned a lot about the fundamentals of Swift in this book — and had some fun in the process! Swift is filled with language features and programming paradigms, and we hope you now feel comfortable enough with the basics of the language to move on to some more advanced concepts.

Understanding the fundamentals of Swift is not only about how to compute answers with expressions and statements but really about understanding types: tuples, functions, structures, enumerations and classes. Then using protocols and generics to *really* take those concepts to the next level. You are ready to dive into more advanced topics and frameworks with *Swift Apprentice: Beyond the Basics* to see how types are used in more complex ways to build frameworks and entire subsystems.

If you have any questions or comments as you continue to use Swift, please stop by our forums at https://forums.kodeco.com.

Thank you again for purchasing this book. Your continued support is what makes the tutorials, books, videos, conferences and other things we do at Kodeco possible — we truly appreciate it!

Wishing you all the best in your continued Swift adventures,

– The *Swift Apprentice: Fundamentals* team

Made in the USA
Middletown, DE
07 August 2023

36294012R00212